REBECCA BELLINGHAM & VERONICA SCOTT

THE ARTFUL APPROACH TO
EXPLORING IDENTITY AND FOSTERING BELONGING

REBECCA BELLINGHAM & VERONICA SCOTT

THE ARTFUL APPROACH TO
EXPLORING IDENTITY AND FOSTERING BELONGING

HEINEMANN
Portsmouth, NH

Heinemann
145 Maplewood Avenue, Suite 300
Portsmouth, NH 03801
www.heinemann.com

© 2025 by Rebecca Bellingham and Veronica Scott

All rights reserved. No part of this work may be reproduced or transmitted in any form or by any means, electronic or mechanical, including photocopying or recording, or by any information storage or retrieval system, without prior written permission unless such copying is expressly permitted by federal copyright law.

Requests for permission to reproduce any part of the work or queries regarding subsidiary rights licensing should be submitted through our website at https://www.heinemann.com.

> *Heinemann's authors have devoted their careers to developing the unique content in their works, and their written expression is protected by copyright law. You may not adapt, reuse, translate, or copy portions of their works and post on third-party lesson-sharing websites, whether for-profit or not-for-profit.*

Acknowledgments: Naomi Shahib Nye, excerpt from "One Boy Told Me" from *Fuel*. Copyright © 1998 by Naomi Shihab Nye. Reprinted with the permission of The Permissions Company, LLC on behalf of BOA Editions, Ltd., boaeditions.org.

"Jacket flap text" by Penguin Random House LLC, copyright © 2018 by Penguin Random House LLC; from THE DAY YOU BEGIN by Jacqueline Woodson. Used by permission of Nancy Paulsen Books, an imprint of Penguin Young Readers Group, a division of Penguin Random House LLC. All rights reserved.

Donovan Livingston, excerpt from "Lift Off: From the Classroom to the Stars." May 25, 2016. Copyright © 2016 Donovan Livingston. Used with permission.

Pádraig Ó Tuama, excerpt from "A Poem Is a Made Thing," from *Poetry Unbound*, December 11, 2022. Copyright © 2022 by Pádraig Ó Tuama. Used with permission.

Library of Congress Control Number: 2024949157

Printed in the United States of America on acid-free paper
ISBN-13: 978-0-325-16080-1
1 2 3 4 5 6 7 8 9 10 VP 29 28 27 26 25 24

4500904641

Editor: Zoë Ryder White
Production: Vicki Kasabian
Permissions: David Stockdale
Cover design: Veronica Scott
Text design: Suzanne Heiser
Typesetting: Gina Poirier Design
Manufacturing: Jaime Spaulding

For my parents, Johnnie and Rebecca. Thank you for all of those trips to our local library, for tolerating an entire summer of BSB on repeat, and for showing me how to look beyond what is in order to imagine what could be. And for Jose, everywhere is home with you by my side.

—VS

♥

For my parents, Rick and Bobbitt. Thank you for always loving me exactly as I am (even when I was in my Nellie Oleson impression phase). And for Ben, you make my life sweeter, steadier, funnier, and more delicious. Your support is unwavering and your tuna noodle casserole is a midwestern girl's dream come true. I love you all so much!

—RB

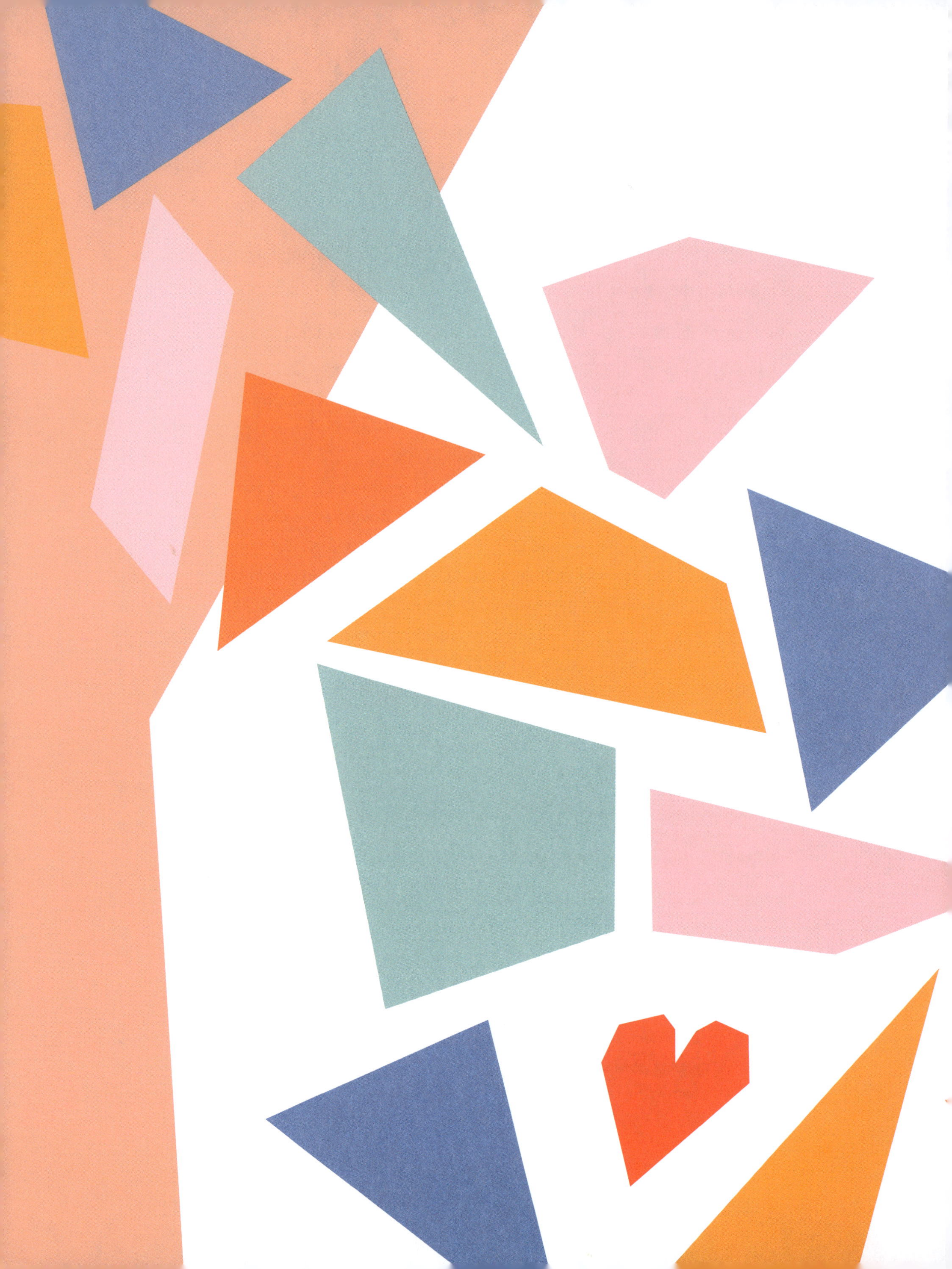

CONTENTS

Acknowledgments x
Introduction xiv

CHAPTERS

1 Learning for Self-Growth
Picture Books, Poems, and Pop Culture 1

2 Launching the Year Artfully
The Power of Beginnings 34

3 Dreaming Up Engaging Cultural Months
An Artful Approach That Affirms and Invites 54

4 Connecting with Your Students Through Artful Read-Alouds
How to Partner with Books to Explore Identity 80

5 Harnessing the Power of Poetry
How to Create and Reflect as a Community 95

6 Teaching Honest History Artfully
How the Artful Helps Us Disrupt the Myths and Humanize the Past 120

7 Responding with Care
How to Empower Students with Letters of Love and Upstander Skills 146

8 Designing Your Own Belonging Lab
A Space for Student Leaders, Poets, and Public Speakers 163

9 Meeting for Windows, Mirrors, and Coffee
A Children's Literature Book Club for Parents and Caregivers 179

10 Reflecting Artfully
The Power of Closing Moments 191

Works Cited 202

ONLINE RESOURCES CONTENTS

OR 1-1 Learning for Self-Growth Artfully

OR 2-1 Identity Map Starter

OR 3-1 Cultural Months Planning Guide: Year-at-a-Glance

OR 3-2 November: Native American Heritage Month

OR 3-3 February: Black History Month—Look to the Stars

OR 3-4 March: Women's History Month

OR 3-5 Cultural Month Planning Template

OR 5-1 Online Mentor Poems

OR 5-2 Our Promises

OR 5-3 Planting Seeds in Third Grade

OR 5-4 At This Table

OR 5-5 Our Something Beautiful

OR 5-6 Food Is Love

OR 5-7 The Song I'll Sing This Year

OR 5-8 My Friend Is Sad Today

OR 5-9 Soundsuits: Nick Cave Found Poem

OR 6-1 Initial Brainstorming for Research Topic and Creative Project

OR 6-2 My Project Proposal

OR 6-3 Thoughtful Representation Checklist

OR 6-4 I, Too Poem Starter

OR 7-1 Words That Sting Lesson Visuals

OR 7-2 Being an Upstander Template

OR 7-3 My Line for the Poem Template

OR 8-1 Design Process to Develop a Belonging Lab Campaign

OR 8-2 Sample Campaign Script

OR 9-1 WMC Planning Guide

OR 9-2 WMC Planning Guide: Ways to Make Sunshine

To access the Online Resources for *The Artful Approach to Exploring Identity and Fostering Belonging*:

1. Go to http://hein.pub/bellscott-login.

2. Log in with your username and password. If you do not already have an account with Heinemann, you will need to create an account.

3. On the Welcome page, choose "Click here to register an Online Resource."

4. Register your product by entering the code IDENTITY (be sure to read and check the acknowledgment box under the keycode).

5. Once you have registered your product, it will appear alphabetically in your account list under "My Online Resources."

Note: When returning to Heinemann.com to access your previously registered products, simply log in to your Heinemann account and click on "View my registered Online Resources."

ACKNOWLEDGMENTS

Here's to the teachers we've met from San Diego to Montgomery, Brooklyn to Boston, and everywhere in between. One of the gifts of this project is having the chance to connect with and learn alongside all of you. It's your glorious scrappy spirits that keep us forever inspired, energized, and hopeful.

Here's to the educational leaders who believe in the brilliance of teachers and the importance of exploring identity even with our youngest learners! To leaders like Cindy Marten, Russ Sperling, Desiree Ivey, Jacqui Getz, Maria Paula Ghiso, Tim Farsen, Cat Corral, and Caroline Blackwell: You are shining lights in the world of education and your artful leadership empowers teachers and students all over. And, to two local shining lights in San Diego who made so much of the work in this book possible, Heather Gray and Theresa Tran. As far as school leaders go, you're purrfection.

Here's to the community of educators, leaders, families, and students who continue to advocate for equity and uplift the work of belonging at Francis Parker School in San Diego.

Here's to the fifth-grade teachers who helped bring History Con to life. Your dance moves, your endless support for our student historians, and your unbelievable lemon bars kept us going and helped us "stick the landing" every year.

Here's to all the teachers on the D-Team who brought their expertise in science, media, design, EdTech, visual arts, and theater to our school-wide projects and cultural month experiences.

Here's to the alumni and current students of the Belonging Lab. We loved eating lunch with you every month, watching you show our community what "belonging feels like," and partnering with you to inspire a new generation of upstanders each year.

Here's to all the parents and caregivers who joined us for Windows, Mirrors, and Coffee Book Club over the years. Your willingness to talk about big issues using books for little people made it possible (even over Zoom) to create a community built on honest and open-hearted exchange. And here's to one special dad, Voltaire Sterling, who recruited every other dad he could and never missed a single meeting.

Here's to Horizons at Parker and the luminous Erika Assadi who is creating space for educational equity and doing it in style. Your teaching team is proof that excellence and inclusivity go hand in hand.

Here's to the phenomenal team at the WNET Group. Your commitment to public media makes it possible for us to spread stories that educate and inspire into communities across New York City and beyond. To Beryl Harold, your enthusiasm and *joie de vivre* always elevated the energy in our workshops. To Eugenia Harvey, your powerful vision and leadership are a model for how to work toward a community where everyone can bring their full selves.

Here's to the Heinemann team: Catrina Swasey, Kim Cahill, and Suzanne Heiser for your expertise, artistry, and support of this project. And here's to editor and poet Zoë Ryder White, for shepherding us through this project from day one. You never cease to amaze us with your wealth of knowledge and boundless patience. Your kindness and generosity kept our spirits up even in the midst of deadlines and rewrites—we always looked forward to seeing your smile on Zoom! You're our dream editor and we couldn't have asked for a better partner and fellow artist to help us bring this book to life.

And finally, here's to all the readers of this book, whether you are an educator or a supporter of educators, thank you for fighting the good fight and for dreaming up a world where every child can create—where every child can belong.

FROM REBECCA

Here's to my Lark Street crew (Ben, Annie, and Ezra!), who cheer me on, make me laugh, and share my dreams for a world where everyone belongs. Each of you has the biggest heart and I love you with all of mine.

Here's to my parents, who are the most generous listeners and who taught me how important it is to always listen, to carefully notice, to stay curious, and to lead with compassion.

Here's to transcenDANCE, an arts-based organization that raises the bar when it comes to supporting young people and creating a community of belonging. Your work lifts young people up like no other and exemplifies the way the arts can transform lives. It's an honor to collaborate with you and support your vision.

Here's to the ladies of *The Raft* who have helped me keep my artist heart alive, which fuels my work in the classroom. I'm always dreaming about the next chance to be back onstage singing and harmonizing with all of you!

Here's to my students at Teachers College, who inspire me every year with their dedication to learning, to teaching, and to creating classrooms of belonging for young people everywhere.

And finally, here's to Veronica! Thank you for continuing to stretch and deepen my thinking, for lifting me up and cracking me up, for always being willing to entertain yet another big idea, and for infusing everything you do with your extra-special Veronica magic. I see the way you make everything and everyone around you shine brighter, but you are the brightest star of all! What a gift to collaborate with someone who inspires me every day with her extraordinary creativity, her capacious heart, and her wholehearted devotion to creating a more beautiful, just, and equitable world.

FROM VERONICA

Here's to Jose whose love, laughter, and cafecitos kept me going from the first page to the last. I'm convinced that in every wrinkle of space and time, there never was and never will be another you. Thank you for dreaming with me, love, even when we were only kids.

Here's to my parents who taught me how to rise up with humility and grace. And here's to Trey (insert secret handshake). Your company is still the best antidote for any gray day.

Here's to the fam. To Grandma who taught me how to see the world like an artist. To Grandpa who taught me how to sing along to a guitar and how to lead with heart. To Tía who taught me about Selena and Tejano music. To Uncle Carlos who taught me to believe in myself. To my aunties who taught me the joy of the Stevie Wonder birthday song. To Grandma Thelma and Grandaddy who taught me to look to the stars. To Maria, Monica, and Julian for being my second family. And to Chloe and Lori and all the little cousins who will dare to dream beyond what we could.

Here's to the boutiques in San Diego who kept my artist dreams alive every time they put one of my designs in their shop windows. You are a town that supports, uplifts, and inspires me to keep making.

Here's to the team at Learning for Justice, Jey, and the members of the Ambassador Collective who are empowering educators to work together to create more just communities all across the Deep South and beyond. Thank you for being my guiding light at so many stages of this work.

Here's to Christen Tedrow-Harrison who is a powerhouse, a wonderful boss, a visionary, and a forever friend with the best *vibras*. I'm raising my espresso martini to you, CTH. A bit of my heart will always belong to our Radical Love Team. Here's to all the things.

Here's to a group of future Black intellectuals and creatives—the students and alumni of Nia (which means "purpose" in Swahili). And here's to the Nia families and facilitators who continue to inspire those little hearts and minds. Being in community with you all is what belonging feels like.

Here's to the extraordinary feat that is the People of Color Conference. Thank you for creating a place where we can come together every year to retreat, grow, and feel connected to each other.

Here's to Emily Fritz, a real-life Ms. Frizzle, for letting me share all of my project ideas with you and for being the first teacher to join my first Diversity and Inclusion team. Here's to "no bad days."

Here's to the coffee shop on West Fourth, the bookstore on East Third, Double Dutch Espresso, the NYPL, the Apple Store in Soho, the shaded bench near Bethesda Fountain, and all of the public Wi-Fi places in between where this book came to life.

And here's to Rebecca! To my writing partner, my overthinking partner, my laughing so hard it hurts partner, my no dream too big or too small partner—thank you for every chat, every check-in, every text, every follow-up text, every walk to Kettle, and every day we shared in our little office (aka the DEIB dorm). You always made our space and our work together feel so full of life and possibility. As the kids once said, you are a true "freedom teacher." Thank you for inspiring me to hold on to my artist heart, for grabbing me food when I couldn't make it to the cafeteria on time, for serenading me with *Hadestown*, and for being a kindred spirit. Here's to endless possibility with you in the room.

INTRODUCTION

For the poets, dreamers, visionaries, and risk takers who planted light in the field of darkness so we could rise up.
—Joy Harjo, "Perhaps the World Ends Here"

Without fail, whenever we are knee-deep in planning mode, whether we're working on a poetry workshop for teachers or an artist studio for second graders, there's this inevitable moment of doubt that arises and we realize we're both thinking the same unhelpful thing: Is this going to be enough? Will another one of these projects even make a difference? As lifelong educators, there's nothing we want more than to offer something of value, something practical and inspiring, something hopeful to lift up the teachers or students we're supporting. But as much as we try to hold on to that hope, especially on days when the headlines are particularly horrifying or when communities seems even more divided than usual, the world's *capital-P* Problems keep pushing their way into our optimistic lesson plans. For every creative light bulb that goes off, there's a parenthetical "what about" lurking in its shadow: Maybe we can write a community poem! *But what about the literacy crisis?* Maybe we can paint a neighborhood mural. *But what about basic needs?* Maybe we can take time to reflect as a team. *But what about teacher burnout?* Maybe we can bring our school together with a song! *But what about the upcoming election?* Maybe we can have a dance party to celebrate Women's History Month! *But what about pay inequity? And the growing threat against women's rights?* Before we know it, we're headed for a what-about downward spiral.

Maybe you've been there. Maybe you've had a similar experience or train of thought: If we can't solve the big stuff, then what's the point of all these smaller efforts? And the truth is, a community poem is not going to fix our broken world. But where would we be, if in our toughest times, we didn't have songs to turn to? Movies to transport us? Poems to unite us? We only have to look back at some of the most pivotal moments in recent history to notice a link between movements and music, or art and activism, or literature and enlightenment. As Amanda Gorman (2021) says, "Poetry and language are often at the heartbeat of movements for change." The arts empower people to rise up. They make space for the harmonious and the discordant. They offer us moments of beauty and joy in the midst of turmoil and glimpses of hope in the midst of uncertainty. They can help us share who we are and who we mean to be, honoring all our distinct complexities and glorious particularities in between. The arts move us, sustain us, and awaken us. And if we're not connecting or creating, it can often feel like we're doing little more than surviving. Even if we don't see ourselves as artists we are probably more creative than we realize. Whether it's writing the next great novel or making a luscious omelet out of the leftovers from the fridge, our lives are full of opportunities to create. And these moments of creating, both big and small, bring us alive. They fuel our work and uplift our spirits and they can do the same for students too.

Our classrooms can be hubs of connecting and creating as well. When we invite the arts into our school day, we help students learn how to pay close attention and listen generously, how to speak up when it matters, even how to find their own brief moments of beauty and joy when they need them the most. Every time we bring out the crayons or lead the song, invite the class to paint a self-portrait or write their first line of poetry, we're breathing life into our classrooms. We're shining a light on what could be and inspiring our students to shine it right back at us, into their projects, into the hallways, and out into the world.

A COFFEE BREAK: LET'S GET TO KNOW EACH OTHER

Before we dive into how this book can help you harness the power of the arts in fresh ways, we thought we'd take a little coffee break for you to get to know us a bit. Here's the origin story of how we met (our very own mini meet-cute!). By sharing this backstory we hope to provide insight into how our friendship and partnership inform our work. How we lean into our different backgrounds and perspectives as a way to model honest conversations and lead collaboratively.

When it comes to making new adult friendships, options can be limited. There are book clubs and coffee shops. The gym and the crafting aisle. One can hold out hope for a new neighbor or an organic run-in at the park. And of course there's always the awkward setup from a well-meaning colleague, or if you're up for it, the apps. Our story, however, is a bit more unlikely. If we were sitting on the *When Harry Met Sally* couch, our friendship story might be closest to the couple with all the odds against them. Different generations. Different cultural references. Different upbringings. Different races. Different households (one with twins, one with a visiting neighborhood cat). And, as would become clear in our shared office space, different organizational habits—one of us likes books arranged a certain way, which she would say is the right way, and one of us takes what she would say is a more *laissez-faire* approach.

Not only were we from seemingly different worlds—Rebecca is a white Jewish woman with small-town, Midwestern roots and Veronica is a Black Chicana from the multicultural sprawl of Houston, Texas—but the circumstances of our meeting were also weighted with complexity. We met launching equity work. At a new school. Months after an international racial reckoning. In the height of a pandemic. And yet, within days of meeting, we realized we were kindred spirits. We would soon discover we both love Broadway and all things New York City. We both love books, bookstores, and a general bookish vibe. We both love comparing notes on the latest think pieces—everything from the state of Diversity, Equity, Inclusion, and Belonging

An Artful Approach to Belonging 101

What is an artful approach?
An *artful approach* to belonging is one that is inspired by the magic of the arts and informed by culturally responsive practices. An artful approach deepens our capacity for noticing, pausing, and reflecting, and invites us to share the story of who we are, listen generously, and be in community with each other.

What do we mean by belonging?
We like to think of *belonging* as students feeling truly seen, valued, and free to be their unique selves. Belonging work in the classroom goes beyond kindness and surface-level inclusivity by embracing differences and lifting up the voices of people who have historically been marginalized.

To learn more about belonging and the positive impact it has on academic excellence for all students and in school communities, we encourage you to look into the research of Claude Steele and Geoffrey Cohen. We have also both been inspired by the work of the Othering and Belonging Institute at UC Berkeley: Research Center for a Fair and Inclusive Society, which reminds us that a key part of belonging is "having a meaningful voice and the opportunity to participate in the design of political, social, and cultural structures that shape one's life . . ." (Othering and Belonging Institute 2023).

(DEIB) in education to who is most deserving of this year's "Best Picture." We are both children's-lit fangirls and have strong opinions about classroom decor. And we both remember thinking at the end of our first epic text exchange, "thank god, you overthink everything too!" As we got to know each other better, we realized that we had some deeper connections as well. We both believed in the power of the arts to create classroom magic. We both wanted schools to be places where students felt free enough to be their unique selves and teachers felt inspired and supported enough to make that possible. We both dreamed of classrooms where children could express themselves not only with words, but with color, song, and movement too.

In those first few months, we would find ourselves meeting in the office or waiting in the school lunch line, deep in discussion about these ideas. We wondered if our two roles, literacy specialist and DEIB associate director, could work together toward building this dream of belonging for all students. In these conversations, we soon realized another deep connection: not only were we both educators but we also were artists. Rebecca, a performer and playwright, and Veronica, a fashion designer and stylist, had

An Artful Approach to Belonging in Schools

An artful approach to belonging is not equity lite. This approach does not shy away from honest history, is not color-blind, and does not ignore the painful realities of systemic oppression. For educators and educational leaders to use an artful approach effectively, we must also expand our awareness of the structural and historical context that has led to inequity in our classrooms and communities.

If you're new to belonging work in the classroom, this book is full of tips, ideas, and artful practices to get you started, but you might also consider a paired read with *Culturally Responsive Teaching and The Brain* by Zaretta Hammond (2014), *Start Here, Start Now* by Liz Kleinrock (2021), or *Belonging: The Science of Creating Connection and Bridging Divides* by Geoffrey Cohen (2022a).

Getting Started with an Artful Approach

Questions to ask yourself as you begin planning artful experiences that help foster belonging with students or colleagues:

1. How might I use the opening and closing moments to set a tone, create a feeling, and invite connection or reflection?

2. How am I incorporating the arts into the experience? Is there a story at the heart of this experience?

3. How might I invite participants to open up and share about their identities by starting with low-stakes options and moving toward deeper, more complex topics?

4. How is this experience informed by culturally responsive practices?

both witnessed the impact of the arts firsthand. And, as teaching artists, we had also witnessed the way the arts could transform the lives of young people. We decided we would integrate our creativity and love for theatre, music, and poetry into our work. In these early conversations, we began to dream up what would become our artful approach to exploring identity and fostering belonging.

Given our love for the arts, we just had to stuff this book full of some of our favorite stories, cultural references, artists, and icons. Alongside practical, user-friendly guides, you'll also discover the Cholita Climbers, Nick Cave soundsuits, Ashley Bryan puppets, and how to use Nikki Giovanni's poem about chocolate to launch an "Express Yourself" themed Black History Month. We also want to lift up people, places, and movements that rarely make their way into elementary classrooms: Yuyi Morales, Afrofuturism, Pow Wow remixes by Halluci Nation, Sean Sherman aka "The Sioux Chef," Duke Halapu Kahanamoku ("The Father of Surfing") all make an appearance. And we had to include a few mic-drop moments by Ta-Nehisi Coates and, well, of course, Beyoncé. Alongside these new and familiar voices, you'll find poems about everything from fearlessly swimming with sharks to rolling out masa with Grandma. And full disclaimer, there's also one-minute dance parties, a quick mention of *The Bachelor,* and theater kid energy sprinkled throughout.

In addition to all these spotlight stories that students will love, we also share teacher tips for launching the year artfully, checking in at every season, and responding to challenging moments that arise throughout the year. Every chapter includes charts to guide your planning as well as mini "scripts" that you can adapt to help you frame some of these big ideas in developmentally appropriate ways. You'll also find samples of lesson plans and student work to help you envision how these ideas come to life at different grade levels.

While we encourage you to begin with the first chapter, "Learning for Self-Growth: Picture Books, Poems, and Pop Culture," you can definitely read this book out of order. For instance, you might find it useful to dip into specific chapters that can help you think about upcoming units or how to support student conversations around identity as they arise. Or maybe you'll want to pull an idea from one of our go-to lists to use for an upcoming project or meetup, like "True for Me," a game for connecting with students, or "Elevated Water-Cooler Conversation Starters," which has fun questions for connecting with your colleagues, or "Identity Maps with a Twist," which can be adapted to explore identity with students or adults.

Like a pep talk with a work friend at just the right moment, we hope this book leaves you feeling energized, supported, and inspired. We hope it leaves you feeling like you have allies and co-conspirators in this work. Like you're ready to bring a whole new

Three Things to Look Out For!

1. **I-Perspective Moments** (Rebecca's Version or Veronica's Version): Not only is this book about an artful exploration of identity, it is written by two people from different backgrounds. As a result, sometimes you'll notice a break in the text in which we speak directly to the reader from each of our unique perspectives and identities. When we write from the "I-perspective," it'll look like this:

   R: Hi! I'm Rebecca, a white woman who grew up in a small town in New Jersey, but NYC will always feel like my forever home. I am the mother of twins and feel very connected to the Jewish rituals, traditions, and life cycles my husband and I pass on to them.

   V: Hey y'all! I'm Veronica. I identify as Black and Chicana (my dad is Black and my mom is Mexican American) and I'm originally from Houston, Texas. While I grew up in Houston and spent much of my adult life in San Diego, I'm finishing this book in my dream town, NYC!

These I-perspective moments help us make space for nuanced conversations and illustrate how our work is constantly informed by ongoing self-reflection and learning. We always teach from the inside out. And that means giving insight into who we are in life to show how that shapes the way we connect with students in the classroom.

2. **Handle with Care:** Occasionally, you'll notice this heart symbol alongside the text. We hope these "Handle with Care" tips remind our readers to pause and proceed with care as they adapt lessons, projects, and content that could potentially result in tricky or harmful moments if led hastily. For example, when you are reading a book aloud and you can't speak from the I-perspective of the main character, we provide tips for how to handle that moment with care.

3. **Closing with a Poem:** We wanted to provide an artful twist on the chapter summaries that typically recap key points throughout the book, so we decided to close out each time with a poem. Some of these closing poems might serve as a mentor text to inspire a new poem by using the stems in bold. Some of the poems, however, don't lend themselves as mentor texts and work better as a read-aloud or a shared reading experience.

INTRODUCTION

lens for the kinds of stories that can spark engagement in your students. Like it's OK to start with small and artful shifts that grow into a more significant impact over time. Like when you draw inspiration from the arts, the possibilities for creating, connecting, and belonging are limitless. Like there is joy in leading in this work and you deserve to take it in. Soak it up! Celebrate the wins! Take a moment to quiet those voices of doubt, to shush those "what-abouts" lurking in the shadows, and to say to them, "*This* is enough. *This* matters." Because a community poem might not fix our broken world, but it sure is a good place to start.

1

LEARNING FOR SELF-GROWTH

Picture Books, Poems, and Pop Culture

> *What artists can do is bring stories to the table that are unshakably true—the sort of stories that, once you've heard them, won't let you return to what you thought before.*
>
> —Lin-Manuel Miranda,
> "The Role of the Artist in the Age of Trump"

EXPLORING THE ARTS TO LEARN FOR SELF-GROWTH

Think about the last time you were blown away by a work of art. Maybe it was a movie that reflected a bit of your own life back to you in ways you had never experienced before. Maybe it was a song that reminded you of home or a special time in your life. Maybe it was a bit of writing that shifted your perception, revealed something new, or stirred something within you that you never realized was there. These moments reveal the power of the arts to inspire deep introspection, which is what we call *learning for self-growth*—a concept that we'll explore in depth throughout this chapter. No matter who you teach or how old your students are, every classroom can benefit from teachers who continue to learn from and feel inspired by the painters, thinkers, makers, singers, dancers, and poets who have dared to dream and create; who have challenged us to imagine and reimagine; and who have helped build new narratives about who we are and who we can become.

Learning for self-growth can happen anytime, anywhere, if you're open to it. But seeking out content that supports your critical awareness, your approach to belonging work, and your historical knowledge takes a little more time and intentionality. So the next time you find yourself feeling transfixed by a work of art—allow yourself to pause. Think about what might have caused this *moving moment* for you. Try not to let the moment pass without fully allowing it to inspire deeper reflection. Take this opportunity to look inward and contemplate what this artful experience is stirring within you and revealing to you, not just about the world but about yourself. This practice of noticing, pausing, and looking inward is something we can keep returning to as we grow in this work. As Dena Simmons, EdD, founder of LiberatED, reminds us, "We can all get better with our practice . . . and for teachers, one way to get better is really to start with self" (Simmons 2020).

Learning for self-growth is something all of us can do because all of us have a story about what matters to us, about the people who have influenced us, and about who we are. Our stories help us make meaning out of our lives, make sense of what's happening around us, and connect with each other. This makes the stories you choose to seek out all the more important.

learning for Self-Growth

We define *learning for self-growth* as any learning experience designed for introspection, especially around historical knowledge and identity development. We intentionally differentiate this type of self-education and exploration from other types of professional development that are typically created for the explicit purpose of developing professional skills and/or classroom content. That isn't to suggest that learning for self-growth doesn't eventually lead to new practices, skills, or curriculum for students—that just isn't the goal. Think of learning for self-growth as something just for you!

Moving Moment

A moving moment is any time a work of art inspires introspection, empowerment, or new ways of seeing the world. In the words of Lin-Manuel Miranda (2019) sometimes that means it "won't let you return to what you thought before."

THE ARTFUL APPROACH TO EXPLORING IDENTITY AND FOSTERING BELONGING

Applying the Windows and Mirrors Framework: Even for Adults!

Like many educators, we rely heavily on the beloved framework of *windows and mirrors*, created by Rudine Sims Bishop: educational scholar, professor emerita at Ohio State University, and widely known as the "mother of multicultural children's literature" (Chenoweth 2019). For years, educators have been beautifully applying the framework of windows and mirrors to grow their classroom libraries, choose books to read aloud, and develop curricular units. Creating classrooms filled with windows and mirrors helps children develop a healthy sense of identity and encourages a compassionate curiosity about the world outside their own. We've come to realize that this framework supports the identity development of adults as well! In other words,

How We Think About Windows and Mirrors

Windows: Stories that are windows into worlds outside of our own. This could include characters and people whose identities are different from our own, settings in places and times that are new to us, and experiences that feel unfamiliar.

Mirrors: Stories that reflect our own lived experiences back at us. This could include characters and people who share our identities and lived experiences and settings in places and times that feel familiar.

Unpacking Our Identities

Dominant Identities are those that set the social norms. These are groups whose values, images, and experiences are most commonly represented and understood as the norm.

Marginalized Identities are those that have historically experienced disempowerment and discrimination.

Identity Complexity: Both dominant and marginalized identities are often on a continuum and present in complex ways. As Diane Goodman (2001) writes in *Promoting Diversity and Social Justice*, "Our particular constellation of social identities shapes our experiences and our sense of self. When we're part of an advantaged group, our subordinated identities may mitigate but not eliminate our access to power and privilege just as additional privileged identities may enhance it" (8).

Intersectionality: We all have multiple intersecting identities. Our different identities are not in silos but are actually interconnected—often overlapping each other. Legal scholar Kimberlé Crenshaw (2016) invites us to use the "simple analogy" of an intersection to help us visualize the ways that intersecting identities might result in unique oppressions. If you picture one road for gender and then you imagine another road for race, age, or ability—the intersection is where those two identities overlap, creating a unique experience for the individual.

windows and mirrors can be applied outside of the classroom too—in our own lives as we consume media and share stories with friends, and especially as we continue to learn for self-growth.

Windows can be powerful experiences for anyone, but they are especially helpful for people who house dominant identities. This is because marginalized identities have historically been underrepresented in the media landscape. While representation in movies and books has shifted over the years, a recent study of Hollywood representation found bleak results. This study revealed that the increase in leading roles for girls and women was "almost a flatline from 2007 to 2022," speaking characters who identified as LGBTQ accounted for "only 2.1 percent," and while there were "five transgender characters in the top 100 films of 2022 . . . four of these five characters appeared in a single film: Bros" (Dockterman 2023). These stats reveal how important it is for people in dominant identities to seek out windows intentionally. In the same way that you might pause when you are experiencing a *moving moment*, you might also pause when you notice that you're experiencing a window, especially for the first time. We recommend allowing these initial window experiences to lead you to explore more "own voices" content centering this identity (see "Own Voices" box on p. 26 for more information on this topic).

Sometimes window experiences can feel uncomfortable. When you notice this happening, it can be helpful to pause and interrogate what's causing these emotions to surface. Are you unfamiliar with the cultural references being used, so you feel a bit like an outsider? This might be new for you, depending on your identity and lived experience. Sometimes this discomfort can inspire curiosity and sometimes it can cause us to shut down or dismiss the movie, song, show, or book. In her book *Once I Was You: A Memoir*, Maria Hinojosa (2020) writes about starring in *Zoot Suit*, the first Chicano play on Broadway in 1979. The show played weekly to sold-out audiences in Los Angeles but in New York City, the *New York Times* panned the production and it closed after just a few shows. Hinojosa initially blamed herself but it turned out that not a single reviewer understood the cultural references or significance of the show. This story underscores the importance of pausing to consider whether we are rejecting content because it is not worthy of our attention or because it was simply an unfamiliar window. Being able to discern between the two can help us expand our worldview and continue to pursue "window" content in our lives.

Window Experience

One of my most powerful window experiences happened in the first few weeks of my first year of college. I was a young, white, suburban girl eager to dive into all the cultural offerings posted on flyers at the student center. Along with several of my dorm-mates, I attended a late-night Stepping performance and from the very first moment I was transfixed. The synchronicity itself was some kind of miracle. The power and the energy in the room were overwhelming. How had I never known about this art form? As it was only weeks into the new school year, it dawned on me that these women had arrived on campus carrying this cultural knowledge with them.

In that moment, I was just starting to understand something that is much clearer to me now. I had been surrounded by mirrors for practically my entire life: the teachers I had in school, the characters I read in books, the characters on popular television shows, and the leaders and heroes promulgated in textbooks and stories. I had virtually never experienced being on the margins because my world had always been reflected back to me. Suddenly, here I was experiencing a window I didn't even know existed. It wasn't an instant aha!—but it was the beginning of a long journey to understanding all the ways I needed to *catch up*, an idea Ta-Nehisi Coates spoke about in 2017 at the Chicago Humanities Festival:

> *If you're Black in this world, and you are gonna become educated on what is considered mainstream art in this world, mainstream traditions, nobody slows down for you. Nobody is gonna hold your hand and explain* The Brady Bunch *to you. Nobody's gonna do that. Catch up. Catch up. Some people live like this. I know it's not what's around you, but some people live like that. Catch up. And that's just how it is. You gotta be bilingual. You gotta figure it out. (Coates 2017)*

Mirrors can be affirming, especially when they reflect a part of your identity that hasn't often been represented thoughtfully—or at all. These experiences can feel rewarding, uplifting, and empowering. Even though a mirror might reflect historical trauma and pain, it can still be affirming to feel seen in a way that is honest and authentic, especially when those stories are thoughtfully told. You might also find while watching a film about a family whose identity differs from your own that there is a dynamic that feels familiar. Maybe the mother–daughter relationship is similar to yours or the small-town setting reminds you of your own hometown. These mirror moments are often unexpected and can connect people across identities.

Although mirrors can be affirming, they can also challenge us to recognize aspects of our identities that we might not have otherwise paused to consider. For example, when Veronica watched *Mean Girls* for the first time she noticed all the insidious ways "mean girl" culture could seep into everyday life. Rebecca had a similar experience watching *Wicked* when she had the overwhelming feeling that she never wanted to be the kind of blonde that Glinda was, acting entitled to all kinds of unearned perks and popularity! These kinds of mirrors often challenge us to confront aspects of our identities and experiences that can be linked with privilege, status, or dominant culture. They can serve as little warning signs—helping us to make internal shifts and pay better attention to what's happening around us.

VERONICA

Mirror Experience

As a biracial (Black and Mexican American) woman from the South who navigated multiple socioeconomic spaces growing up, I've never seen a family that looks or acts quite like mine on TV. I've rarely read a book whose protagonist was navigating a world that felt familiar to me and I've never seen a movie plot that felt like it was pulled right from my childhood. As is likely common for many people who house historically marginalized identities, I grew up loving stories in spite of the lack of representation they offered me. I just always did the work of adapting, of attempting a sort of cultural transposition to empathize and relate. I became so fluent doing this that sometimes I didn't even notice how outside of my experience most of these stories were. And, if I'm being honest, I usually sought stories, especially those found in books, specifically for their power to help me explore, to travel, to learn, to experience the world through someone else's eyes. In other words, I actually loved consuming stories as windows. But I also didn't know what I was missing. I'm not sure at what age it occurred to me that some people, many people, were experiencing not only the enrichment of windows but also the joy of mirrors.

I remember the first time I caught glimpses of my own creative ambition, relentless optimism, and family culture in the characters of Betty Suarez (*Ugly Betty*) and Janine Teagues (*Abbott Elementary*). These weren't perfect reflections, but they were joyful glimpses. Although neither were particularly serious stories, they mattered deeply to me. I continued to intentionally seek out mirrors as an adult, and after years of experiencing the hope, beauty, and introspection they had to offer, I wondered why my teachers had never assigned James Baldwin and Toni Morrison alongside *The Great Gatsby* and *Catcher in the Rye*. As the media landscape, publishing industry, and (at least some) high school reading lists began the long overdue work of "catching up" (see "Rebecca's Window Experience" to unpack this concept), the potential grew for even more glimpses that could reflect a bit of me back at myself. Only every mirror I encountered felt like it wasn't merely reflecting me back but also reflecting back the women in my family who came before me—whose imaginations never graced the pages of a great novel, whose voices never sung out from a Broadway stage, whose lives, as gripping and full of triumph and humor and sadness and joy as they were, had never been written down on a page to be filmed, beautifully lit, and set to a moving score. Every time I experience a mirror moment that feels genuine, even just a glimpse, I think of those women still.

Before searching for windows and mirrors in your curriculum or classroom library, we encourage you to reflect on the window and mirror experiences in your life. Depending on where you are in your journey of exploring identity and fostering belonging, starting with your own self-growth might feel like surprising or familiar advice. But no matter where you are, we encourage you to devote time to learning for self-growth.

Sometimes what you watch, listen to, or read won't perfectly resonate as a window or mirror perhaps because most of the time art is not created to be a learning resource. Works of art are created on their own terms, sometimes for the simple purpose of just existing in the world. But that doesn't make them any less ripe for meaning making, especially if you know how to approach them.

Often we discover window or mirror *moments* within a work of art. Freeing ourselves to think about smaller windows and mirror moments within a work of art leaves room for nuance and complexity. It makes it possible to share what resonates and what we are learning without the piece as a whole feeling like a "perfect" window or mirror.

Artful Identity Maps

One way we can dive deeper into exploring our own identities is by tapping into the potential of identity maps. Many of us begin the year getting to know our students through some form of identity map, heart map, or activity that allows students to share their story and important aspects of their identity. See Chapter 2 for a wide range of artful possibilities for doing this work with children—this chapter is about doing the work ourselves and with our colleagues.

Like us, maybe you have done quite a bit of identity mapping over the years. Or maybe this will be your first time. Either way, approaching each identity map exercise with a "beginner's brain," allows us to stay open to exploring different aspects of ourselves and to getting in touch with what feels most present or activated in that particular moment.

VERONICA

Feeling *Muy* Excited About Identity Maps (Why We Added a Twist!)

As a Diversity, Equity, Inclusion, and Belonging (DEIB) practitioner, I've created more identity maps than you can imagine. At one point in my career I participated in three different workshops within one week that all began with the prompt to make an identity map. On one hand, the frequency with which I found myself writing my name in a circle and adding around it Black, Latina, Woman—all these different identifiers—made total sense to me, given my role. Understanding the ways in which our identities impact our roles as educators or people who support educators really begins with understanding ourselves. On the other hand, by the third identity map that week I had stopped using the time to reflect. As I wrote my name in the middle of the paper, I realized that what I was feeling was (and I hate to admit this) a bit bored.

I decided to give myself a little challenge: I would think of some fun quotes to add to each of my identifiers. Instead of writing Black/Latina, I wrote "Me siento muy . . . excited!" which, as fellow fangirls will know, is a quote from the iconic film *Selena* when she finds herself on tour in Mexico and is trying to get by on her Chicana Spanglish. Instead of writing where I'm from, I copied a line from one of Beyoncé's songs about being from Houston, Texas. What was at first a fun time-filler to keep me from feeling like a bad student quickly became a new way to explore my identity. Each quote offered me a chance to tell a bit more of my story. And as we often remind our students, if you had fun writing it your audience will likely have more fun too. This one experience led to a meaningful and humorous exchange about identity with my group. It also facilitated a real paradigm shift for me: from that moment on, I decided to treat each identity map experience as an opportunity to explore myself in some new way. And this is how I came up with the identity map with a twist!

Identity maps teach us that our journey with self never ends. It's ongoing. It's iterative. It's a lifelong practice. In the same way that your student makeup—their identities and experiences—create new classroom dynamics each year, where *you* are in *your* identity development adds to that dynamic as well. Our students are new each year, but so are we. Much like a favorite book, you can revisit your own identity story at any point and discover something new and interesting to reflect on or think about. You might notice how parts of your identity feel more present at certain times than others or that you're growing into a deeper awareness about who you are and what has influenced your path. Fresh ideas sprout up generation after generation. This ever-evolving social context will continue to bring to light new ways of thinking about your relationship to race, gender, ability, and the world around you. Next time you are invited to make an identity map, embrace the opportunity with an open mind!

LEARNING FOR SELF-GROWTH

Five Identity Maps with a Twist!

The next time you find yourself making an identity map try one of these artful ideas:

1. **Quote Wall:** Use quotes and lyrics to represent your unique identifiers.

2. **Food Story:** Everyone loves food! Add a delicious spin by picking a few foods that tell your story. You might try thinking about foods that represent places important to you, special people in your life, or foods unique to different parts of your identity.

3. **Poem:** Add a poem to your identity map! Try using the starter "I am," or even, "They call me" (get inspired by Charles R. Smith Jr.'s poem "Allow Me to Introduce Myself!" [2018], or "I'm From" by Gary R. Gray Jr. [2023]) to expand on the different aspects of your identity.

4. **Scrapbook Style:** Try incorporating photos and magazine clippings to create a scrapbook or collage-style identity map. Add captions to your visuals to share a bit of your story.

5. **Likes and Loves:** Try theming your whole identity map with something you're really into (movies, hip-hop, musicals, pop culture, decades, fashion, sports, and so on.).

Make It Visual: You can make any of these identity maps visual by adding your own drawings, symbols, illustrations, photos, and captions!

THE ARTFUL APPROACH TO EXPLORING IDENTITY AND FOSTERING BELONGING

Food Story: Sample Identity Map

Breakfast tacos: Quintessential Tejano food. Must be foil-wrapped. Must come with salsita. Must be eaten while hot to be appreciated fully.

Queso: This luscious dip made with chiles is pure Texas gold. Depending on the group I'm with, I might order this by codeswitching to the Spanish pronunciation or I might just pronounce it as many Tejanos do: "kay-so" as in rhymes with "say so." Similar to the thick tortillas de harina used in many breakfast tacos, queso is another hybrid borderlands food that I grew up loving.

Mac and cheese: Good baked mac and cheese is a treasured tradition for many Black southern families. We're not big turkey people in my family (is anyone, really?) so some years we have skipped the turkey but we have never skipped the true highlight in my eyes, the backup singer doing all the work of a lead, the star of any "sidesgiving," mac and cheese. Note: As the only vegetarian/pescatarian in my very carnivore family, I take any opportunity I can to sprinkle in propaganda for the sidesgiving movement.

Sweet Potato Pie: My mom's sweet potato pie is rich. It's velvety. It's coziness in every bite. (Another note: If you didn't grow up in a Southern family, you might not be aware of the annual pumpkin vs. sweet potato discourse that unfolds in our households around the winter holidays. I try to stay bipartisan, but would like the record to show that I side with my mom, always.)

Bluebell (Homemade Vanilla) ice cream: Nothing tastes more like my childhood in Texas than homemade vanilla ice cream. It is the saving grace for scorching summers (on especially hot nights my grandaddy liked to blend his into a milkshake!) and it is still the first treat I go searching for when I'm visiting family in Houston.

Coffee: Sipping a morning coffee quickly became one of my favorite pregame rituals when I first started teaching. My Gilmoresque quest for coffee was often more theater than reality though. Sure, the

LEARNING FOR SELF-GROWTH

caffeine boost made it easier to meet the kids at their energy levels, but it was actually the ritual of it all—the scent, the warmth, and the coffee chats with colleagues that fueled my mornings.

REBECCA

Food Story: Sample Identity Map

Molasses cookies: The family cookie recipe created by my grandmommy that is the perfect combination of sweet and spice. We eat them every year at our family reunion and think of her.

Chicken and rice casserole: My ultimate comfort food. Mom made one every week of my childhood, putting all the leftovers (chicken, vegetable bits) into that rectangular dish to create a cheesy (although some might say bland) midwestern masterpiece.

Pizza: If I had to choose, pizza is definitely my favorite food. I frequent several spots around New York City where I can grab a slice for a late-night snack or quick nourishment on the go. And, it's the best Friday night family meal. Pizza Shabbat is a family fave!

Cherries: I was born in Michigan and both sets of grandparents lived up north in the Cherry Capital of the World. Nothing tastes more like summer than a fresh cherry plucked off the tree.

Throat Coat tea: A miracle worker for singers everywhere. When I am preparing for a concert or a performance, I live on this tea. These tea bags always pop up everywhere—in my purse, in binders of music, or in pockets of clothes.

Latkes: The highlight of Chanukah! We make them from scratch every year (well, my husband and kids do) but we have a few Trader Joe's packages on hand because honestly, they're just as good (and I'm a terrible cook!).

Likes and Loves: Five Female Leads

Elphaba: Just a green girl trying to defy gravity (and cast some spells on the patriarchy along the way). *First played by Idina Menzel in the Broadway musical* Wicked.

Janine Teagues: Young Black teacher with relentless optimism and a quirky wardrobe. *Played by Quinta Brunson in the TV show* Abbott Elementary.

Christine McPherson aka Lady Bird: An artist living in a small-town reality with big city dreams. Desperately seeking fellow dreamers and a bit of drama in her own little corner of the world. *Played by Saoirse Ronan in the film* Lady Bird.

Betty Suarez: Aspiring Mexican American writer who holds her family close as she navigates the fashion world in hilarious ways. *Played by America Ferrera in* Ugly Betty.

Verona: Black/multiracial thirtysomething in an interracial relationship trying to make sense of her past and forge a new path with her partner. *Played by Maya Rudolph in* Away We Go.

Likes and Loves: Musical Numbers

"For Good" from *Wicked*: Anyone who knows me knows how much I treasure my girlfriends and this song is an anthem about friendship and the impact our dearest friends have on our lives.

"To Life" from *Fiddler on the Roof*: I love this song that celebrates Jewish traditions and the phrase *L'Chaim*, which we always say before toasting any special occasion!

LEARNING FOR SELF-GROWTH

"My House" from *Matilda*: This is Miss Honey's song in the musical *Matilda*, and as a teacher, I can't help but identify with Miss Honey. She's the teacher I always wished I could be. When she sings about hanging the picture of her student's work on her walls and being set free by reading, I feel so connected to her.

"Moments in the Woods" from *Into the Woods*: This song is a fan favorite for legions of musical theater devotees, including me. I love how flummoxed the Baker's Wife is, how she becomes swept up in the fantasy of a different life. Throughout the song she wishes life could be more "both/and" instead of "either/or," which speaks to me as someone who wants to be both an educator and an artist and is often struggling to find the balance.

"Everything Changes" from *Waitress*: I've never heard a song that captures the before and after experience of becoming a mother the way this one does. As a mother of twins, I remember how much everything changed once they arrived.

Identity Maps: Always Seeking, Always Learning

When I first began creating identity maps I felt a bit of pressure to get my identity map *right*. I wanted to be sure to name and claim all the things about my identity that felt relevant and honest but also sound interesting, or even a little unique. I felt the impulse to make sure everyone understood I was aware of my privilege but to do it in a way that wasn't cringey. I noticed that I was treating this exercise as a bit of a performance, which made it impossible for me to be vulnerable enough to gain new learning or insight. When Veronica and I began reflecting on how to design more artful identity maps, my relationship to this work opened up and I felt eager to explore, create, and reflect in new ways. Recently, we were co-leading a workshop with teachers using a simple identity map, but I found myself turning each identifier into a line of poetry, repeating the prompt "I am . . . I always . . ."

> I am a teacher. I am always learning and questioning
>
> I am a reader. I am always seeking out recommendations
>
> I am a mother. I am always worried
>
> I am a white woman. I am always pausing to reflect or unlearn
>
> I am a singer. I am always belting out musicals in my car
>
> I am housed and employed. I am seeking out ways to understand and support the housing crisis around me
>
> I am Jewish. I am always seeking meaning out of the yearly rituals and traditions, especially those related to Tikun Olam (repair the world).

In my "I am . . . I always" poem I name aspects about my identity that relate to hobbies and interests but I also explicitly name other identifiers related to race, gender, culture, and privilege. Basically, I am trying to model how to express multiple dimensions of myself without skirting around the dominant aspects of my identity. One thing this exercise taught me is that I don't have to choose between the parts of me that I love to talk about and the parts that feel more challenging—identity maps provide an opportunity to make space for both. You might also notice that I used the "I am . . . I always" framework for every line of the poem except one, which reflects the importance of flexibility. I really liked the rhythm of "I am . . . I always" but it didn't ring true to say I am *always* seeking out ways to understand and support the housing crisis around me but I still wanted to include that part of my identity as part of the poem.

It's OK if not all these identity maps feel like a good fit. There are lots of ways to think about identity and each identity map you create can serve a new purpose. What's important to remember is that these exercises are meant to support meaningful conversation and introspection about who we are. They help us reflect together with our grade-level teams, our colleagues, and anyone with whom we're in community.

What's Everyone Watching? Why Pop Culture Matters

When you return to campus after a long weekend, what are you most excited to talk about with your team? For us, our Monday morning meetings were often catch-up sessions about what we had just watched, read, or listened to. Sometimes, we would feel a little guilty not diving into our agenda right away but as it turned out, those seemingly frivolous chats were an essential part of our work together. We would start by recapping the latest episode of *The White Lotus* but then find ourselves engaged in deeper dialogue about the fluidity and complexity of privilege and status and all the ways that we experience these dynamics in our own lives. What might have started as typical *watercooler* conversation grew into something far more significant. As it turns out, pop culture can be a powerful starting point for a more meaningful exchange about how our identities impact the way we interpret the world or even the latest hit show.

We developed the following check-in questions to help you find organic, authentic (and fun!) ways to reflect on identity and connect as a team (see Figure 1–1). When we ask each other these questions, inevitably we end up laughing. We also end up learning more about each other even after working together for years. We hope these elevated watercooler questions help you to explore identity and connect with the people around you. Note: We've shared some examples in cases where the questions might feel less intuitive.

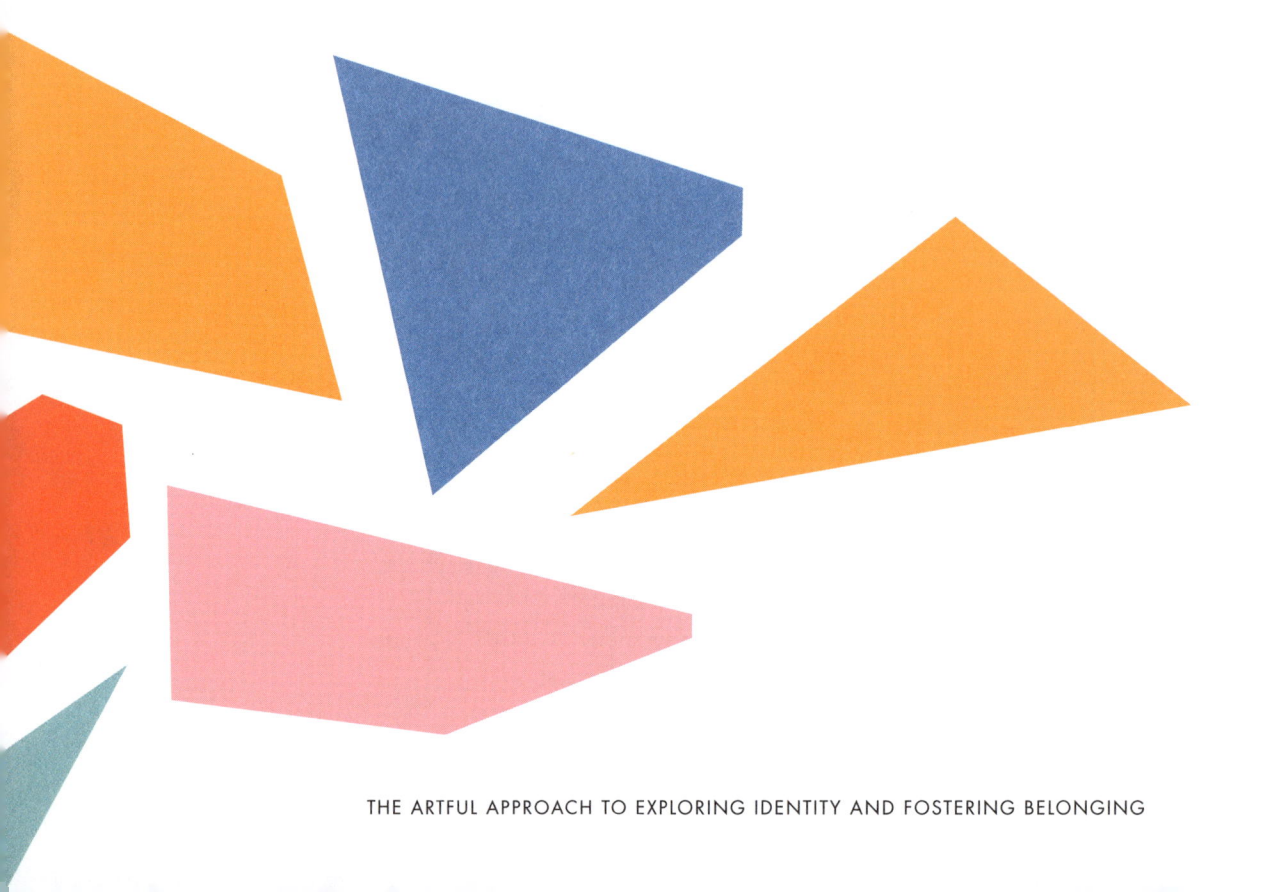

THE ARTFUL APPROACH TO EXPLORING IDENTITY AND FOSTERING BELONGING

Elevated *Watercooler* Conversation Starters

> How to use pop culture moments and the excitement of the zeitgeist to explore identity and connect with your friends, teams, and colleagues.

Quick Check-In *Ideal for openings and closings, team huddles, and sharing aloud with larger groups.*	**Dig a Little Deeper** *Great for when you have more time, a smaller group, or when you're intentionally trying to deepen connections within a team.*
If you could invite any living artist (musician, writer, poet, filmmaker, playwright) to be your sub or thought partner in the room today who would that be?	What's one reason you chose this artist? You might think about their unique experience, identity, and background, or a trait, talent, skill, or value they hold that's important to you.
What's your current anthem?	What's your personal connection to this song or artist? When do you blast your anthem (running, dance party, getting ready to teach)?
What was your last binge-watch?	What drew you to this show? Did the world or any of the characters feel familiar or new? What made you keep watching? If you were in the writer's room, what might you add or change?
Who would you want to play you in your biopic? Or who would you choose to write your story?	What about this artist (actor or director/screenwriter) resonates with you? What about your story makes you feel like this artist would do it justice?

Rebecca: The finale song from the Broadway musical *Jagged Little Pill*, "You Learn."

Veronica: I'm going Broadway, too! "Opening Doors" by the new cast of *Merrily We Roll Along*.

Figure 1-1 *continues*

LEARNING FOR SELF-GROWTH

Quick Check-In	Dig a Little Deeper
Who is a character from a book that you adore or would want to be friends with or get to know over coffee?	Why would they make a good friend to you personally? What would you connect over?
What is your foregiveness genre?*	How did you get into this genre? What's the forgiveness part for you?
What's a book or story you loved as a child?	What does it remind you of (a person, a place, a time in your life)? Does it still hold a special place in your heart?

Rebecca: Murder mysteries. I can't get enough of the *Dateline* podcast (and Keith Morrison's dramatic voice-overs), which is my go-to for running!

Veronica: Costume dramas and dramedies. Give me a plumed hat, a silk cape, and snippy dialogue any day. A murder afoot? All the better! Though I was horrified to find out that Rebecca runs (through the WOODS!) listening to murder podcasts. I'm literally scared for her every time and sometimes will ask her to text me when she makes it back!

*In lieu of *guilty pleasures*, we prefer author and cultural critic Linda Holmes' term *forgiveness genre* (2021). As she says, "a lot of us have . . . a forgiveness genre . . . where you show me this kind of movie, and I'm very forgiving. It doesn't mean I don't know the difference between if it's good or not good. But like, I am fairly forgiving. For some people, those are, like, horror–certain kinds of horror movies. For some people, there are certain kinds of monster movies. For some people, there are certain kinds of romantic comedies."

THE ARTFUL APPROACH TO EXPLORING IDENTITY AND FOSTERING BELONGING

Quick Check-In	Dig a Little Deeper	
What's a quote, lyric, or catchphrase so good you want to frame it or cross-stitch on a pillow? Maybe something unexpected you would never find in a store!	What about this quote speaks to you? When do you return to that quote as a reminder or pick-me-up? Do you think anyone would be surprised to see this quote framed or on a pillow?	
What's the last documentary you watched (or maybe something you read or listened to) that surprised you or revealed some interesting truth? *If you cannot speak from the I-perspective and the content contains trauma, be mindful of how you share.*	What was the headline? What were some of the *moving moments* for you? What felt familiar and what was new? What affirmed, challenged, or deepened your understanding of the experiences and identities centered in the piece?	
What's a cultural moment (a dance craze or style, fashion trend, movie genre, or gadget) that you wish would have a comeback?	What do you remember about this moment? How did this fad play out in your own life? Why was this cultural moment important to you?	**Rebecca**: Leg warmers and parachute pants, because I never got it right in childhood. **Veronica**: Letters in the mail from friends! Scented stickers on the envelope and puff paint doodles still light up my 90s kid heart!
If you received a surprise grant, what dream museum exhibit would you fund?	Why does the world need this exhibit? Who would you invite to the opening?	**Rebecca**: Singing the Tradition: Women in Klezmer Music **Veronica**: From the Screen to the Stage: A History of Black Costume Designers

(Handle with Care)

Figure 1-1

LEARNING FOR SELF-GROWTH

Five 5-Second Check-Ins!

Teachers are always on the go. Sometimes we don't even have time for a watercooler conversation, but it's still important for us to build community together. No matter how pressed we are for time, starting with a check-in matters. And, it's something that practically all artists do: It's the huddle before a show. It's the circle-up before the curtain call. It's all the little rituals—the silly, the superstitious, the meaningful—that provide an opportunity for us to check in with ourselves and connect with each other.

Here are five 5-second check-ins that you can use to bring the group together, especially when time is of the essence:

1. **Group stretch:** *Stretch up to the sky and outward. Reach for the sun, reach for each other, and remember that we're all in this together.*

2. **Affirmation:** *Find a person to make eye contact with around the circle and then say, "You got this!"* This check-in can work by inviting the group to turn to a partner, go all at the same time, or go around the circle and say any fun affirmation that works for the team.

3. **Set the vibe:** *Let's fill the space with all good vibes! Take a few seconds to think of what you want to "add to the vibe" and then popcorn your ideas (jazzy music, bubbly drinks, golden hour, good conversation, cozy fireplace, crisp mornings and the smell of coffee, citrus scents, warm tea, sharing stories, celebrating each other).*

4. **Five seconds of breathing:** *Let's all take one collective breath in and out as we get ready to begin today. And as we're breathing, let's give ourselves a little positive phrase or kind word (either out loud or silently)—whatever is useful to you in this moment.* As a facilitator, you might guide this by echoing the words of a thought leader or artist you want to spotlight to set the tone: *Let's breathe in the words of ____ who said ____.*

5. **Team catchphrase:** *on 3 . . . 1, 2, 3, (insert catchphrase here).* Veronica's DEIB teammates used to say, "All the things," as a way to acknowledge the workload of the day and give themselves grace for trying to manage so many things at once. That team might check in before a presentation by saying "1, 2, 3: All the things!"

A Beyoncé Moment: Two Different Pop Culture Experiences

It can be revelatory to realize that you experienced a pop culture moment entirely differently from a colleague. This applies to interactions with each other as well. As Geoffrey Cohen (2022) writes in *Belonging: The Science of Creating Connection and Bridging Divides,* "Indeed, it can be jarring to realize that some encounter we had was experienced altogether differently by another person." He reminds us that "we bring the past with us. Our memories and expectations [shape] the way we interpret new situations . . . We all have conditioning from life experiences that molds the way we see situations, which can make even ordinary situations different for the different people in them" (22).

The best way for us to illustrate how differently we each experience certain works of art and the world is with a Beyoncé moment. (*Dramatic Pause.*) In 2016, Beyoncé made the world stop when she dropped "Formation," the first single from her album *Lemonade*. This is how each of us experienced that moment.

VERONICA

I probably have a particularly strong sense of pride in Beyoncé. Not only is she unapologetically Black and undeniably woman, but she is also, though some might not realize, quintessentially Houston. She sounds like Houston. She moves like Houston. For me, so much of her art is inextricably linked to the world I knew growing up in Houston: a world full of baby hairs, creole food, and hot sauce. Given this personal connection, the first time I watched the "Formation" music video and heard those lyrics, that voice, that beat, I knew that I was witnessing something seismic. Beyoncé's artistry had always been, in my mind, steeped in Black southern culture, only now the subtext had become text—and just in time as the world was watching. Taking this moment, the day before the Super Bowl, and using it not for a (well-earned) victory lap, but to lift up the voices of the Black South was like a hug for my soul. Sharing the mic with bounce musician Big Freedia and bringing to the stage dancers who could freely shake their braids and kinks to every beat made this moment even more iconic.

VERONICA

A few months later, Beyoncé would release the full *Lemonade* album, in all its grandma-quoting, Serena-Williams-dancing glory. This was a celebration of Black southern womanhood, of "Souf with an F" (Ngugi 2016) as one reviewer named it—and the Houstonian in me couldn't get enough.

REBECCA

While my response wasn't quite as dramatic as the SNL (2016) sketch, which hilariously calls this moment a day "white people never saw coming," I definitely was aware that this groundbreaking work of art was way outside of my experience. First of all, I wasn't as tuned into it given my preoccupation with music that is more indie folk and Broadway than pop, and I had just moved to California with four-year-old twins so I was pretty much not caught up on anything. But I was aware that the world was having a huge cultural moment that was decidedly not about, for, or meant for me. Watching "Formation" was mesmerizing, yet there were so many references and images that I couldn't speak to or fully understand. I loved the music on the album but there was so much I was missing. I have to admit, after *Lemonade* dropped, I became much more attuned to Beyoncé's songs and albums, and it inspired me to learn more about what was behind some of these artistic choices to better understand her as an artist. And now that she is a staple of our dance party playlist at home, I have even more appreciation for her brilliant artistry and legendary status. Though try as I might, I'll never keep up with those key changes in "Love on Top."

The way in which we each responded to this major cultural moment reveals just how unique each person's experience with art, and thus the classroom and the world, can be. Maybe one of our stories resonated with you or maybe you had an entirely different Beyoncé moment of your own. Depending on your identity, you might have noticed new phrases or ideas in either of our reactions to the album drop. You might have found yourself searching for, what the podcast *Code Switch* (NPR 2016) coined, the *explanatory comma*, which is basically a way of providing cultural context for your audience. For example, depending on your experiences in the world you might not have a cultural reference for baby hairs or indie folk. Noticing when you need an explanatory comma, especially for identities and cultures that have been historically marginalized, can help guide where to seek out more windows in the content you consume.

To reiterate, *indeed, it can be jarring to realize that some encounter we had was experienced altogether differently by another person.* This is the power of windows and mirrors. Growing our awareness around this concept and realizing that we each bring our own identities to these moments can help us to welcome new ways of being so that we can better connect with each other. What's a pop culture moment that you couldn't stop thinking about or that impacted you in some significant way?

If you are reading this book you are likely eager to incorporate arts-based modalities into your curriculum or into your efforts to make your community more inclusive. It's tempting to jump in immediately to doing this work with students. But we encourage you to take time to explore just for you. We encourage you to explore resources that are not only informative, but perhaps musical, cinematic, poetic, colorful—stories that, "once you've heard them, won't let you return to what you thought before" (Miranda 2019).

Finally, we encourage you to think about topics that will broaden your horizons and inspire you to look inward and reflect. The Learning for Self-Growth Artfully chart (see OR 1–1 in the Online Resources) can help guide you. In our example (see Figure 1–2), we started with the topic "Indigenous music" because both of us love music and it's a history we are both learning more about. Our interest in music provided an entry point into Indigenous history. Learning for self-growth should not feel like a chore! Think of this process as a low-stakes, often fun or interesting, opportunity to explore a mix of what you're already into and what you'd like to learn more about.

> **The Explanatory Comma**
>
> On an episode of the NPR podcast *Code Switch* (2016), the hosts introduced the idea of an explanatory comma by exploring the question, "How much cultural context should you have to provide when talking about race and culture?" We think of the explanatory comma as a shorthand for providing cultural context. For example: Beyoncé shared the mic with Big Freedia, (explanatory comma) → a gay music icon and pioneer of bounce music, (explanatory comma) → a subgenre of rap invented in New Orleans. The explanatory comma can be an act of generosity because it's a way of helping you, as Ta-Nehisi Coates (2017) would say, "catch up."

Learning for Self-Growth Artfully

My Learning for Self-Growth topic is: Indigenous music in the United States

I want to learn more about this topic because I'm curious about:
- Connections between the music I love and the music that comes out of Indigenous tradition.
- Contemporary Indigenous artists—I was mostly taught about Indigenous people as living and existing only in the past and I want to disrupt that narrative.

A personal connection I might have to this topic (some possible connections might be identity, interest, and shared history or culture):
- I love music and am interested in the role of music in community building.

Phase	**Reflecting:** Reflecting on your watchlists, playlists, and the books on your nightstand.	**Exploring:** Seeking out media intentionally. Brainstorming a list of go-to content sources, thought leaders, and contemporary voices.
Question	What stories and whose voices have shaped my understanding of this topic so far?	Where can I find thought leaders and artists connected to this topic? (Think: directors, journalists, podcasters, authors, historians)
My Response	No specific stories come to mind. My sense of Indigenous music stems from generalized images and content.	• Google "Indigenous musicians" • Search YouTube for contemporary Indigenous songs • Search for Indigenous culture podcast • Look for Indigenous music documentaries
Question	Does this topic feel familiar or fresh and new to me?	How can I continue to return to these sources that are new to me?
My Response	Mostly fresh and new. As a musician, I'm familiar with the world of music, but not with Indigenous musical traditions or specific artists.	I plan to bookmark my faves! I'm subscribing to Lyla June's website.

Figure 1-2

After exploring these resources, I'll reflect using the prompts and questions below.*

My Resources

After reflecting and exploring, I've chosen these resources to learn for self-growth:
- *Rumble* documentary (2017)
- Lyla June music videos and TED talk (2022)
- Great Big Story "How a First Nations Musician Is Creating 'Pow Wow Techno'" [short video] (2022)
- Soundtrack to *Reservation Dogs* (2021)
- "Wahzhazhe (A Song for My People)" by Osage Tribal Singers (2023)

Phase	**Noticing:** *Developing a critical lens for media consumption. Paying attention to the voices, characters, and identities that are centered or missing.*	**Growth:** *Applying this learning to your own experience, understanding, and way of showing up in the world. This might include: shifting language, rethinking assumptions, listening more, discerning between when to pause and hold back or use your voice to speak up, and reflecting continuously.*
Question	**Whose voices are being centered in this content? Is it authored by "own voices" meaning someone who can speak from the I-perspective for the identity centered?**	**How has this story helped me shift or grow my thinking around myself, my positionality, and the topic?**
My Response	*I'm trying to seek out art that lifts up Indigenous voices (like Lyla June and the Osage Tribal Singers).*	*The film helped me see, and really hear, music that I thought I knew in a completely new way. I never realized that so many of the rhythms and beats that flowed through music everywhere were shaped by Indigenous culture and singing styles.*
Question	**Where am I noticing window or mirror moments? Where did I need an explanatory comment? Where am I noticing stereotypes?**	**What lingering thoughts and questions do I have now? What am I hoping to explore next?**
My Response	*As a singer, I saw myself in the moments of connection among the musicians. The culture at the center was all window for me.*	*Lingering thoughts: How else has Indigenous culture influenced our world?* *Next, I'm watching* Reservation Dogs! *I'm going to keep seeking out contemporary Indigenous voices.*

*****Note:** If you've already selected a shared read, watch, or listen for your team, just start with this page (Noticing and Growth) since you've already chosen a resource and topic to explore.

LEARNING FOR SELF-GROWTH

Binge TV and Picture Books: How to Deepen Our Noticing

We can consume content all day long, but developing a critical lens, especially around identity, requires deepening our noticing and paying closer attention to our own ability to discern the dynamics at play. As we become more intentional about the windows we're seeking, it's important to ask: *What might I be missing? How is my identity and experience informing my interpretation?* For example, you might have been one of the many people tuning into the HBO fantasy show *Game of Thrones* and wondering, "Why are there no Black people in this made-up world?" or you might have been distracted by all the dragons and never noticed. If *The Bachelor* is more your thing, however, you might have been one of the fans who wondered why it took twenty-five years for there to be a Black "Bachelor" on network television. For both of these examples, your experience with race likely informed which observations you made or questions you asked. Similarly, you might be a horror movie fan and depending on your gender identity, you may or may not groan at the screen every time there's a new movie without a female lead. Or, depending on your sexuality, you might be acutely aware of the fact that romantic comedies tend to center heterosexual couples.

We once invited an entire faculty of K–12 educators to watch a clip of *The White Lotus*, a wicked satire that explores wealth and status. We asked them to pay careful attention to what they were noticing using the following questions: What do you notice about body language and tone (any "coded language")? What do you notice about your own reactions and feelings toward different characters? What do you notice about the setting (especially considering its colonial and Indigenous context)?

Own Voices

When we use the term *own voices*, we are referring to any work of art created by someone who can speak from the I-perspective for the identity centered in that work.

It's important to note, however, that the label of "own voices" can also be complicated. For one, this label is broad. The group of changemakers known as We Need Diverse Books recommend the use of specific descriptions for authors and characters whenever possible (for example, "Korean American author," or "autistic protagonist") (Lavoie 2021). It can also be helpful to remember that content created by "own voices" is still worthy of critique and should never bear the burden of speaking for the experience of an identity in its entirety. Keeping all of this in mind, if a story centers an identity that has been historically marginalized, we recommend paying closer attention to who is telling it.

Before sharing out as a whole community we provided the following context to help make the connection between social identifiers and how that impacts what you notice:

- Depending on your identity and experience with **Gender** you might have noticed the way some genders take up more space or how the tone used in conversations differs by gender.

- Depending on your identity and experience with **Race**, you might have noticed how some characters pretend to be color-blind or how for some characters race is an obvious and ever-present factor.

- Depending on your identity and experience with **Class** or **Socioeconomic status**, you might have noticed the upstairs/downstairs dynamics at the resort or have laughed when certain wealthier characters describe having a job as limiting.

- Depending on your familiarity with **Intersectionality**, you might have noticed the ways in which multiple identifiers created unique challenges for certain characters, like Paula, who is navigating her access to a world of privilege as a guest of her friend's family and her identity as a young person of color.

Honing our noticing skills and realizing all the ways in which our identities impact our perceptions can lead us to new ways of seeing and understanding not only the stories we consume but also the world around us. When we think about what this looks like in practice, a little boy named Milo comes to mind. In Matt de la Peña (2021) and Christian Robinson's book *Milo Imagines the World*, readers follow Milo on a subway ride. We soon learn he is headed to visit his mom who is incarcerated—a story that was inspired by Christian Robinson's own life experience.

Like Christian, Milo is an artist, and on this subway ride, he notices the people around him and draws pictures of what he imagines their lives to be. He sees a boy in a suit and imagines him going home to a castle. He sees a whiskered man and imagines him going home to a lonely apartment full of rats and cats. He sees a bride and imagines her marrying a groom. Only, at the end of his ride, the boy in the suit gets off at the same stop as Milo. They're headed to the same place. Milo begins to question all his other imaginings. Maybe the whiskered man has a family at home. Maybe the bride is marrying a bride. Maybe there is more than one way to imagine each person's story and maybe, as the book jacket says, "you can't really know anyone's story just by looking at them."

While Christian Robinson's experience informs the story at the heart of *Milo*, Matt de la Peña is the author of the book. This partnership underscores the complexity of "own voices" and how essential it is to make space for nuance. Researching the relationship between Robinson and de la Peña gave us context for the collaboration and the history between these two artists. What we learned was that a deep trust exists between them. In an interview about their partnership, De la Peña shared how important it was for him to "figure out how to honor" Robinson's story (Colorin Colorado 2022). And Robinson shared that de la Peña's "writing gave me an appreciation for my own story" (Robinson 2021a).

The more you get into the practice of noticing with art, the more attuned your critical lens will become: you'll notice moments, characters, stories, and social dynamics in ways you never had before. Before we interpret, before we disrupt, before we launch into action, we start by noticing. And that work begins with ourselves. Taking a moment to pause and notice intentionally is just one small way we can continue learning for self-growth and begin to (re)imagine the world.

Tips for Learning for Self-Growth

1. **Explore what you are already into!** If your interest is in food or fashion, find windows and stories with that lens because you'll connect with it more deeply, and more consistently.

REBECCA

Exploring What You Are Already Into: Memoirs

I love memoirs and when a writer performs their own audiobook I usually choose to listen to it in their voice instead of reading the text. I can absorb even more about a person's identity by hearing their intonation and how they tell their story. Some standouts: *Memorial Drive* by Natasha Tretheway (2021), *The Light of the World* by Elizabeth Alexander (2016), *Between Two Kingdoms* by Suleika Jaouad (2021), *Somebody's Daughter* by Ashley Ford (2021), *Know My Name* by Chanel Miller (2020), *Crying in H Mart* by Michelle Zauner (2023), and finally, *Finding Me* by Viola Davis (2022), which is an absolute tour de force. Memoirs are a perfect way to combine what you're interested in (food, music, travel, pop culture) with authors who have identities outside of your own.

Exploring What You Are Already Into: Movie Night

As a child of the 90s, I grew up in the golden age of home video rental, so I love a good movie night. The browsing. The popcorn. The coziness of it all. And, of course, the discourse. One of my favorite things about movie night is the complex conversations that a good or even good-ish movie can spark. *How do we feel about that complicated character? What surprised us about the ending? What felt deeply familiar? What felt new?* As soon as the credits are rolling, I'm dying to ask all the things and know what everyone thought about it all. Maybe this is why seeing a movie together is such a popular first-date choice. It's such a low-stakes way to get to know someone and hear about their ideas and perspectives in nuanced ways that often stretch beyond the limitations of the social frameworks and political paradigms of the current moment. And because there are a seemingly infinite number of films to choose from, there are infinite post-film conversations to embark on, too.

So where do you start? Don't underestimate the joy of browsing as a group. My husband and I love to browse, or at least I love to browse and he doesn't (always) complain (too much). As we come across titles that interest us, we each make a case for a potential feature film. We might take turns sharing trailers in hopes that the other person will find them just as gripping or funny or intriguing as we did or we might just send vibes urging: *pick this one, pick this one*. After some subtle negotiating (or spirited debate), we press play. Soon we're deep in conversation. Sometimes we try to wrap our minds around how we could each have experienced the same movie in such entirely different ways (see the Beyoncé Break part of this chapter to unpack this phenomenon further). Wherever the conversation takes us, it's often revelatory and fascinating. And it often sparks a hunger for more knowledge or even leads to more research around the topic at the heart of the film.

Tip: Try Movie Night as a Team!

When I was on my first DEIB committee, we led our first year of professional development by exploring the concept of windows and mirrors. We were just beginning this work as a school, so I wanted to get people interested and engaged. I decided to launch a "Movie of the Month" with monthly titles that aligned with our DEIB themes as a sort of optional additional PD. We didn't watch the movies together, but we did watch the trailers. I would reveal our monthly pick by playing one new movie trailer at the first staff meeting of each month. Sometimes I paired the trailer with questions for reflection or a spotlight story for a cultural month. After the first few months, some teachers (and admin!) began finding me on campus to tell me that they had watched the month's movie (sometimes over break!) and what it had made them think or feel. Though we had technically never watched a full movie together, the stories and characters started to make their way into our conversations and professional learning. It was kind of like we were all experiencing movie night as a team.

2. **Pay attention to the moments when you need an "explanatory comma."** As you read, watch, and listen to more window content where you can't speak from the I-perspective, you may encounter references (styles, foods, places, traditions, and so on) that are unfamiliar to you. Take a moment to notice that confusion and explore further to uncover more information or context especially when the content centers identities that have been historically marginalized.

3. **Meet yourself where you are.** Remember that learning for self-growth and seeking out windows is a lifelong process. Once you come into an awareness about a particular issue you might feel a sense of urgency to learn all that you can. But you don't need to read all the books and see all the movies right away. You can give yourself time. Try to quiet your inner critic and notice your defensiveness. In a talk at the New York Public Library, Christian Robinson (2021b) shares the way he embraces mistakes! He says, "I also think it's really important to not be afraid to make mistakes. That is the big part of just being creative or . . . *just being a person* . . . And that's okay. We all make mistakes!" And finally, in the words of Brené Brown, "We're not here to **be** right. We're here to **get it right**. We're not here to be **knowers**, we're here to be learners. And that's the bottom line, to be better people" (Hempel 2021). We think these reminders are such a relief, because "having to be the 'knower' or always being right is heavy armor" (Brown 2020).

4. **Bite-size is key!** Quick podcasts, articles, and YouTube clips can be invaluable resources in an age where everything is calling for your attention. Maybe you haven't yet gotten around to reading Isabel Wilkerson's tome *The Warmth of Other Suns*, but there are plenty of podcast interviews with her that you can download for your commute! This is true for so many authors and contemporary books coming down the pike.

5. **Practice generous listening**. Pay attention to how you're listening and to whom you're listening. Is this an issue that feels familiar to you or new? It's especially important to seek out voices who can speak from the I-perspective when you're learning about something outside of your own experience. While you're in the learning phase be willing to listen a lot more than you talk. As Krista Tippett (2017) says, "Generous listening is powered by curiosity, a virtue we can invite and nurture in ourselves to render it instinctive. It involves a kind of vulnerability—a willingness to be surprised, to let go of assumptions and take in ambiguity" (29).

6. **Bookmark your faves**. When you find a voice that you trust, that resonates with you, has an impact on your intrapersonal growth, or stretches your thinking, try to find ways to stay connected to what they are offering (subscribing to newsletters, mailing lists, weekly columns,

YouTube channels). Those voices will often lead you to other voices that can grow your thinking as well. This is true for places as well (local theaters, bookstores, community centers, museums). These places offer curated resources that lend themselves to exploration and discovery.

CLOSING WITH A POEM

You might use this poem to launch your own year of learning for self-growth. Think: *What am I hoping to explore? What movies could I stream? What podcasts might I tune into to learn more about the world around me? What books will be my guiding light and inspiration?* Use the bold stems to get started in your own writing and feel free to mix and remix so it feels just right for you. This is a fun poem to share with a partner, team, or at a faculty meeting to connect with each other and share resources!

A Year of Learning for Self-Growth

This will be a year of *music, movies, and memoirs*

A year of checking in, *sharing binge-watches, current anthems, and forgiveness genres*

A year of taking in *own voices, journalists who lift up untold stories, and the world of kidlit*

This will be a year of *reading with a critical lens, watching with an open heart, and listening with a generous spirit*

A year of tuning into *CodeSwitch and Pop Culture Happy Hour*

A year of bookmarking the pages of *Maria Hinojosa, Viola Davis, Brené Brown, and Matt de la Peña*

A year of streaming *romcoms with queer leads, artful documentaries (like Homecoming and Rumble!), and movies that can inspire the richest movie night conversations*

A year of dancing to *Pow Wow Techno, Selena, and Big Freedia*

A year of noticing when *something is more window than mirror, when I might need an explanatory comma, or when I experience a moving moment*

A year of seeing myself in *the foods from my home state, the family traditions I keep alive, the female leads on the big screen*

This will be a year of *embracing mistakes, exchanging ideas, and taking time to catch up*

Of imagining a world where *we are always seeking, always learning*

Where *we can connect and share who we are*

Where *we can let loose and dance to Beyoncé*

Where *all of us have a story and all of our stories matter*

LEARNING FOR SELF-GROWTH

2

LAUNCHING THE YEAR ARTFULLY

The Power of Beginnings

> *Having a safe space to imagine and dream and (re)invent yourself is the first step to being happy and successful whatever road you choose to pursue.*
> —Ashley Bryan, *We Rise, We Resist, We Raise Our Voices*

For musicians, there's the Grammys. For designers, there's the Met Gala. And for teachers, there is nothing like the first day of school. We love the back-to-school vibes, the fresh braids and fades, the enormous backpacks they haven't grown into yet. And we love seeing our students in person for the first time. At the school where we met, one of our favorite back-to-school rituals was the weekly community gathering that would typically happen every Monday morning. This was a time for announcements, student spotlights, and birthday celebrations. Each week, students with birthdays would run up to the stage to be serenaded with "the birthday song."

One year, we decided to mix things up! Veronica had recently suggested that our school consider trying something new by singing the Stevie Wonder version of "Happy Birthday" that she had grown up hearing at so many birthday celebrations throughout her life. To this day, when one of her aunties calls on her birthday, she knows that when she picks up the phone, she'll be greeted with that iconic and immediately familiar, "Happy birthday to ya!" like a hug from home. She thought that this song, that many call a "beloved cultural artifact" (Harris 2016) of Black American identity, might be one simple, yet meaningful way to signal to many of our Black students and families that our community is just that—ours. This would be a place for us too, to be joyful, to be ourselves, to be valued, and to belong.

As Rebecca, with her musical background, invited the students to join in on the singing, people slowly started to find the rhythm, clap along, and by the end of the song the crowd was moving, the kindergartners were jumping and dancing, and there were smiles all across the courtyard. One of the Black parents pulled out her phone to take a video, occasionally looking around seemingly in awe that this moment was really happening, perhaps thinking, *especially in this predominantly white community*.

Week after week, this small shift for a big moment in our community brought so much joy to our Monday mornings. Although a birthday song might seem insignificant, this ritual carried considerable cultural weight. As the culminating event for our school's only weekly gatherings with the entire community, the birthday song was a ritual that had the attention of all—and before we changed it, it had likely been sung the same way for over forty years. The change did not go unnoticed. In the days following this new tradition there was a bit of buzz. Lots of students beamed with excitement as they anticipated the new anthem, some started singing the song in the hallways, and some asked us if we wrote it ourselves (we wish!). Of course we had introduced it as Stevie Wonder's birthday song, and even shared a bit of history around how he wrote the song to celebrate Dr. Martin Luther King Jr.'s birthday and advocate for that day to be honored as a national holiday, but we don't blame them for being distracted by all the fun.

After a month of celebrating birthdays with Stevie Wonder's version, we decided to introduce the song "Las Mañanitas," a gorgeous ballad made famous by Pedro Infante and later Vicente Fernández, and a traditional birthday song for many Mexican and Mexican American households. The first time we sang "Las Mañanitas" one grandma walked up to a teacher teary-eyed and shared how much that moment meant to her and how much she enjoyed singing that song with everyone at her grandson's school. All of this goes to show that one should never underestimate the power of windows and mirrors in music or the impact of a (seemingly simple) community ritual like singing "the birthday song."

IDENTITY WORK STARTS ON DAY ONE

While this chapter will provide tools, resources, and insights for planning cultural months across the year, identity work starts from the moment your students enter your classroom and, whether we are conscious of it or not, is integrated into every aspect of our teaching and our classroom environments. In fact, identity work can start even sooner than that: as you begin to set up your classroom, plan your first few lessons, and get ready to welcome a new group of families.

What Do We Mean by Identity?
Things That Make Us Unique

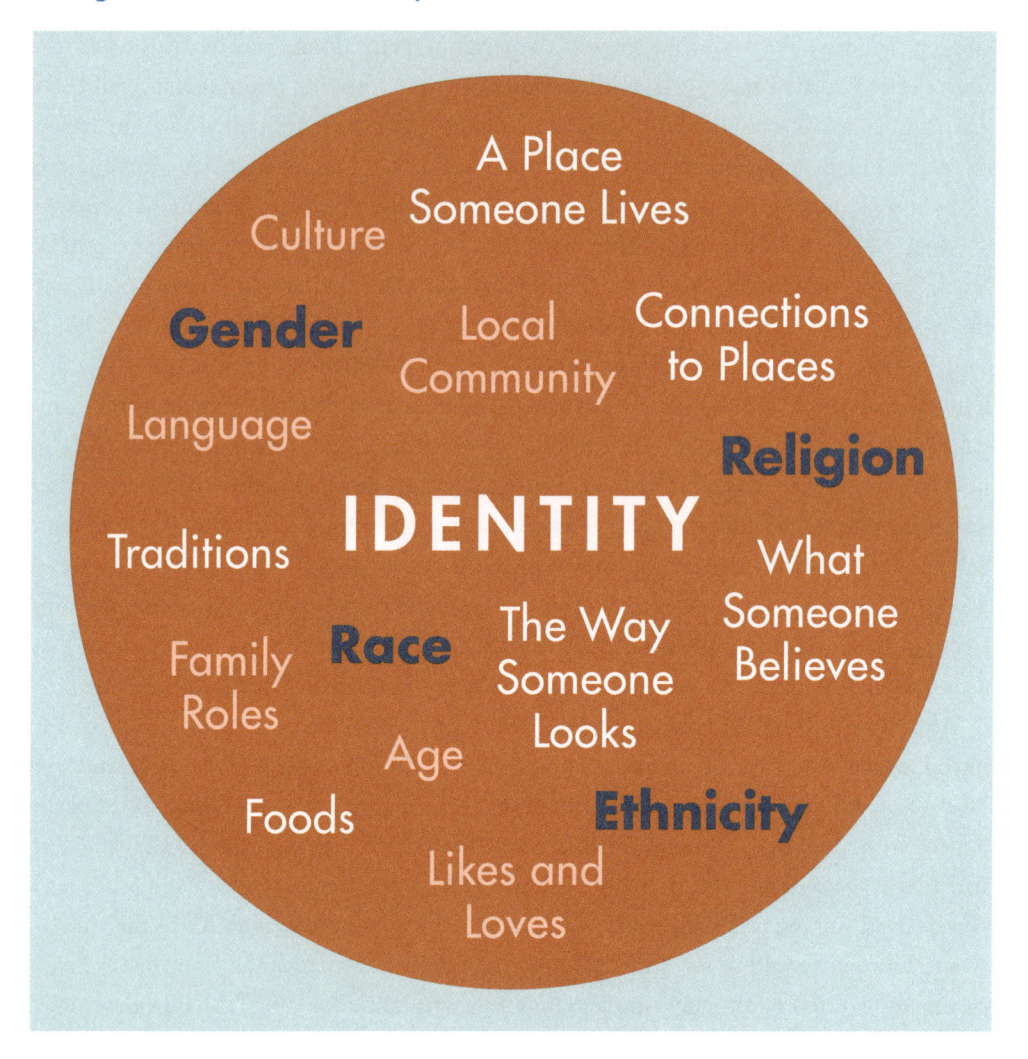

Identity (inside circle): Culture, A Place Someone Lives, **Gender**, Local Community, Connections to Places, Language, **Religion**, Traditions, **Race**, The Way Someone Looks, What Someone Believes, Family Roles, Age, Foods, **Ethnicity**, Likes and Loves

Figure 2-1 Defining Identity for Young People: This graphic illustrates identifiers that will work for all students in light blue with more specific terms (for some) that will likely work in grades 3–5 indicated in dark blue.

Zaretta Hammond, author of *Culturally Responsive Teaching and the Brain* (2014), reminds us, "The only way to get students to open up to us is to show we authentically care about who they are, what they have to say, and how they feel" (75). Singing Stevie Wonder's "Happy Birthday" was one simple (and fun!) way to affirm Black students and families in the community, especially during such a meaningful gathering at the beginning of the school year. The activities and rituals that we facilitate in our classrooms,

THE ARTFUL APPROACH TO EXPLORING IDENTITY AND FOSTERING BELONGING

Identity Development: Meeting Students Where They Are

As students grow into their identity development, their awareness of social identifiers will also grow and become increasingly sophisticated. For example, older students might be aware of the iceberg model (visible, less visible, and invisible) or the ways in which identities can be marginalized or privileged. However, to meet younger students where they're at, it's helpful to make space for them to share about the identities they feel most connected to and proud of sharing. In other words, it's important for us to model flexibility and not be too rigid when inviting students to reflect about who they are and what makes them unique. This will also support students as they learn more about the fluid and intersectional nature of housing multiple identities.

which might seem less visible or high stakes, are equally important.

The experiences you create around beginning-of-the-year activities have a huge impact on the way students feel about sharing who they are in your classroom. All of us have our favorite activities, rituals, and read-alouds for starting off the year and the way we develop and lead these activities are crucial to helping students feel safe, supported, and seen. As every classroom teacher knows, the first few weeks of school are crucial to setting the tone, establishing community, and forming authentic connections with students. Setting aside time to intentionally explore and celebrate identity is essential to fostering belonging all year long.

Tip 1: Start with Low Stakes

Jacqueline Woodson's (2018) picture book *The Day You Begin* reminds us how intimidating the first day in a new classroom can feel. Maybe you've even experienced this yourself. From joining a team mid-season

Six Tips for Launching the Year by Exploring Identity

1. Start with low stakes
2. Look for small, meaningful opportunities to make a big impact
3. Take time to build community and trust
4. Establish short, kid-friendly community agreements
5. Think outside the box (literally!)
6. Design like the fab five (Do it as a team!)

to being the only Black student or Spanish speaker or adopted child in a classroom, there are so many ways that a newbie might feel like an outsider. This experience often leads to a feeling that Geoffrey Cohen calls "belonging uncertainty," which happens when you feel like an outsider of the group and aren't sure if you belong there. It's common amongst students of all identities and you can imagine why it's likely to be especially common at the beginning of the school year (Cohen 2022a).

This makes those first few classroom community moments when identity is centered even more crucial. As we begin to build trust and provide opportunities for students to share who they are, we should start small and with low stakes. If we delve into identity too quickly, we risk pushing students to be too vulnerable before they feel the psychological safety needed to share their story with the room. We also risk inadvertently heightening belonging uncertainty for the very students we're attempting to support, especially if we aren't mindful of how we spotlight differences or if we miss an opportunity to treat those moments with care.

One way to begin with low-stakes sharing is to invite whole-group sharing. Playing a "this or that" game with fun options like "movie night or game night" or "sweet snacks or salty ones" is an easy way for students to share in the first few days of school without going too deep, too soon. This is also a great way to incorporate introverts in the classroom who aren't quite ready to share solo in front of the whole group. With this game, everyone can share about themselves and the spotlight won't be on any one student or identity.

Belonging Uncertainty

"Belonging Uncertainty is a feeling of not fitting into a particular social group or environment. People who experience this may feel like an outsider, isolated from those around them, or unable to connect with people in their environment" (Cohen 2022a).

Starting the year with a book like *Your Name Is a Song* is one way to invite all students to share their names and feel affirmed in hearing their names said back to them with love. This book, a "celebration to remind all of us about the beauty, history, and magic behind names" (Thompkins-Bigelow 2020), does not lean too heavily into the pain or microaggression of having one's name mispronounced or spotlight one identity. Instead, this book spends most of its pages celebrating the musicality of a diverse array of beautiful names that sing like songs. The author has also provided a helpful video guide that you can watch beforehand, in addition to phonetic spelling throughout the book, that will help you honor the names featured throughout the story. After reading the book with a group of third graders, we invited them to each say their name (either by simply saying it or singing it as a song or rapping it to a beat) and then hear their classmates repeat it back to them. This was a wonderful chance for students to feel affirmed and

You can return to these activities and these moments across the year. It might be nice to create opportunities for kids to add onto their journals or nameplates throughout the year as their identities evolve. As you continue to build community your students will likely open up in new ways and feel more comfortable revealing aspects of their identity that are important to them, or that they are growing into as the year progresses. If a student is struggling with what to share, take a note of that too. Just like number sense and grammar, identity work is a skill you're teaching students, and it takes time to build identity awareness, confidence, and vulnerability.

Finding time for this ongoing work might seem overwhelming, which is why we rely heavily on the power of the check-in! Check-ins don't have to take long, especially if you continue to model both brevity and bravery in ways that make sense for the moment. Even with just 5–7 minutes each morning, you can create opportunities for students to share important aspects of their identity. We encourage you to establish a routine around checking in so that students become accustomed to listening generously, reflecting on themselves, and sharing with one another. Check-in moments, however, are only as powerful as the questions you ask. The timing of when you ask questions matters too. Remember to start with low stakes and ease students into sharing more about themselves. When we introduce the check-in question, we usually model one or two possibilities to give students an idea for what they might share and a feel for how the sharing should go (just a reminder: make these brief!).

The following list includes questions you could use across a year. We like to incorporate seasonal themes and food in our check-in questions because these things tend to unite us and help us share our unique stories at the same time. Many of us have special connections and cultural traditions around seasons and food that reveal aspects of our identity. Finding ways to acknowledge the change of seasons or connection to family is a simple way to include everyone's experience in your classroom.

> **Handle with Care**
>
> Given that food is such a great unifier, many of our check-in questions are all about food. One thing to note, however, is that we don't include food questions that would put kids on the spot to recall specific meals of the week (What did you have for breakfast this morning? Dinner last night? Bring for lunch today?) or that assume access to certain types of meals (What's your favorite restaurant?). The kinds of food questions we're asking are connected to identity, culture, and imagination (What's your favorite family meal? or What's your dream ice cream flavor?). If you have students in your classroom who might be experiencing food insecurity avoid any questions that might make them feel excluded or left out.

LAUNCHING THE YEAR ARTFULLY

Questions for Each Season: Check-Ins for Your Whole Year

Beginning of Year or Anytime

- What's your favorite pizza topping?
- What's your dream pet?
- What do you get most excited to eat at a family gathering?
- If you could be a "collector" of anything, what would you collect?
- What's something you hope to be this year? (examples: courageous, kind to my classmates, loving to my family, adventurous!)

Middle of the Year

- What's something you hope will happen one day but hasn't happened YET? (This pairs nicely with *The Magical Yet* by Angela DiTerlizzi [2020].)
- What's one wonderful thing you noticed this week? (the leaves changed colors this week, my big brother was in a good mood this morning, we all danced our best in rehearsal today)
- If you could invite a guest star for show and tell, who would you bring? (my grandpa who grows his own tomatoes, my cousin Moriah who sews her own clothes!)
- What's an artifact you would bring to your own family museum? (a copy of the *Black Panther* DVD because we've seen it a million times, a box of mac and cheese because it's our favorite Friday meal, our beloved cat George's favorite squishy toy).
- My _____ skills/muscles have really gotten stronger this year! (multiplication tables, paragraph writing, counting, chapter book reading, back flipping)

THE ARTFUL APPROACH TO EXPLORING IDENTITY AND FOSTERING BELONGING

End of the Year

- What's something you love seeing (or smelling, hearing, doing, tasting) when spring comes around (flowers blooming, rainy days, March Madness)?

- Who is a character you've read about in a book that you wish you could meet or even be friends with? What would you want to do with them?

- What are some words of wisdom (or an important lesson) that you have received from one of your elders (someone older in your life: grandparent, a neighbor, an auntie)?

- What was something you learned this year that you hope to never ever forget?

- What's one moment you would add to our classroom scrapbook? (You could imagine yourself snapping a photo of the moment and tell us how you would caption it)

Tip 4: Establish Short, Kid-Friendly Community Agreements

It is essential to establish community agreements at the beginning of the school year, especially as we want our classrooms to be spaces where identity is centered and honored. After years of facilitating this work in classrooms we've found these five agreements (see Figure 2–3) have served us well. You might start with these and invite your students to think about what resonates with them and what they might like to add or change. Keep your final agreements short and sweet with language that is kid friendly.

1	**LISTEN FIRST**	Listen with an open heart and mind.
2	**SHARE FROM THE I-PERSPECTIVE**	Speak from your own point of view. This means I share my story and my experience.
3	**REMEMBER IT'S OK TO DISAGREE**	Remember that we all have different ideas, identities, and experiences that help us understand the world.
4	**TAKE A PAUSE**	Think about how and when you share. This won't be your last chance to ask questions or talk about big issues and feelings.
5	**SPEAK UP WITH CARE**	Speak up with care when you hear or notice harmful words and actions. Remember that our words matter.

Figure 2-3 Community Agreements

Tip 5: Think Outside the Box (Literally!)

Poetry is another way to create opportunities for students to share about who they are at the beginning of the year and "I am" poems can be perfect for launching that work. Some of the templates available for the poems, however, can feel more like Mad Libs™ or include simplistic options that limit possibilities for students to share who they are. Sometimes, these graphic organizers with their predesigned boxes and categories are an efficient way to get to know your students, and sometimes students need something heavily scaffolded. But formulas put everyone in the same box and sometimes they're even harmful. We've seen formula poems with fill-in-the-blank lines like "friend to

_____" or "loves to play with _____," which often leaves some kids out, even though the intent behind lines like this might be to encourage kindness and support classroom friendships. When these poems are displayed, sometimes children don't see themselves reflected back or included in the list of friends. We've also seen phrases like "loves the sport _____" on these poetry graphic organizers, but what about students who might not be into sports? To open these poems up for all students to share about what they love and who they are, we encourage you to allow them to make their own choices around design, order, and content as much as possible.

You might also brainstorm a variety of possible titles for their poems, instead of giving each of them the same one: "All About Me" or "Identity Poem." Instead of having students provide exact information (favorite food, activity, color, and so on) include those favorites in a word bank that they can choose from. Rather than creating a premade poem with I Am statements, give them a list of possibilities instead! Let children decide for themselves what to compare themselves to. Let them decide whether to do a poem using feeling words or using food likes and dislikes to share who they are.

Just as formulas can sometimes limit students' ability to express themselves in their own unique ways, the same is often true with identity maps. You can use this template to guide an identity map activity or to inspire your students' I Am poems. Notice how this identity map is not limited to certain identifiers (race, gender, ethnicity), includes invitational language for young people, and each category is open enough to meet them where they're at in their own identity development. Figure 2–4 is meant to be a helpful sample to display for inspiration. Treat this as a "starter" guide to inspire your identity map activities, meaning you might adapt the bubbles here depending on how much or how little you have explored identity in your classroom. Before you begin identity maps, think: *Have I introduced terms that would help students understand identifiers like race or nationality? Have I given opportunities for students to share about deeper cultural connections like religion or ethnicity?* If this is your classroom's first step in exploring identity, you might begin with this "starter" graphic organizer, which keeps identifiers open and uses kid-friendly language. If you're a bit deeper into exploring identity (maybe you've used our *Colors of Us* lesson from Chapter 4 and practiced brave noticing as a class), then adapt this "starter" to meet your needs. You can even use the "What Makes You *You*" bubble to incorporate language your students are already comfortable using. Either way, make this a flexible experience to meet students where they are at. Some students might feel confident saying "I identify as Black" and others might share about their racial identity by saying something like "I have skin like chocolate cupcakes!" Some students might say "I am Jewish" while others might be excited to share "I celebrate Hanukkah!" As students grow into their identity awareness, their fluency with terms will grow as well.

Identity Map *Starter ideas to adapt for students!*

LOCAL COMMUNITY

FAMILY ROLES
Big sister, cousin, sibling, etc.

IMPORTANT FOODS
Important foods to me, foods I love, cultural and family foods

LANGUAGES
What languages do you speak at home? What languages are spoken in your family?

NAME
Nicknames, name meaning, origin language of name

TRADITIONS & HOLIDAYS

WHAT MAKES YOU *YOU*?
What are some unique fun facts? What are you proud of?

HOBBIES & PASSIONS

LIKES & LOVES

Figure 2-4 Identity Map Starter

Instead of distributing this exact template, however, you might offer students more flexible options—something as simple as a blank sheet of construction paper and colorful markers. Students can add their own bubbles (in any size or any shape!) and respond to any of the options in their own style. The more open-ended the format, the more possibilities students can envision for remixing something that best represents who they are.

Notice that these third graders designed their identity maps (see Figures 2–5, 2–6, and 2–7) in their own unique ways, using symbols or sometimes just circles. Also notice that children did not write about the same things. Some children included aspects of their identities that reflected religious, cultural, or racial identity, and others did not. And many of them included aspects of their identity that reflected their passions, favorites, or likes and loves!

THE ARTFUL APPROACH TO EXPLORING IDENTITY AND FOSTERING BELONGING

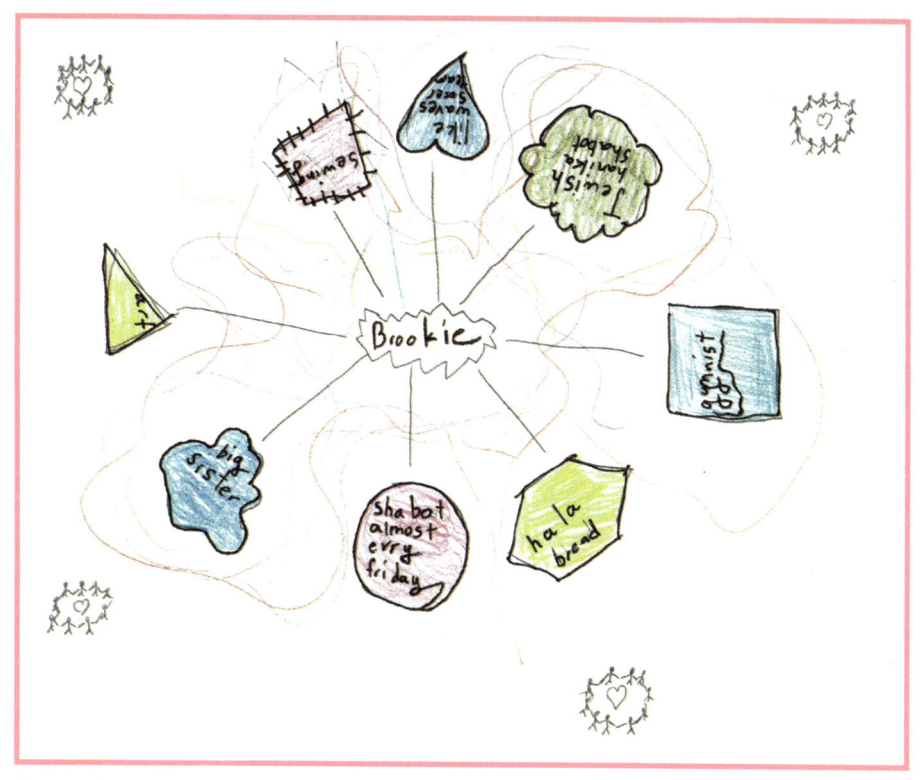

Figure 2-5

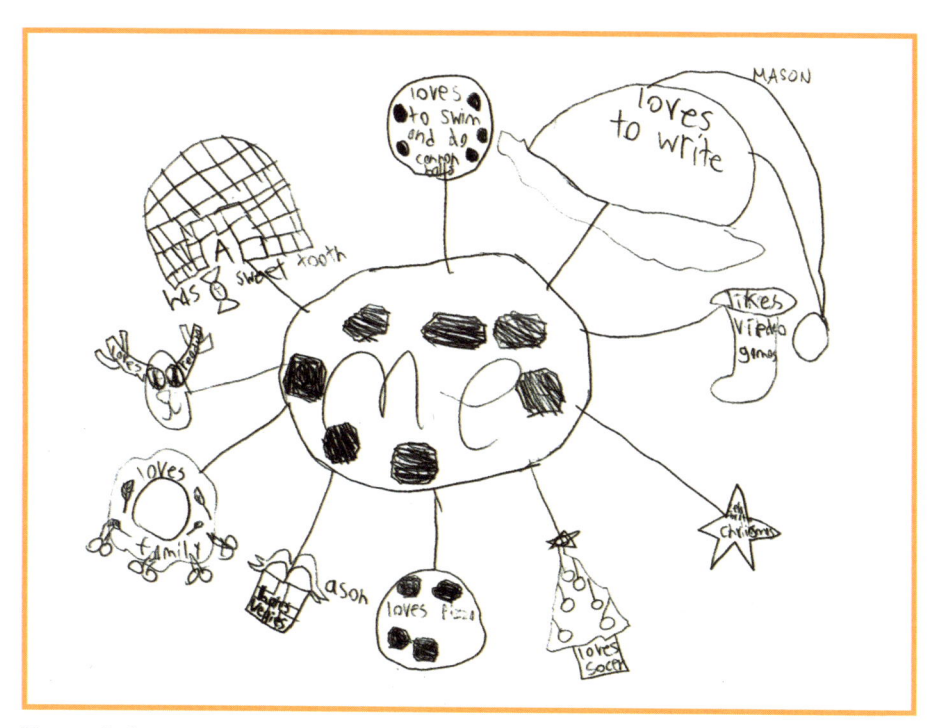

Figure 2-6

LAUNCHING THE YEAR ARTFULLY

Figure 2-7

Tip 6: Design Like the Fab Five (Do It as a Team!)

Setting up a classroom is a lot of work and involves many decisions, both big and small. What will your color palette be? Will there be a unifying theme for the room? Where will student work go? Where will we gather for community conversations? While we can't enlist the actual Fab Five, the Emmy Award–winning *Queer Eye*'s team of advisors, to weigh in on decisions ranging from organization to color palette, at least we can take a page from their playbook, and remember the power of collective action! As you begin to create the vibe for your classroom, you might consider leaving some of the fun for the students. Or you might ask yourself how much of the room has already been decided before students even arrive. Leaving one wall or corner or element for them to decorate, arrange, or name (what will we call our classroom library or reading nook?) is just one way to make a space that is truly inclusive for your students. We both love a theme, and once we get behind an idea, we are all in! But deciding a theme for an entire year might also limit other possibilities for what goes on the walls or in the space. If "cute-ifying" your classroom is your thing, consider going beyond your faves (colors, style, animals, hobbies) and leaving a little space to incorporate the loves and faves of your students (Shubitz 2015). With a little extra planning and intentionality, students can contribute to your shared space and be surrounded by their own hopes and loves and stories as they learn.

Be sure to check out the resources that Learning for Justice (2023) published around centering student experiences: the following questions are a helpful starting guide as you consider setting up and designing your space.

Learning for Justice: Practices for Social Justice

What first impressions are given when entering my classroom?

Who would feel welcomed in this space?

Who might feel uncomfortable here? Why?

What does the arrangement of the room say about how I view my power as a teacher?

HOW TO KEEP IT GOING: IDENTITY ACROSS THE YEAR

Teachers know that the first days of school matter. Building relationships with your students and establishing the routines are a huge priority. The beginning of the school year is the time when focusing on identity is most present in our minds, because this is when we're starting a new year with a new group of students, possibly in a new space. This feels like the closest thing to a fresh canvas in our teacher world, and once we start to fill in the color (start learning aspects of our students' identities and backgrounds), it can be tempting to hang that painting on the wall and move on to curriculum. In other words, after these initial "getting to know you" activities, we might find it harder and harder to make space for ongoing identity work.

While this chapter focused on launching the *beginning* of the year artfully, we hope you find inspiration in the many ways you can continue this work of exploring identity *all year long* with your students, in your daily read-alouds, community gatherings, cultural months, curriculum, and in all the moments in between.

CLOSING WITH A POEM

A Classroom for All of Us

This is a space for all the shades
For Chocolate and Mocha, for coffee and cream
For freckles and speckles and swirls in between
Whatever your flavor, whatever your spice
We've got room for all of it here

This is a space for all of the styles
For buzz cuts and fros, braids, twists, and bows
For frizzy and straight wherever it goes
Whatever you've got, no hair or lots
We've got room for all of it here

This is a space for all of the looks
For sneaks or for sandals, for a headband or hat
For jerseys or dresses, in rainbow or black
Whatever your fit, whatever your vibe,
We've got room for all of it here

This is a space for all the shapes
For bodies that bolt, so fast and so swift
For bodies like clouds that gracefully drift
However you move, however you roll
We've got room for all of it here

This is a space for all that's inside
For slowing it down and taking your time
For loving the quiet or wanting to shine
However you learn, however you think
We've got room for all of it here

This is a space for all that you are
For movers and shakers or readers and bakers
For dreamers and schemers or painters and makers
Whatever you love, whatever's your thing
We've got room for everyone here

LAUNCHING THE YEAR ARTFULLY

3

DREAMING UP ENGAGING CULTURAL MONTHS

An Artful Approach That Affirms and Invites

> *She told me that our stories are ladders that make it easier for us to touch the stars.*
> —Donovan Livingston,
> *Lift Off: From the Classroom to the Stars*

LOOK TO THE STARS: ILLUMINATING NEW STORIES FOR BLACK HISTORY MONTH

VERONICA

I hate to admit this but when I was a young student, I was never that excited about Black History Month. I loved learning about Harriet Tubman, Rosa Parks, and Martin Luther King Jr., but after a while of revisiting the same stories in the same way, it seemed (to my childhood self) there was nothing new to learn. Sometimes the lessons were not only stale but also steeped in trauma, surfacing harsh stereotypes and hard history without leaving much room for Black joy or innovation. Some of my friends even joked that we had been given the shortest month of the year on purpose, and in the absence of a lesson on Carter G. Woodson or Mary Church Terrell, I sort of believed them. And sure, this joke is not historically accurate, but it reveals what so many of my classmates had internalized as students—that Black History Month was just a checkbox for some of our teachers. Award-winning author Jason Reynolds (Petry 2018) refers to this perception of February as the "obligatory academic window to learn about the historic and often overlooked contributions of African Americans" (1).

When the time came to create my own version of a Black History Month experience, I knew that I wanted to dream up something that no student could ever mistake for an "obligatory academic window." I wanted our Black students to feel affirmed and proud. I wanted all our students to feel invited to engage and eager to learn more. I wanted a month that our young people would look forward to year after year. But, as I started to translate my dreams to plans, I also began to recognize many of the challenges some of my own childhood teachers probably faced. *How would I honor the honest (often brutal) past of our shared history? How would I go beyond the icons? How would I find the time to make space for something meaningful? How would I design something for both Black and non-Black students? How would I finally put an end to that tired joke?* I decided that Woodson and Terrell would get an annual shout-out to counter the notion that Black History Month was ever "given" to Black people and to contextualize why February was chosen (to honor the birthdays of Abraham Lincoln and Frederick Douglass). And I decided that we wouldn't limit ourselves to the same few historical figures, because though their impact on our present day can't be overstated, there are countless leaders, movements, and innovators whose stories have yet to be brought to light. By folding new stories into the mix each year, we would keep the month feeling fresh and illustrate the vast diversity within the Black diaspora at the same time.

I decided that we would start with a theme. Each year we could shine a light on a new area of Black history guided by a theme like "Lift Ev'ry

VERONICA

Voice" or "Still I Rise" or "Express Yourself: Celebrating Black Writers, Artists, and Poets." And this annual theme would bring in new spotlight stories, new ways of seeing more well-known stories, and inspire projects that could engage students in a variety of content areas. While all our annual themes had something unique to offer, one that will always hold a place in my heart is the year we asked the community to "Look to the Stars" (Figure 3-1).

The theme "Look to the Stars" created a moment that was not only affirming for our Black students, but invitational for non-Black students to engage meaningfully, too. This theme inspired everyone to get excited for Black History Month! The month included read-alouds of

---

THIS YEAR'S BLACK HISTORY MONTH THEME:
LOOK TO THE STARS
STORIES OF SCIENCE + TECHNOLOGY + HISTORY

Happy Black History Month!

The theme ★★ **Look to the Stars: Stories of Science, Technology, and History** ★★ is an homage to the role the stars have played throughout Black history. From Harriet Tubman, who followed Polaris, the North Star, to lead enslaved people to freedom to Mae Jemison who dreamed of flying freely through the galaxy "surrounded by a sea of stars," this throughline connects a myriad of movements and innovations throughout the constellation of Black history.

"Look to the Stars" is inspired by that history and aims to illuminate the stories of contemporary Afrofuturists who continue to add their sci-fi books, funk music, genre-bending artistry, and STEM innovations to the "ever-expanding reach of Afrofuturist thought across oceans, into land reclamations, up to the stars, through cyberspace and inward as Black visionaries look to the infinite space within." (Smithsonian Afrofuturism Series n.d.)

Figure 3-1 Making an announcement in your class newsletter, on your school or district website, or even in a faculty meeting is a way to elevate the cultural month experience, provide insight into the theme, and share relevant language, terms, and resources.

Mae Among the Stars by Roda Ahmed (2020) and *Tar Beach* by Faith Ringgold (2020) with mini spotlight stories on Benjamin Banneker, Mae Jemison (of course!), and Nick Cave. A Black high school student heard about our theme and offered to share about her work with the DRONe Project ("DRONe or Descendants Recovering Our Names" is a local tech organization with the uber cool mission of empowering young women of color with drone technology to help uncover the untold local history of Black San Diegans). This student's story became our final spotlight story.

    This theme continued to cultivate connections in our community all month. When we led students through a poetry workshop to write their own *My Night Among the Stars* poems, our art teacher offered her expertise to help us teach the history of flying imagery in African American folklore and storytelling and share how these flying figures symbolize a creative way of imagining and enacting freedom and resistance. Our science teacher chimed in with fun space vocabulary like "comet, cosmos, and celestial" that students could incorporate into their poems. A Black high school teacher created AI-generated images of his own favorite leaders in STEM throughout Black history to share with students. And a Black parent shared candidly that as soon as he heard this theme he felt a deep sense of gratitude, relieved that his son would learn about our history beyond the trauma.

    Students for whom the month was not a mirror but a window into an identity outside of their own were still deeply engaged in learning— eager to share their poems and illustrations at our poetry café and to learn more about the intergalactic adventures of Mae Jemison. When we shared a spotlight story on the afrofuturistic soundsuits designed by Nick Cave, second graders were so inspired they asked if they could design their own. The teacher paused what she had planned, took out some blank sheets of paper and markers, and suddenly an entire class was drawing soundsuits inspired by Nick Cave! Even Rebecca and I got in on the fun. Throughout the month, Rebecca and I were often in our office so deep in research for spotlight stories that we often found ourselves tuning out the world around us, glancing up from our screens or books only occasionally to say things like, "Did you know Benjamin Banneker wrote math poems?"

DREAMING UP ENGAGING CULTURAL MOMENTS

VERONICA

As we continued to plan for more and more cultural months, we never forgot the power of the theme or the lessons learned from our year of "Look to the Stars": *If you narrow your focus, even just a bit, the stories you share can inspire endless connections, wonder, and creativity. If you center joy and artful experiences, your students will be excited to engage and share their learning. If you seek out the stories that have yet to be told, your students will find something new to learn, and so, likely, will you.* (See Figures 3-2 to 3-6 for images of students' "Look to the Stars" work.)

Figure 3-2

Figure 3-3

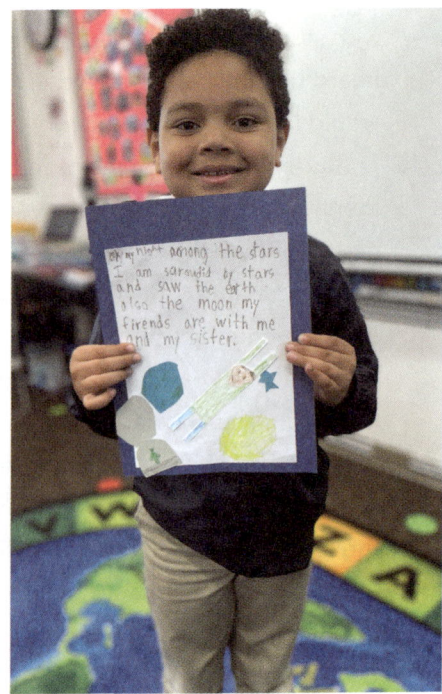

Figure 3-4

THE ARTFUL APPROACH TO EXPLORING IDENTITY AND FOSTERING BELONGING

VERONICA

Figure 3-5 "My Night Among the Stars" poems and Flying Figure artwork inspired by the "Look to the Stars" theme for Black History Month

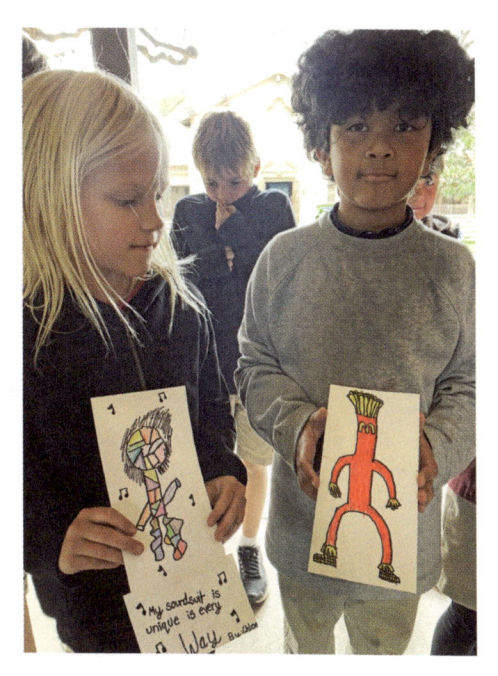

Figure 3-6 Soundsuit design inspired by Nick Cave's Spotlight Story, celebrating "Look to the Stars" theme for Black History Month

PLANNING A YEAR OF ENGAGING AND ARTFUL CULTURAL MONTHS

While we explore identity all year long, taking the time to honor cultural months gives us annual opportunities to celebrate and educate with intentionality. When cultural month experiences are designed with a creative lens, they can also be a time to spotlight contemporary stories, humanize history in fresh ways, and uplift student voices.

When planning, consider how to use each cultural month to affirm students who can speak from the I-perspective for that month and think about how to engage students of all identities in an interactive, hands-on way. Educators who have hosted a "Women's History Month" might be familiar with student questions like "Why isn't

Why Cultural Months Still Matter

Three "own voices" quotes that speak to the enduring power of cultural months:

"Let me conclude by re-emphasizing that Black History Month continues to serve us well. In part because Woodson's creation is as much about today as it is about the past. Experiencing Black History Month every year reminds us that history is not dead or distant from our lives."
–National Museum of African American History and Culture

"The story of Asian Americans led this one woman [Jeannie Jew] to believe that not only should Asians understand their own heritage, but that all Americans must know about the contributions and histories of the Asian-Pacific American experience in the United States."
–Kat Moon (2019) Time magazine

"As we close the month officially designated as Native American Heritage Month, a time when the U.S. engages in national conversations about American Indians, our very existence is a reminder that for us, the conversation never ends."*
–Dina Gilio-Whitaker (2018) Los Angeles Times

*While all these quotes are all in own voices, this last quote surfaces what might sound like dated language to some. See Chapter 6 where we unpack these terms further and share tips for which terms to use!

---

there a men's history month?" or "Why are we spending so much time only learning about women?" Questions like these might surface annually and are often a reflection of students in the dominant identity feeling decentered—a different experience from that of being marginalized, though many students cannot yet discern the difference. We've found that approaching these opportunities thematically, intersectionally, and artfully helps to make cultural months a time that more and more students anticipate every year. And this means that even more students are learning about the stories and the movements, and the historical impact they have on our present day.

Planning Elements: Themes, Spotlight Stories, and Artful Connections

It might be helpful to be able to look across the whole school year as you plan for cultural months. The template shown (see Figure 3–7) allows you to plan thematically, to pay attention to intersectional identities represented (gender, age, race), and to notice how

Cultural Months Planning Guide
Year-at-a-Glance

OCTOBER	Hispanic Heritage Month—Planting Seeds	
Week 1	October 14	Rafael López
Week 2	October 21	Pura Belpré
Week 3	October 28	—
Week 4	—	—
NOVEMBER	**Native American Heritage Month—Food Is Love**	
Week 1	November 4	Kevin Noble Maillard
Week 2	November 11	Joy Harjo
Week 3	November 18	Sean Sherman/The Sioux Chef
Week 4	November 25	—
DECEMBER	**Celebrating Holidays and Each Other**	
Week 1	December 2	Celebrating Each Other with Compliments
Week 2	December 9	Ezra Jack Keats and *The Snowy Day*
Week 3	—	—
Week 4	—	—
JANUARY	**Shining Lights**	
Week 1	January 6	Shining Lights (New Year Theme)
Week 2	January 13	Service (MLK)
Week 3	January 22	Lunar New Year
Week 4	January 27	Fred Korematsu
FEBRUARY	**Black History Month—Look to the Stars**	
Week 1	February 3	Nikki Giovanni/Ashley Bryan
Week 2	February 10	Stevie Wonder
Week 3	February 17	Alma Thomas
Week 4	February 24	Nick Cave
MARCH	**Women's History Month: Fearless**	
Week 1	March 3	Cholita Climbers
Week 2	March 17	Eugenie Clark
Week 3	March 24	Mary Anning
Week 4	March 3	Aisholpan Nurgaiv (Eagle Huntress)
APRIL	**Arab American Heritage Month—Mosaic of the Arts**	
Week 1	April 7	Arab American Music and Dance
Week 2	April 14	—
Week 3	April 21	Mosaics
Week 4	April 28	—
MAY	**AAPI: Soaring/JAHM—Tikkun Olam**	
Week 1	May 5	Jeremy Lin and Sunisa Lee
Week 2	May 12	Duke Kahanamoku and Chloe Kim
Week 3	May 19	Albert Einstein
Week 4	May 26	Hedy Lamarr
JUNE	**Pride—We Are Family**	
Week 1	June 2	"We Are Family" Stories

Figure 3-7
Cultural Months Planning Guide: Year-at-a-Glance

DREAMING UP ENGAGING CULTURAL MOMENTS

many of our stories are contemporary or historical. A blank template of the Cultural Month Planning Guide is available as OR 3–1 in the Online Resources.

When we sit down to brainstorm and plan how we will celebrate an upcoming cultural month, we start with these three elements: Theme, Spotlight Stories, and Artful Connections.

- **Theme:** What theme will bring this month together? What standout phrase will be our refrain for the month? (For example: "Lift Ev'ry Voice" for Black History Month or "Rise Up and Shine On" for Pride.) What will tie our stories together for the month (sports, music, activism), and what colors and fonts will we use to express this month's theme and feel?

- **Spotlight Stories:** What stories, people, places, and movements are we spotlighting? Is there a historical throughline we're attempting to illuminate? Are there contemporary voices included? What picture books, texts, poems, or videos will we use?

- **Artful Connections:** What cross-curricular connections might we explore? Will students create, perform, write, or reflect? Will there be a listening gallery, a window display, a collaborative bulletin board, a poetry café?

Tips for When Time, Funds, and Support Are in Short Supply

- **When You're Low on Time:** Start small and look for existing places in your curriculum and schedule to incorporate cultural month content. Sharing one spotlight story with an artful read-aloud is all it takes to bring a person, place, or movement to life for your students. Keep one theme going the whole year (like music or food!) if you don't have time to change it up each month. If you want to incorporate the arts but don't have time for more extensive artful connections, we have plenty of suggestions for quick mindful moments and turn and talks. And everyone loves a one-minute dance party.

- **When You're Low on Funds:** For free spotlight story books: check out resources like Libby, YouTube channels for authors and publishing houses, and the We Need Diverse Books Educator Grant. When you don't have a physical copy of a book on hand, you can almost always find a read-aloud video online. But make sure to mute the reader so your students can hear the story in your voice! Adjust the settings to go slower or faster to match your pace and pause when necessary to invite conversation. And sometimes a spotlight story is a free video, a podcast clip, or one you've pieced together from bits of information online. For free artful connections: readers theater, community poems, and movement are all artful connections that require little to no materials.

- **When You're Facing Pushback:** We have both been at schools where this work is supported, even championed by admin, and we've also both been at schools where there is a range of implicit and explicit resistance. If you are facing pushback in your community, know that we've been there, we're rooting for you, and we hope you can use the artful approaches outlined in this chapter to work in your favor. We have found that the arts bring people in and open people up to experiences around identity and belonging. Songs, dance, and poems tend to bring communities together and make for a great entry point into this work—especially in an age of book bans, dishonest history, and anti-DEIB legislation. And sometimes, family education can go a long way in garnering support. Consider incorporating programming like Windows, Mirrors, and Coffee (Chapter 9) to engage families in cultural months throughout the year.

Before diving into the details of planning each of these elements you can look at three complete sample cultural month plans that we have included in the Online Resources (OR 3–2 [November: Native American Heritage Month], OR 3–3 [February: Black History Month], and OR 3–4 [March: Women's History Month]). These plans include ideas for spotlight stories, artful connections, and examples of student voices and responses. Note that because we do an all-school project for Black History Month, we kept our weekly artful moments brief to make room for the larger "Look to the Stars" schoolwide project. The Online Resource for February, OR 3–3, includes a sample lesson with mentor texts.

Even if your goal is to start with one spotlight story a month or you host only one event a year, we hope these charts are a helpful starting point for leading your own cultural month celebrations. Included in the Online Resources is a blank planning template (OR 3–5 [Cultural Month Planning Template]). Taking time to craft these moments thoughtfully makes a real difference to our students and often inspires a ripple effect in our communities.

Remixing Resources

Handle with Care

As you plan for upcoming cultural months consider curating materials that feel just right for your grade level, your class dynamics, and your unique students. Remember that there is no one perfect resource, so if there's one page of a dated packet or just a few minutes from a video (maybe not entirely created with young people in mind) that you want to share, don't be afraid to unpack the packets (or trim down the video) and make them work for you! We love the abundance and simplicity of a download but not all materials are classroom-ready. By taking a little time to preview and edit as needed, you can customize the experience for your community needs. Try supplementing with music, engaging media, and contemporary stories to bring these materials to life and keep things fresh and fun.

Occasionally you may find some of the picture books you want to share contain an image or passage that references hard history or delves into a topic too complex or too painful for your age group. In that case, you might simply skip that part or intentionally not linger on a particular image. By doing this, we are still able to give kids access to an important story or author in a way that is developmentally appropriate. Additionally, developing this lens for sourcing materials opens possibilities for so many sophisticated resources (New York Times articles, podcasts, and movie trailers to name a few!) that you might otherwise overlook.

Dreaming up a Theme

When Walt Disney was designing Disneyland, he apparently studied lots of places that welcomed crowds of all types like "carnivals, national parks, museums, and even the streets of New York City" (Henry Ford Museum 2020). According to legend, these studies led him to his first "break" from "traditional amusement parks: the single entrance." Although his team worried about congestion, Disney pushed for what he knew a single entrance could provide. He wanted visitors to "experience a cohesive story." And anyone who has ever visited any theme park—like LEGOLAND® with its LEGO®-shaped ticket booths or the San Diego Zoo with its iconic flamingos—knows just how powerful this entry point can be.

As you begin to plan a cultural month experience for your students, think: **What will be our entry point?** What cohesive story am I hoping to tell? What theme will connect all my individual spotlight stories? This could be a theme inspired by one specific subject area (music, literature, or STEM), or one inspired by geography (local Indigenous artists or AAPI [Asian American and Pacific Islanders] activists in our state), or even inspired by a specific movement or time (the Harlem Renaissance or Afrofuturism). It's important to note that a theme or cohesive story is not the same as a single story (i.e., stereotypes) as it aims to paint a fuller picture and shine a light on lesser-known voices. In fact, when done thoughtfully, a theme can challenge single stories.

THE ARTFUL APPROACH TO EXPLORING IDENTITY AND FOSTERING BELONGING

One Theme, One Community

Every year public radio station KPBS and the San Diego Public Library partner to select a community read for "One Book, One San Diego." Maybe your community has something similar or maybe you've even organized one of these shared reads for your own community through a grade-level team or local book club. There is something about a shared experience that unites people from different age groups, backgrounds, and identities and celebrates their differences, unique ideas, perspectives, and stories in the loveliest ways. A theme can serve this purpose for your school community as well. When Veronica was tasked with leading her first cultural month experience (which involved creating a school's first-ever Black History Month celebration) she wasn't quite sure how to approach it in a way that brought as many people into the celebration as possible. Should she create a unique activity for each grade level? Should she provide separate materials to teachers who weren't familiar with the history behind this cultural month? What about parents?

She ultimately decided on the theme "Lift Ev'ry Voice" and came to realize that organizing any events under one theme would on its own create some sense of community across grade levels, identities, and constituencies. This allowed each grade level and ancillary teacher to introduce the theme in a way that made the most sense for their students. She announced the theme at a faculty meeting with a brief explanation of the historical significance and gave some time for teachers to brainstorm and share inspiration.

The music teacher decided to teach the song "Lift Ev'ry Voice and Sing" (also known as the Black National Anthem) to all her classes, the Spanish teacher shared a few spotlight stories of Afrolatino activism, the third-grade teacher connected the theme to a biography unit, and the fifth-grade teacher looked for opportunities in U.S. history. Parents and caretakers from all grades attended a special morning performance of "Lift Ev'ry Voice" led by the third-grade class. And that morning student volunteers and teachers walked through the crowd, handing out little lyric sheet copies so that anyone, no matter their experience with the tradition, could join in the community singing, which is one of the most connective experiences we can have! As musician Brian Eno (2008) says, "When you sing with a group of people, you learn how to subsume yourself into a group consciousness because a cappella singing is all about the immersion of the self into the community. That's one of the great feelings—to stop being me for a little while and to become us. That way lies empathy, the great social virtue."

This is the power of a theme. It allows for scaffolding and differentiation, affirms those who can speak from the I-perspective, invites connection for those who can't, and brings the whole school together. In the end, the theme "Lift Ev'ry Voice" transformed this school's Black History Month from separate, and often unrelated, activities in

Tips for Dreaming Up Cultural Month Themes That Challenge Stereotypes

- **Keep It Open:** Keep your theme open enough to include a variety of spotlight stories that will represent diversity within an identity group.

- **Make It Visual:** Consider how the colors, fonts, and images might be used to disrupt single stories. For example, when we were planning for Native American Heritage Month, we tried our best to find as many color and contemporary photos as possible in order to amplify the Indigenous voices that say "We are still here!" and showcase vibrant life in Indigenous communities today. For Latin and Hispanic Heritage Month, we always start by showing a map to illustrate the vast geographical diversity within Latinidad and Spanish-speaking countries.

- **Lift Up the Underrepresented:** Choose a theme that will bring stories to light that are often underrepresented for the identity you're celebrating. As we planned for AAPI Month, we decided the theme would uplift brave and bold stories of athleticism and strength to challenge the "quiet Asian girl" stereotype that Tae Keller (2020) surfaces in *When You Trap a Tiger*. This theme led to spotlight stories about Jeremy Lin, Sunisa Lee, Chloe Kim, and Duke Kahanamoku, and one super fun community moment where our students whipped and nae-nae-ed alongside a video of Jeremy Lin and Steph Curry. This turned out to be one of our favorite community moments of the year—unforgettable and filled with joy.

- **Go Beyond the Staple Stories:** Jason Reynolds once said, "by ten years old, I had become somewhat of an expert, not on Black history, but on Black History Month" (Petry 2018, 1). Let's stop creating experts in Black History Month and instead, inspire an exploration of Black history. Many of us have told and retold the same handful of stories every year, and rightfully so—these icons, Dr. King, Rosa Parks, and Harriet Tubman have more than earned their place in our textbooks. Even though including these stories in our teaching of American history has always been and continues to be a struggle, they deserve their legendary status in our collective cultural memory. But, in the same way we wouldn't wait until Presidents' Day to introduce the story of George Washington, we shouldn't squeeze this vast history into the month of February. We should bring these stories into the classroom in contextualized ways that help students make connections to the larger story of America. And we should also feel free to expand upon the stories we tell to represent Black history! We can mix it up a bit each year to keep students engaged by letting a theme guide us toward more specific movements (Harlem Renaissance, Afrofuturism!) and fresh stories (Josephine Baker, Nick Cave!).

- **Have Fun with Your Theme!** Our Women's History Month "Stories of Adventure, Discovery, and Exploration" allowed for captivating spotlight stories. Many young girls at our school identified with scientific-pioneer Eugenie Clark, and shark lovers and amateur biologists of all genders were completely enthralled by the interactive read-aloud of *Shark Lady* and gripping video footage of Eugenie immersed in the ocean, surrounded by sharks.

different classrooms to one powerful experience for all. That morning, our voices, both the confident and experienced and the softer and the still-learning, began to sing in synchrony and harmony: "Sing a song full of the faith that the dark past has taught us, / Sing a song full of the hope that the present has brought us; / Facing the rising sun of our new day begun, / Let us march on 'til victory is won" (Johnson 1900).

Resources for Dreaming Up a Theme

Many museums, libraries, and cultural centers have curated gorgeous exhibits, collections, and community events (both virtual and in person) and those are a great place to start for theme inspiration. For example, imagine you visit the website for the Contemporary Jewish Museum and come across their virtual exhibit *Levi Strauss: A History of American Style*. How might this inspire a theme for your Jewish American Heritage Month celebration? You could try incorporating a few specific Jewish designers (in this case Levi Strauss and Isaac Mizrahi) with a theme like: "From Strauss to Mizrahi: Celebrating Icons of American Style" or maybe highlight some style innovations with a theme like "Blue Jeans and Beyond: A History of American Style."

Museums to Explore Virtually for Theme Inspiration

- National Museum of African American History and Culture
- Arab American National Museum
- National Museum of the American Indian
- The Contemporary Jewish Museum
- California African American Museum
- Autry Museum of American West
- The Met (especially the Roof Garden Commissions and Met Stories series)
- The MoMA and PS1
- Centro Cultural de la Raza in San Diego
- The Exploratorium

Searching for Spotlight Stories

Once you have a theme you're ready for our favorite part: searching for spotlight stories! We love combing through picture books, skimming our favorite websites and vlogs (we provide a list of those at the end of this section), and deciding which stories we'll share with the students this time. Whether you have time to plan ahead and are excited about the possibility of doing some research, or you're pressed for time, or you need some inspiration to get started, know that starting with a theme will help to simplify your search.

The specificity of your theme will narrow the scope of your search and give you a place to start including keywords to Google. We recommend narrowing down the number of stories you spotlight to aid this process even further. We like to feature one spotlight story per week, but spotlighting even one powerful, engaging story for the month is a great place to start. There have been months where there was so much going on at school that we only had time to share a couple spotlight stories. Rather than throw more stories in the mix, we took our time thoughtfully honoring the two.

To keep students engaged and help them think intersectionally, you can also try mixing up the types of stories you share. Your lineup could include important people, movements (the Urban Art Trail), places (Angel Island or the Arab American National Museum), art forms (Alvin Ailey Dance or Mosaics), and contemporary connections. For Native American Heritage Month, we celebrated with the theme "Food Is Love" and shared spotlight stories on: Sean Sherman (The Sioux Chef) (Great Big Story 2017), Kevin Maillard and his book *Fry Bread* (2019), and Poet Laureate Joy Harjo's (1996) poem "Perhaps the World Ends Here," which is full of references to eating around a table. As you decide which stories to bring to light consider the following tips.

Tips to Search for Spotlight Stories

1. **Make the First Story Count:** We typically choose a story that feels particularly engaging to kick off a month. If the theme is your entry point, what do you want to show students first? What story best encapsulates your theme? What will get them most excited about learning more?

2. **Think Intersectionally:** We're always looking for stories that represent multiple aspects of identities so that we can share a variety of voices within a cultural month that illustrate how vast and diverse experiences within an identity can be. If we're celebrating Arab American History Month, we'll choose spotlight stories that not only represent Arab American identity, but also showcase diversity in gender, ability, age, nationality, and other identifiers.

3. **Center Own Voices:** Whenever we share stories about identities, and especially identities outside of our own, we like to bring in voices who can speak from the I-perspective. We might make sure to "hand over the mic" by showing a video of the author speaking or quoting them to share their perspectives. We also take the time to learn how to pronounce names, places, and terms that are new to us and try our best to honor them with proper pronunciation. We might not always get it right, but we always make a real effort and we acknowledge when we've made an error.

Writing Your Own Spotlight Stories

Sometimes we can't find a story that fits well with our theme, is engaging and brief enough to hold our students' attention, and is worded for a K-5 audience. When that happens, we take a few minutes to write our own. Here is a sample of one Veronica wrote after sharing a video of an exhibit about Ezra Jack Keats:

> *That virtual tour is just a peek into the life of Ezra Jack Keats. After his book The Snowy Day won the Caldecott medal, Ezra kept writing and illustrating. Throughout his life, he wrote 22 picture books and illustrated more than 85 books for children—many of them inspired by a group of friends growing up in a diverse neighborhood with streets that looked just like where Ezra grew up in Brooklyn, New York.*
>
> *Over the years, Ezra traveled all around the country to visit schools and teach children about illustration. Because he believed that "a love of reading and art was what helped him survive growing up and he wanted to offer younger children the same opportunity."*
>
> *After finding his voice as an artist, Ezra grew into an incredible illustrator and author who used his paintbrush to bring his neighbors and his friends to life in his gorgeous paintings and books for children.*

Some Prompts to Get You Started on Your Own Spotlight Story

- They were/are a _____.
- Throughout their life, they created/published/designed won _____.
- A fun/little known fact is _____.
- They were inspired by _____ believed in _____ grew into _____ were celebrated because _____.

4. **Make It Joyful:** Remember that joy is an act of resistance. Remember that these months alone should not bear the burden of teaching honest history. Remember that these months can be celebratory and affirming and full of joyful moments.

5. **Sprinkle in Contemporary Connections:** How will you draw a connection from the past to the present? Look for moments to bring in contemporary music, artists, and young voices to make the history feel relevant for students.

6. **Be on the Lookout:** Think back to the "learning for self-growth" you started in Chapter 1 and use your own read, watch, listen lists and conversations to inspire ideas for spotlight stories that you can reference later.

7. **Edit to Make It Work for You:** You may come across a story that feels almost perfect for an upcoming cultural month with just one problem—it's clearly intended for a grown-up audience. Don't let this stop you from using (a part of) the story! Edit or play and pause a video, take a quick phone recording of one little section, or copy and paste an article into a doc to edit and incorporate language that works for your students. You can share these stories in a developmentally appropriate way by rewriting and crafting your own version for the grade level you teach. It's like quilting or collaging—piecing together a spotlight story to tell the story you hope to tell, artfully.

Making an Artful Connection

Now that you've dreamed up a theme and chosen your spotlight stories, you can decide what students will do to engage creatively. If the theme is an entry point for students, the artful connection is the experience they'll have once they walk through the gates. It's worth spending time thinking about what feels right for the experience you're trying to create. At the new famous Ghibli Park, a theme park surrounded by trees in Nagakute, Aichi, Japan, and inspired by the animated films of Studio Ghibli, "There are no big attractions or rides," the official site says. Instead, they invite visitors to "Take a stroll, feel the wind, and discover the wonders" (Ghibli Park 2022). Sometimes we will plan an artful project with several *artful* layers: writing a poem then creating an accompanying visual or staging a spoken word poetry café. When you're pressed for time, an artful invitation can be a smaller moment, like a quick movement or imagination exercise (more ideas follow). What matters is making sure the tone fits with the theme of the month or the story being spotlighted. If we are celebrating a joyful theme or story, we might invite students to dance along to music or learn a community song. When honoring a more complex story, we tend to invite students into a more mindful, reflective experience. Consider how to thoughtfully pair the history you're spotlighting with an appropriate artful connection: Should the experience feel more Disneyland or more Ghibli Park?

For students who can speak from the I-perspective, these artful connections are powerful mirror moments that are meant to be affirming and joyful with opportunities for them to learn even more about themselves and their identity. For students who cannot speak from the I-perspective, these experiences provide windows and a different entry point for them to connect with this history. Our hope is that these artful connections are inviting for students of all identities because no matter what their entry point, students are almost always able to connect with a character trait or value that has been uplifted (bravery, persistence, advocacy), a feeling that the story has inspired (hope, gratitude, or fearlessness) or even the artwork or creative process itself.

By allowing an artist's work to inspire poems, movement, artwork of their *own*, we are giving students a way to engage with this history by modeling deep cultural appreciation versus problematic appropriation. We feel this approach ensures that one group's learning does not come at the expense of another group's sense of belonging. These connections can feel fresh, special, and new for all students.

REBECCA

Catching up with Black History Month: Learning Through Artful Connections

Collaborating with Veronica to develop an artful approach to cultural months has given me a meaningful entry point to connect with the stories and histories centered across the year, even when I can't speak from the I-perspective for any given month. This is true for many people at different times of the year, but it is especially true for white educators like myself. As we've developed the themes and artful connections for different cultural months, I have been exposed to many windows while also finding ways to connect with my own creativity.

One of the most powerful examples of this is in our research about Ashley Bryan, who we spotlighted for our "Express Yourself" themed, Black History Month one year. While I loved Ashley Bryan's books and illustrations, I never knew the depth of his story or the extent of his brilliance. Peeking into his artist's studio off the coast of Maine and hearing him give voice through poetry to the puppets he created gave me a fuller appreciation for his artistry and for the history that shaped his life. I learned about his collaborations with Nikki Giovanni and the books he illustrated for her poems for children, which ended up becoming the basis of our Express Yourself Projects. Using the books *The Sun Is So Quiet* (Giovanni 2014) and *I Am Loved* (Giovanni 2018) as mentor texts, Veronica and I modeled poems and illustrations in the bright, bold style of Ashley Bryan paired with the starting lines from many of Nikki Giovanni's poems.

This artful exploration gave me a personal connection to Ashley Bryan and Nikki Giovanni because they inspired my own writing and expression. But more importantly, it gave me a more nuanced understanding of both artists, as well as Black history.

The truth is, I didn't learn a lot about Black history growing up. Although Veronica and I grew up in different times and different states, our experiences celebrating Black History Month were not dissimilar. I vaguely remember lessons around Black historical figures like George Washington Carver, Rosa Parks, and Martin Luther King Jr., but I don't recall opportunities to engage creatively with these stories, and certainly not in ways that would inspire me to make something artful that had a meaningful connection to Black history.

When we were writing this chapter, I had to confirm with my parents, and several of my childhood friends, because it seemed impossible that our schools were not closed for MLK Day, or that we didn't acknowledge Black History Month in any significant way. But, as it turned out, the school district where I grew up, which was a majority white town, only voted to celebrate MLK Day with a school closure in 2017. In fact, one of my childhood friends recalls asking our high school principal why we didn't celebrate MLK with a school closure, and he replied, "If we recognize MLK Day, we would have to recognize others." Similarly to Black History Month, the honoring of MLK took decades of activism and artivism (Stevie Wonder's "Happy Birthday" song!) and proves that progress is not inevitable. As I've learned from Veronica, this is why these holidays and cultural months matter. People fought hard to make sure that the stories and the people who were often left out of the textbooks were honored. Highlighting these days and months helps us remember to reckon with the honest history of our country so that the truth of who we are and who we want to become is possible.

Examples of Artful Connections: Project Inspiration and Ideas

- **Bodies in Motion Free Draw:** During Native American History Month we invited students to draw a picture of themselves doing something where they feel their "bodies are poetry in motion" inspired by ballet dancer, Maria Tallchief. Sometimes we combine this with a word cloud or poems that describe the movement or activity.

- **"This Little Light of Mine" Sing-Along:** During the winter holiday season, our theme tends to be "Celebrating Our Holidays and Traditions!" so that students can share their special traditions with each other. Many of these traditions (Christmas, Hanukkah, Kwanzaa, New Year's Eve, and Lunar New Year) involve lights, candles, and bringing light to the darkest months of the seasonal year. We love to use the song "This Little Light of Mine," an African American spiritual that was "transformed by the nation's civil rights movement into something more" (Deggans 2018), to invite students to think about the ways they are sharing their light or their traditions with each other. Once children know this song, you can return to it time and again to celebrate Martin Luther King Jr. or Black History Month, and to celebrate the ways people of many identities have "shined" their light to fight for justice.

- **Mindful Movement Inspired by Alvin Ailey Dancers:** During Black History Month we watched a clip of the Alvin Ailey Dancers moving through the streets of Paris and then invited students to wake up their bodies with the following mindfulness practice: *Let's all take a deep breath and wake up our bodies as well! Let's start by waking up our arms with some gentle taps. Now let's wake up our shoulders. And let's take another deep breath. Make sure you take a breath from deep in your bellies. Now let's lift up our arms and make a round shape over our heads. And let's close out by breathing our arms down and rolling our shoulders back.*

DREAMING UP ENGAGING CULTURAL MOMENTS

- **"Moments of Beauty": Drawings Inspired by Alma Thomas:** During our "Express Yourself" Black History Month, we celebrated the work of Alma Thomas, who painted the world around her by using tiny bright rectangles and vibrant colors. We invited students to paint something in their environment keeping her signature style in mind and using the same bold colors. *Pay attention to the everyday beauty around you and bring what you notice to life with bright colors!*

- **"Huddled Masses" Song and Poem:** During Jewish History Month, we invited students to listen to Shaina Taub's (2018) chorus of "Huddled Masses," which features Emma Lazarus' famous lines, "Give me your tired, your poor, your huddled masses on the teeming shore, yearning to breathe free." Afterward, we invited them to imagine what lines they might write for the Statue of Liberty today.

Artful Connection Examples: Student Work Samples

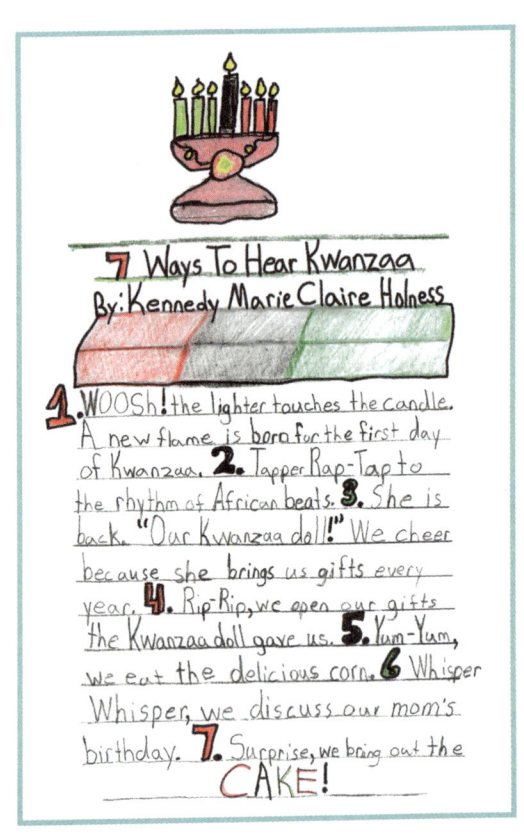

Figure 3-8 Poems inspired by "10 Ways to Hear the Holidays" Inclusive Holiday Celebration

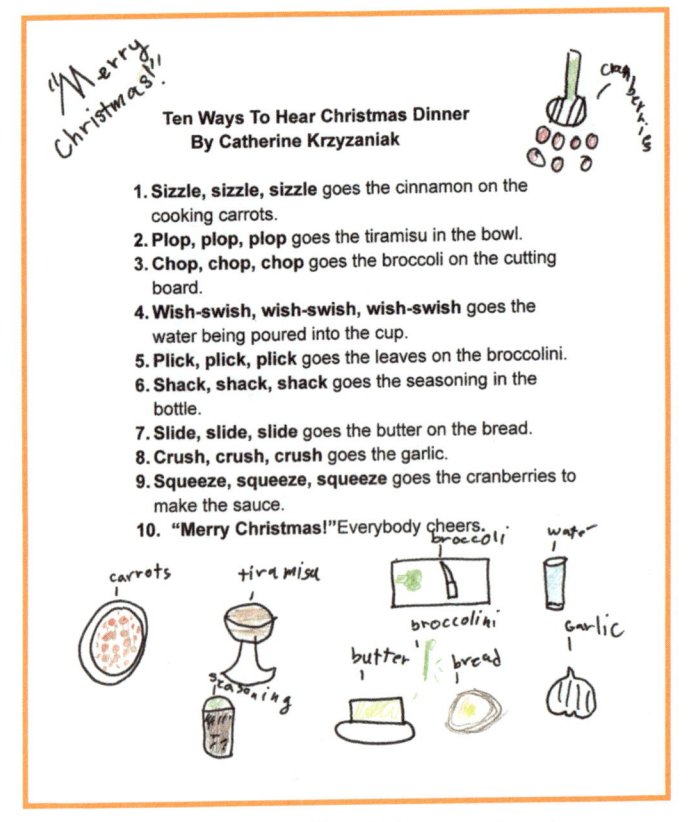

Figure 3-9 Poems inspired by "10 Ways to Hear the Holidays" Inclusive Holiday Celebration

THE ARTFUL APPROACH TO EXPLORING IDENTITY AND FOSTERING BELONGING

Figure 3-10 Poems inspired by "10 Ways to Hear the Holidays" Inclusive Holiday Celebration

Figure 3-11 Fifth-grade poem inspired by "Soaring to New Heights" theme for Asian American Pacific Islander Heritage Month

Figure 3-12 Student Scrapbook Postcards inspired by "We Are Family" theme for Pride Month

DREAMING UP ENGAGING CULTURAL MOMENTS

Figure 3-13 Student Scrapbook Postcards inspired by "We Are Family" theme for Pride Month

Figure 3-14 Student Scrapbook Postcards inspired by "We Are Family" theme for Pride Month

THE ARTFUL APPROACH TO EXPLORING IDENTITY AND FOSTERING BELONGING

RISE AND SHINE: CELEBRATING THOSE WHO RISE AND GIVING OPPORTUNITIES FOR STUDENTS TO SHINE

When we first met, the pandemic was in full swing and all of our teaching was online. To acknowledge the cultural months, Veronica would prepare a short spotlight story related to the cultural month to share with the community on Zoom and Rebecca would support children's learning with a picture book, a poem, or even a song. Eventually, we began to leave the virtual world behind but our principal wanted to find a way to keep sharing stories with our community because the integrated work of literacy and DEIB was engaging for students and teachers alike.

Ultimately, we came up with the idea to deliver a weekly "virtual show" every Friday called *Rise and Shine*—where we would "celebrate those who rise" and give opportunities for students to "shine"! In other words, share a spotlight story and make an artful connection. We call the stories we share during cultural months, "spotlight stories" because they are exactly that: a brief spotlight on a person, a movement, a place, or art form. Usually we incorporated student voices (the shine part!) in the form of individual student or classroom poems or a line or two from multiple children, photographs of student artwork, or photographs of students at work. The framework of "celebrating those who rise" and encouraging children to "think about ways they can shine" also helped us create a throughline across the year and a consistent time for delivering content around the cultural month themes.

We decided *Rise and Shine* would be a five-to-seven-minute show where we would teach students from all grade levels, at the same time, about important historical figures—and read aloud poems or portions of picture books that fit with the themes of the month. We would share prompts or ideas for artful connections that teachers could implement in their classrooms, using whatever scaffolds they needed to support learning for their students.

We realized that students of all ages needed a mindful moment as well, which led to the creation of short "Friday Feel Good" moments! Each week, Rebecca would lead a Friday Feel Good that incorporated the themes of the month and supported belonging-informed, social, and emotional learning. Aligning social–emotional learning with the content and themes felt important. As Dena Simmons (2021) points out, "to be effective equity-centered educators, we cannot be emotionally intelligent without being culturally responsive." Friday Feel Goods were as simple as inviting students to take a breath and imagining a food that brings them comfort (inspired by Native American History Month's theme "Food Is Love") or to think about a person who matters to them and helps them feel supported (inspired by the "We Are Family" theme in Pride Month or the "Mountains We Climb" Women's History Month theme). Other Friday Feel Goods might involve inviting them to think about words or phrases that help them feel like they belong, and then sharing them with a neighbor (inspired by "Shining Lights" in January).

Rise and Shine moments can happen in any number of spaces or contexts. Perhaps you set aside one morning meeting a week, or even one a month, for a Rise and Shine–themed gathering. Or maybe you have a once-a-month all-school assembly where you share a spotlight story, incorporate student voices, and invite everyone present to have a mindful moment. Whether you call it by our very extra name "Rise and Shine," or come up with your own spin, we hope this chapter gives you ideas for sharing the stories of people who have found ways to rise in the face of injustice, often against all odds.

CLOSING WITH A POEM

How We Rise and Shine

Let's make the first story count
And honor the honest past
Let's go beyond the icons
And sprinkle in the fresh
Let's lift up the stories
Of movers and shakers
Even the ones that aren't so famous
Even the ones that have yet to be shared
Let's look to the leaders, the movements, the innovators
And make space for something new
This is how we rise
This is how we shine

Let's make our voices soar
And express ourselves
Let's create as a community
And remember to make it joyful
Let's make an artful project
Maybe something beautiful
Let's be on the lookout for the shining lights around us
And the music living inside us
And the hopes and dreams that guide us
Let's look to those who came before us
The artists, the writers, the poets
Let's look to each other
Our classmates, our family, our friends

Let's look to the stars
And never stop looking
This is how we rise
This is how we shine

DREAMING UP ENGAGING CULTURAL MOMENTS

4

CONNECTING WITH YOUR STUDENTS THROUGH ARTFUL READ-ALOUDS

How to Partner with Books to Explore Identity

> *Children need to see themselves in books. They need to see their gender. They need to see their color, hair texture, their disability, themselves. Picture books especially are like many children's first introduction to the world. Seeing yourself is almost like a message. It's saying, you matter, you are visible, and you're valuable.*
>
> —Christian Robinson,
> "Christian Robinson Illustrator"

"Let's put our hands together, too!" That was the response from a kindergarten class after a read-aloud of *The Colors of Us* by Karen Katz (2012), a book that celebrates the many shades of skin color that make up "the colors of us." In the story, a little girl named Lena is painting a self-portrait and she wants to use brown paint for her skin. Her mother reminds her that brown comes in many different shades. As they walk around the neighborhood, Lena notices skin like peanut butter, dark chocolate, and pizza dough. She sees skin the color of caramel, cinnamon, and chocolate cupcakes.

After a read-aloud of this book, we invited students to move into a circle for the second part of the lesson. One student noticed the final illustration in the book—a border of hands celebrating the many skin colors featured throughout the story. This student looked up at the class and immediately invited us all to do the same: "Now let's put our hands together too and look at all the colors!" Another child chimed in, "Hands in, everybody!"

Any of us who read aloud to children have stories about the beautiful, hilarious, magical moments that happen in the midst of sharing a fabulous book aloud. Sometimes a book is so compelling you can predict how students will respond. Every time we have read *Drum Dream Girl* by Margarita Engle (2015), inspired by the incredible story of Millo Castro Zaldarriaga, children are inevitably inspired and outraged all at once! "Everyone should be allowed to play drums!" they cry. "Her father shouldn't say she can't play drums!" And, when we show them actual footage and photographs of Millo, they always scramble into position for a good look. Of course, we also take a moment to have a quick dance party as well, as we listen to the music of her band (easy to find: google "Millo Castro Zaldarriaga Drums" or "Anacaona 1937" for footage).

> Millo Castro Zaldarriaga was a Chinese, African, Cuban girl who resisted the taboos around drumming that existed for girls. In 1932, Millo began performing with her older sisters in a band they called Anacaona, which was considered Cuba's first all-girl dance band! Millo went on to play alongside some of the most famous jazz musicians of her time. She even played for President Franklin Delano Roosevelt's birthday party!

Reading aloud is one of the most powerful tools educators have to build community, engage children in critical thinking and comprehension, grow content area knowledge and vocabulary, and model the work of a sophisticated reader. Reading aloud is also one of the most powerful tools educators have to explore identity in meaningful, affirming ways. We both believe strongly that the work of belonging is inextricably tied to the power of story: to tell honest history, to celebrate identity, and create space for conversation and reflection, all of which is made possible by reading aloud a wide range of children's literature.

For a deep dive into the immense potential of reading aloud artfully, check out Rebecca's book, *The Artful Read-Aloud* (Bellingham 2019). For this chapter, however, we will be spotlighting the unparalleled potential of reading aloud to create classrooms and communities of belonging. Reading aloud literally brings to life stories and voices of all kinds of people, from all over the world, and from different times in history. The impact that artful, meaningful read-alouds can have on young learners in elementary school classrooms is hard to overstate. You are not only giving them access to sophisticated and academic vocabulary and concepts, you are giving

Why Read-Alouds Matter

Access: Read-alouds give children access to academic vocabulary and concepts that otherwise might be beyond reach. Helping children see themselves as readers and thinkers is something that supports reading development in all children, both while they are learning to decode and when they are reading independently.

Reading aloud also supports language development in children's brains, which is tied to their ability to learn to read on their own. In a recent study, researchers compared the activity in the language regions of the brain when children watch an animated version of a story, listen to the same story in audio format, or listen to a caregiver read the story. They discovered that the language centers in the brain light up the most when a caregiver reads the story, and the researchers dubbed their findings as "The Goldilocks Effect" (Klein 2022b). This underscores the importance of trusted adults reading aloud every day to children to support language development and build background knowledge about any number of subjects, which supports reading comprehension. As *Education Week* points out, "Decades of studies have shown that children can understand text better if they have some background knowledge about the topic" (Schwartz 2023), including the Commission on Reading's study that determined "the single most important activity for building knowledge required for eventual success in reading is reading aloud to children" (Brooks 2022).

Modeling: Read-alouds are the most efficient way to model the mind of a strong reader at work. Reading is an invisible process and we need to demonstrate the way in which successful readers make meaning out of all kinds of texts. By inviting children to pause and talk, or by thinking aloud ourselves, we model for students that we read to think, to understand, to question, to build knowledge and insights, and to feel deeply. We model for children that we don't just read to get to the other side of a book, but to let it inform us, move us, open us up, and connect us to ourselves and the world around us.

Joy: Read-alouds create connections and spread joy like nothing else because they make it possible for all children to listen together, laugh together, talk together, and make meaning in community. Gathering around a story, a poem, or a fascinating informational text is one of the most effective ways to build community and share ideas all at the same time.

them access to windows and mirrors. You are not just helping them understand how a sophisticated reader makes sense of text, you are helping them understand how a human being makes sense of the diverse world around them. You are not just lighting up the language centers in their brains, but you are lighting up students' capacity for connection, compassion, and curiosity.

ALL EYES ARE ON OUR READ-ALOUDS!

As educators, we know how engaging and connective the read-aloud can be, and as a result we spend a lot of time reading aloud to children throughout the day, throughout the school year, and throughout all content areas. We also know that teachers spend hours and weeks planning out which read-alouds to choose for their first day back at school, which read-alouds to use to complement and elevate units of study in social studies and literacy, and which read-alouds should be spread out across many weeks to explore themes such as friendship, diversity, and community. In other words, our read-alouds reflect significant investments of time and energy; what we choose matters, and the discussions we have around them impact kids deeply. But it is not enough to just choose the "right books." We always need to consider context, the dynamics of our classroom, and the current moment, especially when reading aloud a book. Equally important is the way in which our own learning and identity informs the choices we make and the way we lead conversations around these books.

When we read aloud a book to children, we are lifting up that story, that author, and that message in a more high-stakes way. We are asking all children to give their attention and their time to the read-aloud text, and we are modeling a different kind of investment in that text than if we were to only include it in our libraries or use it with a small group. Put simply, reading aloud a book to your class is very different from having it on your bookshelves! Given all this, you might decide to include a book in your library but not necessarily read it aloud.

Who Are the Students in Your Room?

Keep the dynamics of your room and your students foremost in your mind whenever you choose to read aloud a book. In the same way that we are mindful of how to pace a read-aloud to meet the reading needs of each student, stopping to pause to provide background knowledge or check for understanding, we are also mindful of how we are centering content that explores identity.

There are lots of books that affirm identity in straightforward ways, but some books require a different level of preparation because of the complex topics they address. Books like *Amy Wu and the Perfect Bao* by Kat Zhang (2019), *Festival of Colors* by Kabir Sehgal and Surishtha Sehgal (2018), and *Thank You, Omu* and *Saturday* by Oge Mora (2018 and 2019) are terrific examples of books that tell an uplifting story without also trying to address a challenge related to identity in explicit, or even implicit, ways. But books that intentionally affirm historically marginalized identities often also address a fuller historical context—which might mean surfacing stereotypes and painful history. When books surface honest history (like *Fry Bread* by Kevin Maillard [2019] or *On the Trapline* by David A. Robertson [2021]) or challenge stereotypes (like *Pink Is for Boys* by Robb Pearlman [2021]) they are often doing a few things at once. For example, *Hair Love* by Matthew A. Cherry (2019) is a love letter to Black hair, but it also pushes back against white, Eurocentric beauty norms at the same time. *Eyes That Kiss in the Corner* by Johanna Ho (2021) serves a similar purpose by celebrating Asian identity while also disrupting beauty norms. Because of the multiple layers that exist in some of these books, we need to be prepared to facilitate the conversations, questions, and responses that emerge around any number of issues related to the story—and to always keep our actual students in mind as we do this. In short, we should handle these read-alouds with care.

In the Moment: Facilitating Tricky Conversations

After sharing a book that addressed unkind words about identity, we invited students to write down their thoughts, feelings, or questions. After a few minutes of reflection, an Asian American student called Rebecca over to share about a time when she had experienced a hurtful comment about her eyes. Another time a Black student shared on his note card that he had been called a hateful term during a basketball practice. Years of facilitating these conversations has helped us anticipate the vulnerable sharing that can be tricky to navigate as a teacher. As a result, we intentionally craft reflections during these read-alouds that aren't whole-group or even partner share-outs. However, we can never control what students might say out loud. When this happens, and a student brings something to light and the whole class is watching, it can feel uncomfortable and the reflex might be to shut the conversation down.

Instead, pause. Think about how to add some guardrails around the discussion (you might recenter a specific community agreement or provide a whole-group reminder) without signaling that talk about identity is inappropriate territory. Before you respond to the moment, be mindful of your tone. Remember that kids don't always have the sophisticated, contemporary language we might use ourselves when discussing marginalization and that they're likely just thinking out loud and asking honest questions, which is a sign that you've built a trusting classroom community and that the read-aloud is resonating with your students.

Finally, we need to be mindful about how to support children who are not in the majority, or who might feel uncomfortable when a book surfaces stories or issues connected to their identity. This is particularly true around books that center hard history (books that grapple with slavery), which we will explore in more detail in Chapter 6: Teaching Honest History Artfully. Remember that identities are not always visible, so we don't want to assume that a child's identity is represented or not by a story that explores or uplifts identity. This is why the beginning of the year matters so much! When we take the time to get to know our students, and the multiple identities they house, we can make informed and nuanced decisions about what, when, or even *whether* to read a book aloud to the whole class.

Some children are uncomfortable sharing aspects of their identity publicly, which means that even if a book is an affirming window, they might feel particularly vulnerable or visible during the read-aloud. Other students welcome the opportunity to share about themselves, and finding a read aloud to support that child's experience will make a huge difference. Regardless, it's always helpful to check in with the student and their caregivers. They might be able to provide more context, resources, or offer helpful language their families use, like "We call ourselves Mexican American instead of Hispanic" or "At home we call my cochlear implant a sound machine!"

> **Handle with Care**
>
> If something egregious is being said to the group or hate speech has been spoken out loud, teachers should interrupt what is being said and name the harm. See the Learning for Justice "Speak Up at School" pocket guide (2012) for addressing harm in a way that is both restorative and direct.

Reading Aloud with Care: Tips for When You Can't Speak from the I-Perspective

1. *Be aware of your own comfort level.* As always, be mindful of your own comfort level around books outside your own identity and places or phrases that might cause you to feel discomfort, which can inadvertently send the wrong signal or message to children (*there's something inappropriate or strange about this character's identity*). Are there moments that are making you feel anxious that you might speed through or stumble on? Are there moments that make you uncomfortable because there are references or moments or experiences that feel unfamiliar, that are not what you grew up with? Is there vernacular, language, dialects that you don't use or feel familiar with? Are there cities, names, or other identifiers

in a book that you need to practice or learn how to pronounce before you read aloud? If so, practice reading those parts out loud to get more familiar with the text or the language. You also might find a colleague and simply talk through your questions or uncertainties. There are many resources and guides online where you can look up how to pronounce a name or place and listen for common usages. It's okay to stumble, but when we center our own discomfort around mistake-making, we are making it about *our* experience. On the other hand, if our stumbling reveals effort and intention and we handle the moment with grace, then we are thoughtfully modeling how to engage with material even when we can't speak from the I-perspective.

2. ***Read the voices in a straightforward way.*** Using voices, accents, dialects or sociolects outside of one's own identity can feel inauthentic and might reinforce stereotypes.

REBECCA

Reading Aloud When You Can't Speak from the I-Perspective

Reading aloud books that center character identities and experience outside of our own is a significant responsibility. As a white educator, I am especially intentional about the way I approach a read-aloud that centers BIPOC (Black, Indigenous, and people of color) voices. To honor the work of these authors and poets, I think about myself as a partner to the text—a vessel of sorts.

This idea of partnership was a revelation to me after hearing Jewell Parker Rhodes, author of acclaimed books such as *Ghost Boys* (2019) and *Ninth Ward* (2010), speak about her work as an author and artist. Rhodes encouraged teachers to see themselves as partners with her, and other writers, when they read her stories or use her work in the classroom. That helped frame the way I approach reading aloud books outside my identity: I am a partner with this book and with this author. It is my responsibility to give kids access to this story, this author, these ideas, this history but I need to be mindful about the way I show up in this moment, the way I use my voice, and the way I create an

REBECCA

environment that makes listening, learning, and conversation possible. I need to be particularly mindful of reading these stories with care. It may be my voice the students are hearing, but it is not my story and it is not my experience. As a result, I do not layer in any additional accents or assumed ways of speaking. I read the story, and the dialogue in a straightforward way. I lean into the *feelings* between characters, but I don't try to embody the identities of the characters, especially if the characters are marginalized *identities*. This was especially true as I read aloud Tae Keller's (2020) book *When You Trap a Tiger*. I read the dialogue between Halmoni and Lily tenderly, but in a straightforward way. I didn't try to embody Halmoni, but I did infuse the dialogue with her love for her granddaughter.

3. **Anticipate questions and tricky comments.** Be prepared for questions to arise that you might not have immediate answers for, or that might make you feel anxious or uncomfortable. That's OK. It's important to model taking a pause when you're not ready or prepared yet to dive into a potentially fraught or complicated conversation. For example, you might be reading a book like *Eyes That Kiss in the Corners* (Ho 2021) and a student could comment that the character in the book looks just like a classmate. As an adult, knowing stereotypes about Asian and Asian American identity being viewed as a monolith, you might be eager to shut this conversation down and respond to the student in a way that signals to them that their comment was shameful and wrong. Instead, you might try interrupting with care and educating at the same time by saying, "Hmm. I can see you're trying to make a connection. But every person is different in their own way, and if you look closely, we all have our own unique look."

4. **Shake up your traditions and take inventory of your classroom library.** As you grow into new awareness, you can begin to review your read-aloud picks with a fresh lens. We all have a shelf with

> **Handle with Care**
>
> **How to Interrupt Tricky Read-Aloud Moments**
>
> When a student asks a question or shares a comment that feels problematic, here's a helpful guide for navigating these kinds of moments: (1) Pause calmly (2) Push back without shaming (3) Teach into a skill (maybe the skill of noticing, being an upstander, or other skills that could support the student and group's growth).

CONNECTING WITH YOUR STUDENTS THROUGH ARTFUL READ-ALOUDS

our favorites, and we all have books we love reading aloud each year, but that shelf can get dusty! We encourage you to look at your annual favorites and consider mixing it up a bit, sometimes swapping out or letting go, and sprinkling in a few new ones hot off the press.

5. *You are a mentor text.* Remember that you are modeling and teaching how to navigate conversations around identity. The book and the content within the book is only one part of the process. Students will be watching and learning from you as you facilitate the conversation that grows from the read-aloud. There will be times for interrupting with care (as in the previous tip) while other times you might need to opt for more firm interruptions to support the students in your classroom who house identities that have been historically marginalized. We are not only modeling strong reading skills, but also a willingness to embrace

Where to Find Your Next Great Read-Aloud!

1. **Award Winners and Short Lists:** We all love the Newbery and Caldecott award-winning books but make sure to check out the books that have been honored, or short-listed by these organizations: Stonewall Award, Pura Belpré Award, Coretta Scott King Award, Walter Dean Myers Awards, Sydney Taylor Book Award, American Indian Youth Literature Award, Asian/Pacific American Award for Literature, among others

2. **Bookstore Newsletters and Multicultural Publishing Houses:** Check out local BIPOC bookstores or sign up for their newsletters. Shout out to the bookstores Cafe con Libros in Brooklyn and Rep Club in LA and the publishing house Lee and Low!

3. **American Library Association and School Library Journal:** This journal lists the winners of multiple children's literature awards.

4. **Your Local Library and Librarians** (who deserve their own shout-out on this list!): For generations, many librarians (like Pura Belpré!) have been curating beautiful collections of lesser-known authors and their work. Pop into your local library to see what they have on display!

5. **Curated Lists:** ADL Books Matter™ (n.d.) allows you to search by topic or find children's books; WNDB (We Need Diverse Books); 1000BlackGirlBooks (Dias 2015).

a learner's stance, which helps children understand that learning about the world is continuous—that it's OK to acknowledge what you don't understand or know yet, and that all of us, even adults, sometimes get it wrong. The important thing is to stay open and keep learning.

6. *Think about intentional pairing.* Consider curating materials and media that can help you contextualize the story you're sharing and engage in a deeper dive into the identity and culture being centered in your read-aloud. This could be as simple as sharing a photograph of BIPOC authors and illustrators whenever you read their stories. For example, after a read-aloud of *Fry Bread* (Maillard 2019), consider displaying a photo of Kevin Maillard (and sharing that he is a Black member of the Seminole Nation) along with an intentional pairing, like a video clip of Sean Sherman who talks about the history of Indigenous foods and creates dishes that represent tribal diversity.

ALL HANDS IN! AN ARTFUL READ-ALOUD EXPERIENCE OF BEING COLOR BRAVE

The book that we opened this chapter with, *The Colors of Us* by Karen Katz (2012), is one of our favorites. We love to launch the school year with this beautiful picture book that affirms the kinds of noticing children are already doing—what Melody Hobson calls being "color brave" (Hobson 2014). Being color brave encourages us to move from color-blindness to "speaking openly and honestly about race." And *The Colors of Us* empowers students with positive language (mostly delicious foods!) for naming what they notice. We often invite teachers to read this book aloud at the beginning of the year because it sets children up to talk about identity and skin color all year long, but it also gives adults a positive and readily available construct for noticing differences and skin color as well.

A Black mom at our school once shared that her kindergarten daughter was experiencing exclusion by her classmate and was told that the classmate didn't want to play with her because of her dark skin. The girl's teacher approached us to seek guidance in leading a conversation that would support the class after this incident. We decided that this would be a perfect time for our annual read-aloud of *The Colors of Us* to engage students in a developmentally appropriate conversation about skin color, celebrating differences, and being inclusive of all. We intentionally designed the read-aloud to affirm dark skin color and model brave noticing of differences. To prepare to read aloud, we read the book together and looked for moments where we might intentionally pause to notice and affirm dark skin color. And, while we read aloud, we made sure to spend time with each illustration to demonstrate how beautiful and special each different character is in their own way.

Another time, when we were prepping for this lesson in the hallway, a young white boy overheard us naming out some of the foods and chimed in with, "I LOVE chocolate brownies!" This was another reminder of how affirming it is to offer students beautiful words about things they love (delicious foods) to describe skin colors, especially those as gorgeous (and yet all too often underappreciated) as dark chocolate brown.

Before we begin reading this book aloud we remind students about our community agreements and reinforce the first two: "Listen First" and "Speak from the I-Perspective," which can be adapted for younger children to "Speak from your own heart." While reading the book aloud, we pause at a few places to intentionally affirm a few characters who have "chocolate brown" and "bronze and amber" skin: "Look how beautiful those jewels look against Candy's bronze and amber skin," we say. Or "I just love chocolate cupcakes." We do this to implicitly push back against colorism and wrap a little extra love around any students in the room who have dark brown skin.

After reading the book, we might reinforce the message with a poem (we have one you can use at the end of this chapter) or go straight into the noticing part of the lesson. After reading the poem, we model noticing:

> **Veronica:** *So now we are going to look around and notice all the beautiful and different colors that are in this classroom. When I look around, I see the color of dulce de leche. Ms. Bellingham, what do you see when you look around?*
>
> **Rebecca:** *I see the color of my morning coffee, which is one of my favorite colors to see! So students, now it's your turn. When you look around this classroom, what colors of the world do you see? What beautiful shades do you notice? It could be your own skin color, or it could be a skin color you're noticing in the classroom!*

Before we invite children to share out loud, we display a slide (see Figure 4–1) that includes many kinds of food to make it easier for students to make a comparison. The foods that are represented on the slide are purposefully chosen. We want to make sure to include foods that reflect a wide range of children's backgrounds because the foods we eat are so closely tied to our homes, our families, and our identities. Designing a slide with foods that are affirming takes a small amount of effort but makes a huge difference to children. And thanks to platforms like Canva, it is easy to design slides that are both artful and representative of your community.

Figure 4-1 Delicious ideas for *The Colors of Us*

If you need some inspiration or ideas for what you're noticing, you can look at this board for some ideas!

When you get an idea, give us a quiet thumb. When we're already we will go around the circle and share the colors of us that we see.

It looks like we are ready, so when it's your turn you can say, "When I look around, I see the color of _____."

After we share out our noticing, we close out this experience by asking students how it makes them feel to notice all these different colors of skin.

Here are some of the responses we have heard over the years:

When I see all the colors I feel calm and joyful.

I feel grateful and excited.

I feel happy because we all have different skin colors.

I see all different colors and all these different colors are really important.

I feel brave and excited and everything sounds delicious.

We chart the children's noticings, which makes it possible to create a class poem that reflects the observations and feelings of each group. Figure 4–2 is a poem by first graders that would be displayed next to the Delicious Ideas poster in the classroom.

1st Grade Poem

When we look around we see the colors of us
The colors of bread and bao
Tortilla chips and churros
Hot cocoa and cinnamon
How delicious all these colors are

When I look around the classroom
I see beautiful shades of skin color
I see cotton candy, sugar cookies, and chocolate cake
I see vanilla ice cream and fudge topping
And my sister is caramel—a little darker than me!
So many beautiful shades!

When I look around the classroom
I see all different colors
I see skin as brown as hot chocolate
I see peanut butter and pancakes
Gingerbread cookies and whipped cream
All different, all important, and all really beautiful
When I notice all these colors
I feel happy, I feel brave and excited
And I think to myself 맛있어 (Mas-iss-eo)
Which means . . . DELICIOUS!

When I see all the colors I feel calm and joyful
I feel grateful and excited
And I don't feel lonely at all
I don't feel lonely at all!

Figure 4-2

You might notice one of the lines is written in Korean. During our class discussion comparing skin colors to different foods, a first grader named Jonny saw a picture of bao on our food list and responded enthusiastically saying, "mas-iss-eo!" (Korean: 맛있어) out loud to the class. Veronica privately asked him if he could share what this word meant and he happily shared "*Mas-iss-eo* means *delicious*!" We asked Jonny if we could include his special word in our class poem and he was thrilled. This was particularly special because Jonny had sometimes been reluctant to share his Korean language with the class, but maybe due to the affirming nature of this experience and hearing the support of his classmates, he felt proud and comfortable to do so.

We also want to underscore that the point of this lesson is to give students language for the noticing they're already doing and help them realize that there is nothing wrong with noticing differences. Being color brave isn't about encouraging students to constantly name out their noticing, which could be overwhelming for students in the classroom whose visible differences might be in the minority, it just means being comfortable naming and talking about identity!

CLOSING WITH A POEM

As we wrote our closing poem for this chapter, we imagined all the children you teach and all the ways they show up in your room and in the pages of your read-alouds. If you do choose to read this poem with your class, we hope it inspires your students to share in their own community moment of celebrating who they are and what they notice about each other. And don't forget to look around the classroom and just marvel, for a moment, at the magic of our differences—"Hands in, everybody!"

The Colors We See
MS. BELLINGHAM AND MS. SCOTT

There are lots of different shades of brown
There are lots of different colors to see
These are the colors of us
These are the colors of you and me

I see the color of nilla wafers and butter rolls
I see the color of caramel corn and cinnamon tea

I see the color of honey and milk
And colors dark and chocolatey

I see skin that's butterscotch sweet
And skin that's peachy and tan
I see skin like hot cocoa
And skin like a gingerbread man

I see cheeks that are sunset pink
And toffee colored too
I see cheeks like warm spice cake
And skies like nighttime blue

What colors of the world do you see?
What beautiful shades are here?
What colors of the world do you see?
When we take a look around
So many colors appear!

5

HARNESSING THE POWER OF POETRY

How to Create and Reflect as a Community

> Poetry and language are often at the heartbeat of movements for change.
> —Amanda Gorman, "Amanda Gorman and Michelle Obama in Conversation"

EXPLORING THE ARTS TO LEARN FOR SELF-GROWTH

When we were growing up we both had friends who aspired to be writers, actors, and artists, but we never knew anyone who wanted to be a poet. Poetry seemed, for many in our circles at least, like something you learned about, not something you did. Certainly not for a living, but not even as a practice for reflection or connection just for yourself. But as many of you might have noticed in your own classrooms and school communities, this has started to change. Thanks to a new generation of talented bards like Elizabeth Acevedo, Jason Reynolds, Clint Smith, Ocean Vuong, Jericho Brown, and of course, Amanda Gorman, poetry has been elevated to a new place in our cultural imagination. Novels in verse like Kwame Alexander's Crossover series (2019), Lisa Fipps' *Starfish* (2021), and Jasmine Warga's *Other Words for Home* (2021) are not only winning awards but are also developing a new cultural currency among young people. It's like poetry is having another renaissance, only this time the Beyoncé kind with silver sparkles and dance hall energy (everything comes back to Beyoncé).

The power of poetry is certainly nothing new. For centuries people have gathered to share stories and express themselves in verse. As evident in this book, the poetry of today would likely not be possible without the brilliant minds of poets like Nikki Giovanni, Langston Hughes, Mary Oliver, and Maya Angelou. But for us Gorman Fangirls at least, the 2021 inauguration marked a turning point for the status of poetry in our zeitgeist. We both remember the moment in the inauguration when Amanda Gorman took to the stage and performed her now-famous piece, "The Hill We Climb" (Gorman 2021). Commentators reflected that Gorman had given voice to this historical day in ways that no other performer had been able to that morning, which was quite the statement given she followed world-renown pop stars Jennifer Lopez and Lady Gaga. Millions of people tuned in to witness what few poetry moments had ever achieved—pop culture status.

It was almost as if, when she climbed those steps of the U.S. Capitol, Gorman was not only honoring the passing of the presidential torch but also ushering in a new poetry era. And young people were paying attention. Gorman's closing lines would soon be turned into posters and quoted by little voices in classrooms across the nation. Her iconic gold blazer and red velvet headband would soon become a Halloween costume favorite of aspiring poets who hoped to one day follow in her footsteps. Not long after, Gorman would become the first poet to grace the cover of *Vogue*, making the subtext text, that in case you weren't paying attention poetry was now en vogue.

Now we are in the midst of this surge in which poetry has new relevance and significance. More and more people are recognizing that language matters, that the way we use language has enormous potential to repair, heal, honor, and transform. For too long there have been gatekeepers to the world of poetry and the last thing many people would identify with is being poets, of all things! *I don't get poetry, poetry is not for me, poems are too complicated and inaccessible.* But using poetry to build community, share stories, explore identity, and foster belonging is one of the most accessible and impactful tools we have because poetry makes it possible to write yourself into being on the page even with a few very simple words arranged in just the way that you want!

Pádraig Ó Tuama, host of *Poetry Unbound*, writes,

> *As I think of poems as a "made thing," I wonder, who is making whom? Often, I only discover what I'm feeling when what I write tells it back to me. The made thing makes me back . . . I know that others are the same: artists of all kinds are made back by the art they make. And by artists, I mean us all. Who isn't an artist? (2022)*

THE ARTFUL APPROACH TO EXPLORING IDENTITY AND FOSTERING BELONGING

Jason Reynolds echoes this idea when he describes writers and poets such as Langston Hughes and Maya Angelou as "word-makers." When asked why he used that term in his first-ever picture book *There Was a Party for Langston* (2023), Reynolds replied, "When we talk about making something, we're talking about the creation. Usually when we say it, we're talking about the creation of a tangible thing. To me language is a tangible thing; it leads to the tangible nature of our lives" (*CBS Mornings* 2023).

Both Ó Tuama and Reynolds remind us that writing poems isn't about being lofty or clever or using perfect meter, but about creating and making something new. We write poems to *make ourselves back*, to make meaning out of our lives, to give (tangible) form, even with something as effortless as a list, to our experiences. We write poems to wrap language around our stories, our memories, our hopes and dreams, our identities. When we invite children to write poems, we are inviting them to declare themselves on the page, to be seen, to be heard, to be embodied, to be made worthy and significant and whole. We invite children to write poems so they can honor and perhaps reveal who they are to us and to themselves.

POETRY IS A WAY TO START SMALL

As poets, we work in a line. We start really small. We start with a syllable. We start with a sound.

Ada Limón (Klein 2022a)

While poetry may seem complicated, we think it's one of the easiest ways to dive into identity work with young people. Poetry is easy to find (see "Where to Find a Poem"). Poetry sets a tone. Poetry is lyrical, rhythmic, and creates a space for movement. Poetry can serve a big need in a short time. Poetry gives you a chance to start small, which can make it a more invitational literary art form than an essay or even a free-write. And because poetry is meant to be read aloud, it's inevitably an opportunity to express ourselves and share our stories in community with each other. In even the briefest bit of time, poetry connects us all.

When asked about why she chose to cowrite her book *Born on the Water* (Hannah-Jones and Watson 2021) in verse, Renée Watson said that poems can act as "containers for young people to process their emotions . . . each poem kinda acts as a small vignette so you can pause and kinda breathe through . . . and take it in bite size pieces. . . . " (Pulitzer Center 2022). While this is certainly true for the experience of reading and sharing *Born on the Water,* we find this to be true about poetry in general. Poems can act as containers for all sorts of complex conversations and content, whether that be marveling at the vastness of our universe, grappling with hard history, or navigating friendship troubles in third grade. As a rhythmic art form, poems have the pauses and breaths built in. We can use those pauses to remind ourselves to slow down, listen more carefully, and reflect little by little, line by line.

Because of their brevity, poems make it easier for students to express themselves without the pressure of writing a perfect paragraph or an entire essay. In the same way

Where to Find a Poem!

While we have several books of poetry collections that we return to frequently, most of the time we collect poems in other ways. Here are a few suggestions for finding poetry that is both fresh and responsive to your needs:

1. **Picture books are often written as poems!** We often type up the words of a picture book to create a poem that can be used to inspire children to write their own. Be on the lookout for picture books that have a repeating refrain or only a line or two per page and allow it to inspire you to create a prompt or invitation for your own students. Some of our favorite picture books that read like poems are: *You Matter* by Christian Robinson (2020), *Love* by Matt de la Peña (2018), *Fry Bread* by Kevin Maillard (2019), and *Autumn Peltier, Water Warrior* by Carole Lindstrom (2023).

2. **Songs are also written as poems!** Study a song, even just a refrain, that might spark an idea, conversation, or an invitation for writing.

3. **Books told in verse have scores of poems to use with young people,** even if you don't read the whole book aloud, or use the whole book for a particular age group. We've used "Mami Works" from Elizabeth Acevedo's book *The Poet X* (2018) to teach how precise action words can reveal so much about a person, which inspired our "Mountains We Climb" Women's History Month project.

4. **Broaden your searches to include poems not written for kids!** When we google "poems for kids," we don't often find a poem that suits our needs. Lots of times the poems that come up are limericks and rhyming poems, which are fabulous for fluency, vocabulary, morning meetings, and any number of important academic areas or daily moments. Most of the

that pauses can serve us well, refrains are also a common element in poetry that signal to us *look again.* They're an invitation to think, see, and make meaning in new ways every time they appear. Refrains remind us that even the smallest thing contains multitudes—one line, one phrase, one word can be—just like us—many things.

In this chapter, you'll find original poems written by the two of us and some of the young people with whom we work. You might use these poems to build community at the beginning of the year, or to celebrate identity and cultural months throughout the year. You'll also find prompts that make it easy for you and your students to get started with your own poems, but of course feel free to mix it up and use the prompts however the creative spirit moves you!

time we are looking to share something that invites deeper thinking about identity, or that offers us a lyrical phrase that we can use as a prompt or starting point to build upon creatively. Even just sharing an excerpt from a poem whose target audience is not young people, you will open possibilities for expression and connection that might be more inspiring or fruitful than if you just stick with poems tagged for children.

5. **Find a few voices that you love** and whom you can return to again and again for inspiration. Some of our go-to authors and poets are Christian Robinson, Matt de la Peña, Jason Reynolds, and Joanna Ho. These writers are always producing new work and they all write poems that are intended for young people. We also love Joy Harjo, Mary Oliver, Naomi Shihab Nye, Nikki Giovanni, Clint Smith, and Aimee Nezhukumatathil, among others who don't often or always write explicitly for children, but whose work can be used to elevate a conversation, a curricular unit, a cultural month, or even a community moment. We pay attention to what our faves are writing and we watch for other poets they lift up.

6. **There are several websites that we browse for ideas:** Poetryfoundation.org, and poets.org are often categorized by BIPOC voices, cultural months, subject areas, and different times of year.

7. **Get to know your poet laureates!** Even though we have a national poet laureate, states, and even some cities, have "poet laureates" too! This is a great way to get to know local voices in your area and learn about other poets who are writing and sharing new work.

8. **Look out the window:** Poetry is all around us! As Ada Limón, one of our poet laureates, instructs young poets, "Don't forget to look out the window and stare at things, because that's where poetry happens" (Limón 2023).

HARNESSING THE POWER OF POETRY

How to Use This Chapter

You might think of this chapter as an anthology of sorts, one that is organized around times of year and themes that often arise in elementary school classrooms. There have been times when we felt we needed a particular poem to address any number of moments that occur throughout a school year, and when we didn't find the exact poem we needed, sometimes we wrote one ourselves! We try to write poems that are not only artful, but that also set children up to write their own poems, that give them a bit of a scaffold for expressing their own ideas.

We hope these poems will be useful to you as you begin your year and invite students to express themselves through poetry. We also hope the poems that we share that are inspired by picture books will help you deepen your awareness for the possibilities inherent in picture books for poetry invitations and community poems. Finally, we hope you use these poems as a resource as you help children reflect on their learning and their progress and as you build your classroom community throughout the year.

We've collected the poems into one Mentor Poems document (OR 5-1) so that you can access and print copies for your classroom as needed. In addition to the mentor poems and lessons appearing in this chapter, you'll find additional mentor poems and lessons in the Online Resources (OR 5-2 through OR 5-9).

POEMS ACROSS THE YEAR

Following is a table of contents to help you navigate this anthology of poems. We grouped the poems into two categories: "Beginning of the Year Poems" to use to launch a new school year and "Throughout the Year Poems" which includes poems that pair nicely with cultural months, holidays, or seasonal moments, and can also be used any time of the year. While we wrote most of these poems, some were written by children inspired by prompts or invitations we shared with them.

Along with each poem, there is an invitation or a prompt for you to use to help children get started in their own writing.

Beginning of the Year Poems

- First Day Backpack
- Summer Shines
- Our Promises (online only, OR 5–2)
- *Just Like Me* Inspired Poems: I Am Many Things, I Am Many Places
- Planting Seeds in Third Grade (online only, OR 5–3)

Throughout the Year Poems

- My Grandmother Has Knitting Needles/My Sister Has a Song
- At This Table (online only, OR 5–4)
- Our Something Beautiful (online only, OR 5–5)
- Food Is Love (online only, OR 5–6)
- The Song I'll Sing This Year (online only, OR 5–7)
- My Friend Is Sad Today (online only, OR 5–8)
- Black History Month and Express Yourself Poems:

  Express Yourself

  I Wrote a Poem for You Because

  The Reason I Like _____

  Octopus Cave

  Soundsuits: Nick Cave Found Poem (online only, OR 5–9)

- How to _____ Poems:

  How to Love Your Own Little Classroom

  How to Love Your Own Little Family (online only, OR 5–1)

  How to Do Something Small That Makes a *Big* Difference

Beginning of the Year Poems

The first days of school are perfect for creating community poems and sharing aspects of our identities with each other. In addition to poems and invitations below, simple list poems can be an easy and low-stakes way to create community right off the bat. Just about anything can be a list, and therefore a list poem! You could create any number of prompts for beginning of the year list poems including:

- 5 Dreams for First Grade!
- 3 Things I Need This Year to Thrive
- Our Ways to Be a Good Friend

First Day Backpack

Backpacks hold everything you might need for a school day—what a great way to teach metaphor! You could create a Backpack Poem for any special day, theme, or activity: A Field Trip Backpack, A Friendship Backpack, A Baseball Game Backpack, or a Library Backpack! Check out our "Belonging Backpack" poem in Chapter 7: Responding with Care. The poem below brings a little artful twist to first day of school jitters and names out the kind of community we want to create.

First Day Backpack

A good night's sleep

Your favorite outfit

A mini pep talk (from somebody—even yourself!)

Bounce in your step

A few deep breaths

Something delicious in your tummy

A dash of courage

An elbow bump from your new classroom teacher

Familiar faces waving hello

A silly joke from an old friend

A sprinkle of kindness from a new friend

Invitation: What is in your "first day" backpack?

Summer Shines

We wrote this poem to lift the extraordinary ordinary moments of summer, help students notice simple pleasures, and create a more inclusive sharing experience.

Summer Shines

Swimming and splashing in the summer moonlight
Staying in PJ's all day and all night
Ice cream for dinner cools down the heat
A new favorite song and I dance to the beat
Not showering not scrubbing not brushing my hair
Not leaving the couch—a day free of care!
Sleepovers with cousins and friends from the block
We're sleeping in late! Who needs a clock?
Walking with grandpa to buy a cold coke
Laughing so hard when he tells me a joke
Spending all day in shorts and bare feet
Look at the heatwaves that wiggle the street!
Movie-night time when the rain just won't stop
Building a fort with blankets on top
Snuggled together my brother and I
See all the fireflies light up the sky
We'll never let go of this last summer night
We're making this summer shine one last time
Yeah, making this summer shine one last time

Invitation: Sometimes the best moments of summer are the everyday ordinary ones, the ones that you don't plan, or that happen unexpectedly—like a surprise visit from a cousin or a rainstorm in the middle of the day! Let's think about some of those "extraordinary ordinary" moments from our summer and create our very own "Summer Shines" poem together! What was one of your "summer shines"?

"I Am Many Things" and *"I Am Many Places"*

Pádraig Ó Tuama reminds us that even though some think poetry is "an abstract art," most of the time, "a poet is trying to say something about 'I am,' trying to speak of the dignity and the power of their own life, and that they're using that powerful word 'I' and locating it in the poem, to say something that's true for them. And because of that, it's true for many" (Ó Tuama 2020). When we encourage children to write about themselves in poem form, we are giving them opportunities to say something true about themselves. One of the books we often use to help children write their own "I am" poems is Vanessa Brantley Newton's *Just Like Me* (Newton 2020), which includes poems about being many things—like a canvas, a warrior, a city girl, a country girl, an explorer, a little sister, and a negotiator (to name a few). We also share our own poems, "I Am Many Things" and "I Am Many Places" to intentionally model how to celebrate multiple aspects of our identities and give students various entry points for sharing about who they are.

I Am Many Things
REBECCA

I am a Michigan Girl
I pick and pit and pie bright red and purple cherries
I search and skip and save spotted Petoskey stones
I swim out to the rocks
I skip through the pines
And I stay up late with the sun
on midsummer nights

I am a Singing Girl
I wake up with a song on my brain
and a will to sing it all morning long
I sing in the car
I sing in the shower
I sing in the kitchen
I sing on the sidewalk
I even sing in my dreams

I am a Teacher
I read out loud and I share my words
I listen and look closely while children learn
I model and reflect
I plan and research
I learn from all of the teachers
devoted to this work

I am a Mommy
I hug and hold
I comfort and reassure
I drop off and pick up
I wake up and tuck in
I toast and I pour
And sometimes I lose my patience
But mostly I love and I love
And I love and I love
And I love and I love
And I love

I Am Many Places
VERONICA

I am the bluebonnets
Swaying in the Texas sun
My roots branch down
Deep into the soil
But my petals glow indigo
Like velvet faces
Gazing up
Toward the midnight sky

I am the ocean waves

Gleaming on a golden shore

My emerald waters

and crystal surf

Swell with the tides

Like California dreams

Reaching across

An endless sandy coast

I am the snow falling

On the rooftops

And cobblestone

The city winds

Carry me

From park bench

To shop window

And onto the glowing headlights

Of a yellow taxi cab

Here to take me home

Invitation: What parts of your identity do you want to celebrate with a poem? You might choose a few aspects from your "I Am" list or identity map and think about some actions, feelings, and images that help you expand, elaborate, and grow your ideas into a small poem. Or add a twist by incorporating symbols representing places that are important to you.

- Prompt (Many Things version):

    I am a _____ (part of your identity)

    What's a part of your identity you want to share? (*I am a Singing Girl*) What are some things about that part of your identity that you do or feel? (*I wake up with a song on my brain*)

- Prompt (Many Places version):

    I am a _____ (symbol to represent a place)

What's a symbol that represents where you are from, where you live now, or where you dream of going? Maybe you are a peach tree in Grandma's yard, a skyscraper in your city, or a corner deli with your favorite treats. And what's an action you can imagine this symbol doing? It could be something that represents what you love about the place or something unique to who you are! Maybe your peach tree is helping out by providing shade on a sunny day or maybe it's blossoming in the spring with juicy ripe peaches that remind you of home.

Throughout the Year Poems

"My Grandmother Had Knitting Needles" and "My Sister Has a Song"

> *My Papi has a motorcycle.*
> *From him I've learned words like carburetor and cariño,*
> *drill and dedication.*

My Papi Has a Motorcycle by Isabella Quintero (2019) is one of our all-time favorite books to use with young people and teachers, and these beautiful opening lines are a perfect invitation to share about the people in our lives who have impacted us, which is another meaningful way to share about our identities, at the beginning of the year or anytime. You also might spotlight writer Isabella Quintero as part of Hispanic Heritage Month.

Every time we invite people to write a stanza or a poem using the following prompt, we are inevitably blown away by what people share, the feelings that surface in the room, and the way such a simple prompt makes such an affirming community moment possible.

My Grandmother Has Knitting Needles
REBECCA

My grandmother had knitting needles
From her I learned how to pay close attention,
To stay observant and soft,
To wrap myself in the care I need.

My grandfather had a toolbox.
From him I learned how to fix what's broken
To notice the smallest cracks,
Offer what I can to make them whole

My grandmommy had flour, sugar, spices, and oil.
From her I learned to enjoy the moment
To savor the hour that we are in
To always say yes to sweet cakes, a clinking glass
Another round of cards

My mother has a permanent marker
From her I've learned to make a plan (and stick to it!)
To consider the details and the needs of others.
To hold tight to what matters most

My father has a book
From him I've learned to never stop learning
To stay open, to think fresh, to connect
Idea to idea to idea to idea

My husband has an iron pot
From him I've learned to stay steady
To nourish others without fanfare
To stay grounded and strong
One onion at a time

THE ARTFUL APPROACH TO EXPLORING IDENTITY AND FOSTERING BELONGING

My children have a wand
From them I've learned that magic spells
Are less about the magic
And more about the shared delight

- Prompt:

My _____ has a _____

From him/her/them I've learned _____

REBECCA

Incorporating Movement into Poetry

I love incorporating movement into poetry, and I've used this poem to create a spoken-word dance piece with TranscenDANCE students in San Diego. Layering in movement with the words enabled students to embody their connections to family, friends, elders, and ancestors, which elevated the experience, and ultimately the performance of this community poem. I indicated the places in the text when students moved their bodies to help you imagine how this poem came to life. Asking a question such as "How might you add movement to one line of this poem?" opens up possibilities for embodiment and self-expression for any experience, even ones that are with an entire class of children!

My Sister Has a Song
MIDDLE SCHOOL STUDENTS

My sister has a song
From her I've learned to keep dancing (3-second dance move, then freeze in neutral position)
To be graceful and express myself
To do what I love and find happiness

My mother has a yellow mixing bowl ("stir" the bowl with wide circular motions out in front)

From her I've learned

To always share what you have

To share your love with special treats

My abuelito has a tomato garden (slowly sink to the "earth")

From him I've learned that sunlight and love help things grow (one by one begin to rise up until everyone is standing by the end of the verse)

That tasty things take time

That delicious tomatoes are worth the wait

My brother has a baseball bat (in position with your "bat"!)

From him I've learned to keep swinging (swing!)

And keep trying (swing again!)

And always have fun (high-five a neighbor)

VERONICA

Express Yourself: Celebrating Black Artists

"Express Yourself" is a celebration of Black artists, writers, and poets perfect for Black History Month (or anytime!). Inspired by "Majestic" by Kwame Alexander, this poem spotlights and celebrates the work of historical figures like Maya Angelou, James Baldwin, and Alvin Ailey, as well as contemporary creatives like Jason Reynolds, Spike Lee, and Quinta Brunson. By giving each artist their own unique stanza, this poem makes space for diversity within the Black diaspora and illustrates the different ways Black artists show up in the world.

Black History Month and Express Yourself Poems

Express Yourself
VERONICA

Like James Baldwin
Who wrote to the world
And took his typewriter
Wherever he flew
From Harlem to the Swiss Alps
From Paris to Istanbul
Putting words onto pages
From his traveling mind
And reminding the people that
Not everything that is faced can be changed,
But nothing can be changed
Until it is faced.

Lift your voice
Like Nikki Giovanni
Who was born in Knoxville, Tennessee
And grew up to be
A professor,
A poet,
A picture book queen
Using her voice to move mountains
And reminding the people
That we are like snowflakes
That we are like birds
That we can fly
That we are loved

Paint a rainbow sea
Like Ashley Bryan
Who lived to be almost 100
And spent his days
In his artist studio
on a little island
Off the coast of Maine
Bringing his imagination to life
And reminding the people
That we can paint the world
With the sunniest yellows or cloudiest blues
The way we see it
The way we dream it

Stretch your arms up to the sky
Like Alvin Ailey
Who danced to his own beat
And made his own moves
And started his own company
Bringing hundreds of ballets
From his dancing mind
To the world's stage
And reminding the people to
Dance when we are tired
Dance when we are happy
Dance when we are together
Dance, Dance, Dance

Invitation: Who is a Black artist that inspires you and what do they inspire you to do? _____ like _____ (e.g., Maybe you want to Write to the World like James Baldwin or Paint a Rainbow Sea like Ashley Bryan)

THE ARTFUL APPROACH TO EXPLORING IDENTITY AND FOSTERING BELONGING

Poems Inspired by Nikki Giovanni

During our "Express Yourself" themed Black History Month celebration, we explored the partnership between Nikki Giovanni and Ashley Bryan, who collaborated on two books of poetry, *I Am Loved* (2018) and *The Sun Is So Quiet* (2014). We read through several of Nikki Giovanni's poems but focused on three in particular as a way to invite children to write poems of their own: "Because," "The Reason I Like Chocolate," and "Rainbows."

After modeling poems of our own inspired by Nikki Giovanni's work, we created prompts and invitations for children to write their own "Because" poems for people, pets, even foods, and "The Reason I Like" poems for things they wanted to celebrate!

Because You Are My Little Brother
VERONICA

I wrote a poem
for you because
you are my little brother.

I wrote a poem
for you because
whenever we go to the movies
you always share your buttery popcorn
and chocolate covered raisins
and you laugh under your breath
at the same parts as me

I wrote a poem
for you because
you build the biggest forts
and you play the silliest games
but you're never mean about it
even when you win
for the third time in a row

Figure 5-1 The Reason I Like Trees

Figure 5-2 The Reason I Like Colors

HARNESSING THE POWER OF POETRY

I wrote a poem
for you because
you always sing along in the car
and you point out the window
at the most interesting sights to see
because no one understands me
quite like you

Figure 5-3 Because You Are My Pet

Figure 5-4 Because You Are Someone Shining in My Life

Take notice of the way children created illustrations for their poems in the fabulously bright, bold style of Ashley Bryan!

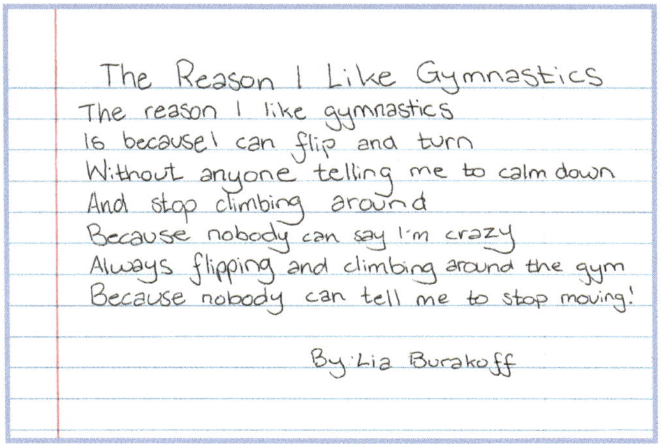

> **The Reason I Like Gymnastics**
> The reason I like gymnastics
> Is because I can flip and turn
> Without anyone telling me to calm down
> And stop climbing around
> Because nobody can say I'm crazy
> Always flipping and climbing around the gym
> Because nobody can tell me to stop moving!
>
> By Lia Burakoff

Figure 5-5 The Reason I Like Gymnastics

If you read Nikki Giovanni's poem "The Reason I Like Chocolate," you'll notice that this student used her poem as a mentor text even more so than we did!

Nikki Giovanni's "Rainbows" is a fanciful poem that starts with the line, "If I could . . ." and involves a little boy swimming through the air to reach a "rainbow boat." We simply borrowed the opening lines, "If I could . . ." and invited children to tap into their imagination. What would they do "if they could"? Where would they go? What would they do? We encouraged them to let their imaginations run wild, and use specific action words, just like Nikki Giovanni did.

We also looked closely at the way Nikki Giovanni ended her poem with a slight shift, starting with the word "But . . ." to acknowledge the reality and the fantasy embedded in the poem. Rebecca closed her poem with a similar turn, using the phrase, "But I am just a lady who lives on the earth."

Octopus Cave
REBECCA

If I could swim

down down deep

Into the ocean

I would find myself a cave

And share it with a friendly octopus

HARNESSING THE POWER OF POETRY

She would show me
How to pluck treasures from the sandy floor
Weave among the coral trees
And squeeze inside the smallest shell

She would show me
How to hold still and hide in plain sight
How to turn from red to blue to green to brown
To change my shape and become something new

At the end of the day
We would invite
All the other fish
To join us for a costume party
Using the crowns and jewels
And magic wands
We found inside
The trunk of treasure
We discovered together
In the shipwreck that lives next door

But, I am a lady who lives on the earth
And who cannot dive down to the sea
For days or weeks at a time
I will just have to close my eyes
And imagine instead

Invitation:
If I could, I _____
Where would you go? What would you do?

Figure 5-6

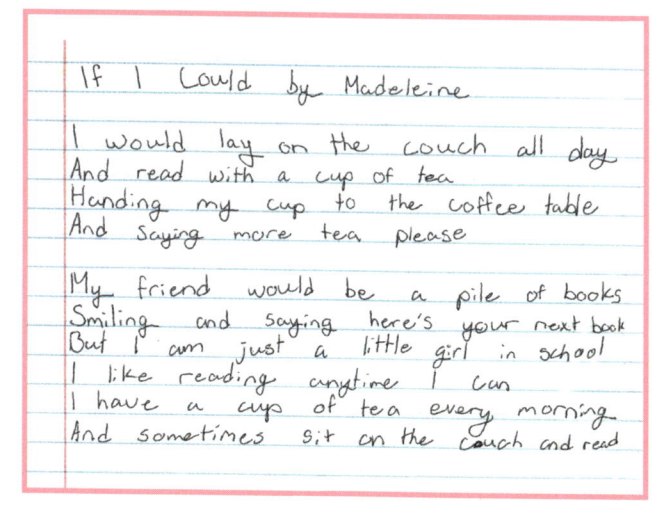

Figure 5-7

How to Love Your Own Little Classroom

The poem "How to Love Your Own Little Corner of the World" by Eileen Spinelli, in *A World Full of Poems: Inspiring Poetry for Children* (Spinelli 2020), can be a wonderfully versatile list poem mentor text. We love a list poem that starts with "How to . . . ," which can be used with practically anything! (See "How to Give with Care" in Chapter 7, and another mentor poem "How to Love Your Own Little Family" in the Online Mentor Poems, OR 5–1.)

How to Love Your Own Little Classroom
REBECCA AND VERONICA

Show up ready to learn

Bring your own ideas

But stay open to the ones

Everyone else brings

Look for the ways

Each person shares their own gift

Listen for the ways

HARNESSING THE POWER OF POETRY

Each person shares their own story

Have a heart that welcomes

Each member of the class

Not just the familiar friends and faces

But the new and fresh ones too

At the end of the day,

Ask yourself:

What does my classroom need?

Maybe a tidy-up?

Maybe a kind note for my teacher's desk?

At the end of the day,

Try to remember:

Tomorrow will always be a fresh start!

Invitation: Think about who or what you want to write a poem for (your classroom, your family, a person, school, library, and so on) and use precise action words!

Figure 5-8

Figure 5-9

THE ARTFUL APPROACH TO EXPLORING IDENTITY AND FOSTERING BELONGING

CLOSING WITH A POEM

Given that this chapter is full of poetry, we thought we might close with a found poem of phrases and words we found upon reviewing this chapter.

Community Reflection Tip: After you or your team finish reading this chapter (or any chapter), try making your own found poem as a reflection and summary of what you learned and what resonated with you. To make your poem, just go back to the beginning of the chapter and highlight or jot down the phrases and words you want to hold on to.

Poetry Connects Us All (A Found Poem)

Write yourself into being on the page

Even with a few very simple words

Start small

Listen carefully

Be on the lookout

Reflect little by little, line by line

Let the creative spirit move you

Invite children to write poems to reveal who they are

to us and to themselves

Model with a poem of your own

Slow down

Use precise action words

Layer with movement

Look again

Mix it up

Celebrate with a poem

Write poems to wrap language around

our stories

our memories

our hopes and dreams

our identities

Poetry connects us all

6

TEACHING HONEST HISTORY ARTFULLY

How the Artful Helps Us Disrupt the Myths and Humanize the Past

How do you tell a story that's been told the wrong way for so long?
—Clint Smith, *How the Word Is Passed*

Teaching honest history is one of the most powerful opportunities we have to honor the stories and identities of the students in our classrooms and communities, which is why much of our early collaborations were steeped in the world of social studies. In partnership with classroom teachers, we would review, revise, and reimagine social studies units across grade levels. And one of our first big projects was a reimagining that informed many of the honest history practices you'll find in this chapter. It was during the pandemic when a fifth-grade team needed our help with updating a tradition, one that we've actually encountered at many schools, called Colonial Faire. A holdover from the days when historical simulations were popular, Colonial Faire is one of those carnival-like festivals (think Renaissance Faire or Medieval Times) that immerses students in activities like butter churning and hoop rolling. As we began to dive into the team's Colonial Faire binder, which held instructions for various game setups, notes about colonial life, and historical recipes—we realized that this could be an opportunity to rethink more than this one day of activities. We wondered: *What if we reimagined not only the culminating event itself but all the social studies curriculum connected to it? And, what if we saw this community moment and connected curriculum as an opportunity to foster an even greater sense of belonging for all our students?*

As we began to outline a process, we realized that once again we needed to start with *learning for self-growth* before making any changes in the curriculum. We decided to create our own mini Windows, Mirrors, and Coffee Book Club (see Chapter 9 for a closer look into the WMC Book Club concept) with this teaching team and read contemporary children's literature to help inform our curricular updates. Our focus would include a handful of units that spanned from the 1600s to the forming of a nation, so we chose the books *Never Caught, the Story of Ona Judge* by Erica Armstrong Dunbar (2020) and *Stamped: Racism, Antiracism, and You: A Remix of the National Book Award–Winning Stamped from the Beginning* by Jason Reynolds and Ibram X. Kendi (2020). The result of Reynolds and Kendi's collaboration is a masterclass in translating lofty concepts and hard history into language that could speak to and engage young learners. And, by starting with children's literature, we would be learning and building our student resource library simultaneously.

Each time our team met, we made time for checking in about our own learning as teachers. We discussed the books, what was coming up for us, what was new and what felt familiar, and what we thought should be shared with students. This became our process. Sharing artful resources (children's literature, and eventually podcasts, poems, and videos), making personal connections to the content, and only after that, considering how our own learning might impact the curriculum. As a result, much of what we consumed for our own learning became the bulk of our supplemental resources for students. We thought if an article felt sophisticated enough for us as adults and inspired our own intellectual dialogue, it might inspire a similar conversation amongst our students. If a poem or a short film moved us to want to know more, it might speak to our students as well. We hoped that by looking to the arts, considering our own unique positionalities, and incorporating contemporary voices we would begin to do the work of telling this story that had been, as Clint Smith says, "told the wrong way for so long" (Smith 2021).

In this chapter, we will guide you through this journey from reimagining the fifth-grade social studies curriculum to launching a new school tradition called History Con. The steps along the way will include: a deep dive into the limits of textbooks, a look at contemporary, inclusive language, an exploration of artful resources like picture books and museum exhibits, a step-by-step chart for disrupting social studies myths, and ideas for facilitating and reflecting based on your identity, your students' identities, and the dynamics of your classroom.

BUT WHAT ABOUT THE TEXTBOOK?

We've never met a teacher who has raved about their social studies textbook. By virtue of being textbooks, they often leave a lot to be desired because no text can serve all the purposes, meet all the needs, or tell all the stories that make up any historical time period.

Our fifth-grade textbook, which had guided most of the units in the past, was fine enough. In its pages, students could find (mostly) useful timelines, maps, oil paintings, bullet points that summarized "life on the plains," and the occasional anodyne anecdote—seemingly stripped of any of those gritty details that tend to make stories compelling. Side note: perhaps this is why Reynolds reminds young readers throughout *Stamped* that "this is NOT a history book" (Reynolds and Kendi 2020). The book wasn't only dry, but also dated in its terminology. As students flipped from Pilgrims and Puritans to life in the Southern colonies, they might encounter language like "slaves," a term we'll unpack later in this chapter, or other terms that students began to question, like the identifier "American Indians" as a catch-all. Given these flaws, searching for a new textbook might have been ideal, but this one had just recently been purchased and replacing it was not yet an option. And even if it had been an option, finding the perfect textbook is practically impossible.

The truth is there is no perfect resource. Even some of the most powerful supplemental videos and articles we've found still benefit from framing or the occasional editing for student eyes. In one video that incorporated powerful testimony of enslaved people, some of the imagery included leaned too heavily into brutality, potentially reinforcing negative stereotypes about Black people, so we pressed pause and didn't share those images. Another time, we found a video that explained the sophisticated concept of "history vs. memory" in a concise and student-friendly way. The video was helpful, but long, so we edited

> ### A Note on Textbooks from Author Steve Sheinkin
>
> From Steve Sheinkin, author of young adult history books, National Book Award finalist, and Newbery Honor recipient: "I was so naïve—I went into textbook writing thinking I was going to help make history fun for students. Sadly, after jamming in all the names, dates, and review questions there's just no room for the types of stories that make history engaging and memorable. And if you do sneak in a story, it'll get cut because textbook makers live in fear that someone somewhere—never a kid, always an adult—will claim to be offended. And that's how textbooks are born!" (Sheinkin 2023)

for brevity and clipped it down to two minutes. If we begin to see our textbooks in this way, as books full of content, some helpful, some dated, some too long, all of it amenable to clipping and curating with a critical lens—then we can make even the most mediocre textbooks work. While we're certainly not recommending you use a low-quality textbook or accept one filled with inaccuracies, we know that abandoning the book in its entirety is simply not an option for so many of us. Figuring out how to do what we can with what we have can be one step toward teaching honest history even with an old book. As Tim Gunn would say, sometimes we just have to "make it work" (Mallenbaum 2015).

We decided that we wouldn't let our imperfect textbook hold us back from honoring the past. We also agreed that we would never use the book to launch any unit, relying instead on our artful resources to do that job, and that we would encourage students to read critically—a task we later learned that students took very seriously. In fact, we once discovered that one student had even taken a Sharpie® to one of the chapter's opening timelines and had not only crossed out "slaves" to write "enslaved people" but had also added a moment on the timeline that the textbook had not deemed significant, *1619: The White Lion Arrives*.

Naming Identities: So Which Term Do I Use?

One of the most common questions we get from students (and educators too) is about which term to use to describe a group of people. Is it Indigenous or Native American? Black or African American? Latinx or Latine? Or they'll notice that the textbook uses

---

Starting the Conversation: Celebrating Black Artists with a Joyful Check-In

Whenever we lead a workshop that centers hard history, we often start with this question: *Who is one Black artist uplifting joy with their art? (This could be a musician, painter, poet, writer, or any artist you happen to love!)*

While this question might seem more rooted in the present than the past, it brings to light the historical throughline of Black resistance through art and the legacy of culture created by enslaved people. When we ask this question, teachers are typically so excited to share their faves like: Whitney Houston, Jon Batiste, Maya Angelou, Quinta Brunson, Tobe Nwigwe (upcoming artist from Houston), Missy Elliot, Justin Cooley (Tony-nominated actor from *Kimberly Akimbo!*), Bill Withers, Beyoncé (of course), Wesley Morris (journalist and *New York Times* critic-at-large), and Jordan Peele. Starting the story with the arts offers us an opportunity to share a little bit about our taste and what we love, and illustrate the diversity within Black identity at the same time. Not only does this framing disrupt the single story of Black American identity, it also sets us up to later disrupt the single story of enslaved people.

a term that differs from what the teacher is using. For example, we led a lesson in which we used the term "Indigenous people," but the textbook header was "California Indians," so our students asked which one was right. Before answering our students, we acknowledged that many people do identify as "California Indians" so that term might still feel accurate for some even though it might feel dated for others.

Sterlin Harjo, co-creator, writer, and director of *Reservation Dogs*, who can speak from the I-perspective, shares his relationship to these terms, "I mean, look . . . my grandma said Indian. So, I'm not here to change what my grandma said. And it's what I know. I'm sorry that Christopher Columbus got it wrong, but that's what we call ourselves, you know? And, like, we also—I also say Native, and I say Indigenous. Just depending on where I'm at and who I'm talking to, those are all interchangeable to me. And Native American's just a mouthful" (Gross 2023).

Educators also want to know what to say when the textbook, a student, or a guest speaker uses dated terms. Much has been written on the most updated terminology and we encourage all readers to utilize the resources in this chapter and engage in their own research as they make decisions about language within curriculum and class discussion. But it's important to note that language, especially language that refers to groups of people, is both evolutionary and fluid. It can be helpful to name this for students. One phrase we offer teachers, and use ourselves, when introducing or discussing terms outside of our own identities, is "As someone who cannot speak from the I-perspective, I choose to use the term because . . ." For example, one of us might say, "As someone who can't speak from the I-perspective for Indigenous identity, I've tried to research and listen to 'own voices' about which term people prefer and what I've found is that many people have their own unique preference and many terms are used within different communities. I try to use tribal affiliation when referring to a specific tribe because that's what I've seen in my resources. And if I'm speaking to a person who identifies as Indigenous, I will use the term that they prefer to honor their identity." This way of speaking about identifiers models being comfortable with ambiguity and listening to "own voices," especially when the identity is one outside of your own.

Honest and Humanizing Terms

Language is always evolving so it's important to stay curious about updated terms and embrace a growth mindset as teachers of honest history.

1. **Enslaved People:** Learning for Justice (LFJ) notes that "Teachers should explain that while 'enslaved person' is preferable, 'slave/slaves' is important contextually because that was the language of

the time and how many enslaved people were identified and identified themselves." LFJ also notes that "*Enslaved person* is preferable to *slave* because a person is not a thing" (Learning for Justice 2018, 5). Using the term *enslaved people* can help us center the humanity of the people who were enslaved because being enslaved was not their core existence. Like all people, they were so much more complex than the worst things enacted upon them. We can think of no better way to explain why this term matters than by Ta-Nehisi Coates' words in *Between the World and Me*: "Slavery is not an indefinable mass of flesh. It is a particular, specific enslaved woman, whose mind is active as your own, whose range of feeling is as vast as your own; who prefers the way the light falls in one particular spot in the woods, who enjoys fishing where the water eddies in a nearby stream, who loves her mother in her own complicated way, thinks her sister talks too loud, has a favorite cousin, a favorite season, who excels at dressmaking and knows, inside herself, that she is as intelligent and capable as anyone" (Coates 2015).

2. **Enslavers**: *Enslaver* is preferable over *master*, *owner*, or *slaveholder*. According to the National Park Service (2022), "An enslaver exerted power over those they kept in bondage. They referred to themself as a master or owner—hierarchical language which reinforced a sense of natural authority. Today, the terms *master* or *owner* can continue to suggest a naturalness to the system while also distancing us from the fact that enslavers actively enslaved other human beings who were entitled to the same natural rights as themselves."

3. **Slaver's Ship**: Instead of *slave ships*, Learning for Justice (2018) recommends that we consider using *slaver's ship*. We think this language assigns ownership to enslavers and makes the practice of enslaving people sound less neutral, or inevitable.

4. **Colony vs. Territory**: While these two terms might not seem directly related to hard history, many students have started to ask us why their textbooks tend to use the term *territory* in place of *colony* when referring to places like the Philippines or Guam. We think that developing a critical lens for language has heightened our students' awareness around which terms are used and why and helped them begin to see the

words in their textbooks less as neutral facts and more as choices made by authors. For anyone interested in the why behind these terms, historian Daniel Immerwahr says the shift from calling some places colonies to calling them territories is part of the U.S. government's effort to use a "gentler" language that could signal the "country's growth" without the "spirit of forthright imperialism" of the term *colony* (Immerwahr 2019). Given the nation's history of slavery, the shift in terms here might be interesting for students to consider at some point. *Why would a country that once engaged in the institution of slavery want to distance itself from the term* colony?

5. **Indigenous People:** In our research, particularly with Indigenous Foundations, we've found that many Indigenous people prefer their tribal affiliation (Lakota, and so on) over generalized terms. And some Native Americans prefer one term over the other, so it is important to use the term with which people self-identify.

6. **Honest History vs. Hard History:** *Honest history* is a term that "refers to all histories" according to the organization Learning for Justice. *Hard history* is a term coined by Dr. Hasan K. Jeffries (2023) that refers specifically to American slavery.

TEACHING HARD HISTORY: DISRUPTING THE MYTHS

We have found that the process of disrupting the myths of hard history depends on the power of our noticing. Once we develop a lens for noticing, we can begin to pause and make intentional shifts that help us lift up the stories that have often been excluded. The following "Notice, Pause, and Consider" chart is a guide for how to use the arts, historical artifacts, and contemporary reads to disrupt common myths about slavery.

Notice, Pause, and Consider: Disrupting the Myths

Common Myths & Single Stories
How we've encountered and experienced this myth both as students and teachers.

TEACHER MOVES to Disrupt and Interrogate the Myths & Single Stories
How to "**Notice, Pause, and Consider**" while your leading a lesson on Hard History.

MYTH: Enslaved People Were a Monolith
Commonly shared imagery of enslaved people is often monolithic, dehumanizing, and lacking any individuality.

TEACHER MOVES

Notice: What images are you displaying throughout lessons on slavery? What imagery does the textbook contain?

Pause: When you notice images that portray enslaved people as a mass of bodies without any individuality, agency, or special details that honor their unique humanity or personality.

Consider: Lifting up narratives written by enslaved people, using contemporary picture books (like *Born on the Water*, *Freedom Over Me*, and *The People Remember*) that use illustrations to humanize enslaved people and highlight specific cultural connections and individual features whenever possible. Consider spending some time noticing the individuality of each person's face in Nikkolas Smith's illustration for the poem "The White Lion." As Smith said of his illustrations in *Born on the Water*, "Countless Black Americans and I share the ancestral lineage, and often without any specifics, so I decided to illustrate a broad range of Central West African details, from architecture to hairstyles, instruments, and clothing" (Hannah-Jones and Watson 2021).

Figure 6-1 Notice, Pause, and Consider: Disrupting the Myths   *continues*

MYTH: Enslaved People Had No Past or Connections to a Specific Place

The story of enslavement commonly told in textbooks typically starts on American soil, leaving out any connections to West Africa, or any specificity about life within the regions most deeply impacted by this history.

> **TEACHER MOVES**
>
> **Notice:** Where are you starting the story? Where do the resources you are using start the story? What countries, regions, languages are you surfacing in connection to enslaved people and their unique cultures?
>
> **Pause:** When you encounter language that describes Africa as a monolithic culture or enslaved people arriving "from Africa."
>
> **Consider:** Sharing maps of West African regions and countries and pointing out specific places that are mentioned in the text and resources you use. Reading poems from *Born on the Water* like: "What Grandma Tells Me," "They Had a Language," "Their Hands Had a Knowing," "And They Danced," and the opening pages of "The People Remember."

MYTH: Enslaved People Had No Culture of Their Own

There are rarely any mentions in textbooks of the contributions enslaved people made to food, music, culture, and democracy.

> **TEACHER MOVES**
>
> **Notice:** How are you making space to learn about the cultures of enslaved people and honor their cultural contributions that continue to live on?
>
> **Pause:** When you see the culture of enslaved people described as something they "left behind." We can honor the devastation of leaving behind, *and* the resistance of holding on to culture—culture that lives on today in the descendants of enslaved people.
>
> **Consider:** Incorporating the work of scholars like Michael Twitty, a food historian who specializes in the cultural creations of enslaved people, and Faith Ringgold, a Black artist who has incorporated quilting and African folklore and imagery into her work.

Figure 6-1 *continued*

THE ARTFUL APPROACH TO EXPLORING IDENTITY AND FOSTERING BELONGING

MYTH: Enslaved People Didn't Resist

Although this is changing thanks to the groundbreaking work of Learning for Justice's *Teaching Hard History Framework* (2018), historically, stories of resistance have rarely, if ever, been told in social studies textbooks.

TEACHER MOVES

Notice: Is there an absence of stories that depict collective action, creativity, resilience, or individual resistance?

Pause: When you read through text that describes enslavement in a passive voice or locates all the power with the enslavers. For example, when you read sentences like, "Sometimes plantation owners freed their slaves," which assigns all the power and agency to the enslaver without acknowledging acts of resilience, creativity, and courage on the part of the enslaved.

Consider: Teaching into the LFJ *Teaching Hard History*: "In every place and time, enslaved people sought freedom" (Learning for Justice 2018, 15). This is a good time to share how creating art can be an act of resistance in difficult times by telling the stories of potter David Drake, who signed and inscribed his work despite harsh anti-literacy laws, and George Moses Horton, who resisted by learning to read and write and later became a poet. You could even share a few lines of Horton's poems (available online).

MYTH: Slavery Was Common and Seen as Morally Ambiguous or Just a Product of the Time

Some textbooks depict slavery as so common it was like the default option (enslavers were just a product of their time and didn't know what they were doing was morally wrong).

TEACHER MOVES

Notice: Does the textbook acknowledge the conscious decision of enslavers to choose economic growth and prosperity over the humanity of people?

Pause: When stories describe the enslavers' choices as a matter of fact, or even as a sense of patriotic duty, or a necessary evil with sentences like *wealthy plantation owners used slaves to keep their huge plantations running. These people thought that the economy would suffer without slaves. Most people in the Southern colonies accepted this as true.*

Consider: Reading closely and critically. Taking a moment to look closely at the language in passages like this is crucial. Who is the subject of the sentence and who is the object? Who or what is "suffering"? Dr. Hasan Jeffries, historian and contributor to the Learning for Justice *Teaching Hard History Framework*, also draws attention to the architectural design of some prominent plantations that seemed to make an effort to hide the quarters for enslaved people (Learning for Justice 2018). You can look up photos of Montpelier that illustrate this and invite students to think critically about why these design choices might have been made. Why might a wealthy (and in this case famous American president) enslaver have chosen to arrange the buildings on his plantation in this way?

TEACHING HONEST HISTORY ARTFULLY

MYTH: Slavery Only Benefited the Southern Colonies
Many textbooks only mention slavery in the "Southern Colonies" chapter.

TEACHER MOVES

Notice: Does slavery only come up when you are teaching about the Southern colonies?

Pause: When you encounter texts and resources that frame the origins of the early colonies without including information about the role of slavery in all of them.

Consider: Incorporating supplemental resources throughout your lessons for teaching about the early colonies.

These are only a few examples of how the Northern and middle colonies profited and participated directly and indirectly in the institution of slavery:

- New York's Wall Street was originally a market for selling enslaved people.
- Aetna, located in New York, participated in the institution of slavery by insuring enslavers for the enslaved people they owned, which reinforced the concept that enslaved people were property and created wealth for the enslavers and the corporation.
- The famed Faneuil Hall in Boston was named after the wealthy merchant, Peter Faneuil, who enslaved people himself, and a market for selling enslaved people also existed alongside Faneuil Hall.
- Brooks Brothers built some of its wealth and reputation selling "servant" clothing designed for enslaved people to wear. This clothing was meant to reflect the wealth of the enslavers and enslaved people were forced to wear it. There are even two coats in the permanent "Historic New Orleans Collection" that some historians say might have been designed for young enslaved boys.

Figure 6-1 *continued*

THE ARTFUL APPROACH TO EXPLORING IDENTITY AND FOSTERING BELONGING

MYTH: Our Country's Wealth Is Unrelated to the Highly Skilled Labor of Enslaved People

Our country's tremendous wealth is rarely linked to the highly skilled labor and expertise of enslaved people.

TEACHER MOVES

Notice: How are you connecting the stories of enslaved people with the early economies and foundational wealth of the United States?

Pause: When you encounter stories that belittle or minimize the contributions made to the country's economy by enslaved people.

Consider: Describing the labor of enslaved people as not only difficult and laborious but *highly skilled* as well. Consider telling the story of the hundreds of enslaved "stone cutters, axemen, carpenters, and brick makers" who helped build the White House between 1792 and 1800 (Williams 2021). You might also explore the history of products with deep connections to the labor of enslaved people. For example, you might share research around sugar, which has created immense wealth for our nation: "The United States sugar industry receives as much as $4 billion in annual subsidies" and Louisiana's sugarcane industry alone is worth $3 billion, "generating an estimated 16,400 jobs" (Muhammad 2019). Learning for Justice and C3Teachers are great resources for this topic area.

MYTH: Indigenous People Were Not a Part of America's History of Slavery

The story of Indigenous slavery is almost never a part of the narrative.

TEACHER MOVES

Notice: Is there any acknowledgment of the story of Indigenous slavery in the texts and resources you are using?

Pause: When you hear or read about Indigenous people only existing in the past. When you're teaching about the past, obviously you will be speaking in past tense. It's just important to also note that Indigenous people did not only exist in that time, and make sure to amplify the Indigenous voices that say, "We are still here!"

Consider: Sharing the video "The Forgotten Slavery of Our Ancestors" found on the Learning for Justice website, which could be paired with the book *We Are Still Here!* by Traci Sorell (2021).

Teaching Hard History with Picture Books

Picture books are incredible resources for teaching hard history. We encourage you to be on the lookout for contemporary releases that are crafted with care, artistry, and attention to humanizing detail—and that feel right for your particular students. As Jason Reynolds says, "it's very hard to take a big big thing and make it very very small and still allow it to be nuanced and sophisticated for our young people" (*CBS Mornings* 2023). This is the power of picture books. As Reynolds also reminds us, the "economy of language is very different in this particular space because you are only using a few words." Every page (every word!) of a picture book is written with intention, and these words and images combined have the potential to name, disrupt, expand, and affirm all at once. And as works of art themselves, picture books are often sophisticated enough to elevate not only our children's understandings, but our own understanding, too.

As you gather resources, we encourage you to remember these practices:

1. Look for books that are humanizing and honor the specificity and dignity of enslaved people with both their illustrations and text.

2. Give yourself time to *handle with care*. Remember to read the text closely on your own first. Pay attention to what you are noticing, feeling, wondering before you facilitate conversation with others.

3. Plan for and practice your read-aloud. Research how to pronounce names and places and remember to make space for noticing, pausing, and reflecting.

4. Choose your reflection methods carefully. Sometimes you will want to invite participants to journal without sharing aloud, and other times you might create opportunities for people to share in pairs, in small groups, or with the whole community.

5. Use the content of the book to intentionally disrupt the common myths of slavery. Incorporate any supplemental materials or teaching moments you might need to underscore the disruption of these myths.

The Story of Born on the Water

In the fall of 2019, which marked four hundred years since the arrival of the first slaver's ship on the coast of what would become America, many American journalists were publishing projects that sought to illuminate the ongoing legacy of slavery. One of those journalists, Nikole Hannah-Jones, published her groundbreaking initiative *The*

1619 Project, which had a simple yet profound goal, "to reframe the country's history by placing the consequences of slavery and the contributions of black Americans at the very center of our national narrative" (Hannah-Jones 2019). What began with a collection of essays and podcast episodes on everything from the history of Black activism to the relationship between capitalism and the brutality of work on plantations to the "The Birth of American Music" (Morris and Hannah-Jones 2019) eventually led to a myriad of books, scholarship, and creative outpouring that all served to reshape this narrative in their own ways.

One of those creative works was a picture book that we have leaned heavily upon ever since its release to support teachers who are seeking ways to reshape how hard history has been taught in a K–5 setting. *Born on the Water*, written by Nikole Hannah-Jones and Renée Watson and illustrated by "self-described artivist" Nikkolas Smith, was written to intentionally affirm young Black people and descendants of enslaved people, and it also serves a purpose for all readers because it tells the story of not only Black history but American history as well (McMurdock 2022). As Smith says, "We want people to grow up having an accurate understanding of what happened in this country. I feel like it's really not until we address all of these things openly and honestly that we're gonna really grow and move forward as a nation" (McMurdock 2022).

When read with care, this robust resource has the potential to humanize the enslaved people at the center of this history, disrupt common myths about slavery, and engage students in thought-provoking conversation about what this shared past might mean for our future. It's important to spend time with this book yourself before engaging in the work with children. In the following section, we will walk you through a teacher workshop we lead using *Born on the Water*. The questions we ask, the way we highlight the artists' voices and process, the way in which we take time to pause, and how we choose to share and reflect are all intentional teacher moves that you could borrow or build upon for other texts, other times.

We begin by inviting teachers to look closely at the cover and think about what they notice in the artwork: *What do you notice about how Smith has drawn the people on the cover? What do you notice about what he has chosen to include or not include? Are any of his choices in imagery surprising (you might consider that this is a book about slavery)? Does this depiction of enslaved people feel familiar to you or does it feel new? As you look closely at this illustration, we invite you to begin naming out what you are noticing.*

After attending several talks about this book, we've learned that Smith did not want to illustrate bondage in the typical way for the cover, which could be why he chose other symbols in place of the typical chains or shackles. Smith has also shared that although he wanted to show the suffering, he also wanted to honor the resilience. After sharing these details, we invite teachers to notice again, and this time we call out specifics (the clouds are reminiscent of cotton; the people's bodies are partially submerged in the water). Next, we share the end papers and the three symbols that open and close the story. We share how Smith says these symbols were inspired by scarification patterns. Referring to the three symbols he says, "It's all there from the beginning. Life. Death. Rebirth. And the book is told in those three sections" (Pulitzer Center 2022).

As we read the book aloud, we allow time for noticing and checking in throughout. When we first read this book, we were struck by the fact that the first poem, "Questions," began in a classroom. For us, this seemed to subtly signal that this book was speaking directly to teachers, reminding us of the impact we can have in our roles as educators. Sometimes the first exposure children have with hard history is in a classroom. And how we tell this story matters.

After reading "Questions," we often pause and invite teachers to think back to their own schooling, the textbooks they remember reading, the movies and TV shows they grew up with, and consider how these experiences and materials informed their understanding of slavery. We ask: *What are some myths or single stories around slavery or enslaved people that you heard as a young person?* We ask teachers to write their ideas down because we don't want to reinforce stereotypes or lift up the harmful myths by sharing out loud, even with adults. Instead, we walk around the room and make note of what we're seeing and then we share out themes and patterns that might be helpful for the group. We use this time to unpack how this story has been "told the wrong way for so long" (Smith 2021). The poems and pictures in this book explore hard history in sophisticated ways—underscoring how enslaved people generated untold wealth for America, illustrating how they used music and poetry to hold on to community and culture, and shining a light on how they demonstrated extraordinary agency to resist and survive. Taking the time to notice deeply is essential. By pausing after each poem and reflecting throughout, we can create a space that isn't only about learning the facts but is also about honoring the humanity of the people at the center of this story.

BRINGING HONEST HISTORY ALIVE WITH MUSEUMS

In 2016, the National Museum of African American History and Culture (NMAAHC) opened its doors. According to its website, it was "established by an Act of Congress in 2003" and remains the only "national museum devoted exclusively to the documentation of African American life, history, and culture."

> When I first visited the museum in 2022, I was overwhelmed by the experience. The journey from floor to floor feels intentionally designed to draw a throughline from African and pre-colonial history to modern times as visitors rise from the depths of the basement level with its galleries on the transatlantic slave trade to the more open-space higher levels with galleries on everything from civil rights to contemporary art and music. As I moved from gallery to gallery, I was struck by the number of Black caregivers with young children. They weren't just passively consuming the exhibits, but were stopping at almost every plaque to read, instruct, and process. These caregivers seemed to be using the museum as a kind of classroom. I noticed them pointing out important places on the museum's many detailed maps and even quizzing their little ones after listening to an audio exhibit together: *And who was Mr. Lewis again? And what did he fight for? And why was that important?*

Museums, when designed with intention and care, can bring history to life, connect the past to the present, and make an indelible impression on our cultural memory. None of this has been lost on educators who have long known about the power of museums—the likelihood that at least one of your elementary school field trips was to a museum is high. However, these spaces simply haven't existed for all areas of study. As Ariana Curtis, curator of Latinx studies at NMAAHC says, "who's telling these stories matters. Museums are human made. There are biases. There are perspectives, and for a long time, I don't think we were honest about that—you know, that there was always this shroud of objectivity, and that's just not true. And so now that we're understanding better who tells the story matters, like, what is the source data from which we're telling these stories—that matters" (NPR 2022).

In fact, the *who* behind many of the stories being told in our nation's museums has only recently begun to include Black voices. Most of the leading museums of Black history have only been funded in the past decade. The National Memorial for Peace and Justice, a memorial to the Black victims of lynching, was established only recently in 2018. The *New York Times* said of its opening, "The Country Has Never Seen Anything Like It" (Robertson 2018). The Legacy Museum, a project by the Equal Justice Initiative to trace the legacy of slavery, also opened its doors in 2018 when the *Washington Post* (Kennicott

2018) named it "One of the most *powerful* and effective new memorials created in a generation." That it has taken this long to document, memorialize, and curate these foundational places of education seems to suggest that our nation has only begun to scratch the surface in telling the honest history of our founding. And while many of us will not be able to take our students on a field trip to the growing number of museums and memorials across the country, many of these places offer robust virtual exhibits, artifact galleries, short films, and articles that we can use both to learn for self-growth and to supplement the materials we curate for students.

A few years ago, planning a fifth-grade unit and browsing the digital collection of the National Museum of African American History and Culture we came across one artifact that wound up inspiring an entire new lesson. There on the NMAAHC website was Harriet Tubman's shawl—delicately made of silk lace and linen, an ornate fashion accessory owned by an icon rarely associated with fashion. We learned from the museum that the shawl was a gift from Queen Victoria to honor Tubman and her life's work of liberation—a fact we both found fascinating. The concrete, tangible existence of artifacts like this one reminds us that these legends were human.

Tips for Using Museums to Teach Honest History

1. **Check out virtual exhibits** to learn for self-growth and explore potential supplemental materials. A good place to start is: National Museum of African American History and Culture (NMAAHC).

2. **Bring a lens of curiosity**: Whenever you visit your own local museums, encourage students to bring a lens of curiosity to these experiences: Who is telling the story? Whose voices are incorporated? Where do they start the story?

3. **Create a digital artifact gallery** for students to explore on their own. This can be as simple as a doc or slide deck with screenshots that link to virtual exhibits or collections.

How Should We Reflect and Share About Our Learning?

Journaling, pair shares/group shares, turn and talks, and whole-group reflections all have their benefits. To engage your class in social sharing be sure that proper guardrails and community agreements are in place. To help guide you in selecting which format might be a good fit, consider the following:

1. **What's our classroom culture like?**

   Think about your identity and the identity makeup of your students as you begin to prepare for student-centered reflections. This is especially important as you engage in reflections around hard history. If you have Black and/or Indigenous students in your classroom, how might you intentionally support them as you facilitate conversation and engage in reflection? How might you avoid racial spotlighting if those students are in the minority? This could be a good time to reflect on the identity work that you have been engaging students in throughout the year. If you haven't yet invited students to share about their identities or want to revisit this work before you launch into a hard history unit, see Chapter 2: Exploring Identity Throughout the Year for inspiration.

2. **What's the content at the heart of what you're exploring?**

   Is the content on which you're reflecting connected to generational trauma, fraught contemporary issues, and/or violence? How far along are you in your units that cover hard history? Have students been empowered with the language that can make a humanizing, thoughtful, and productive social reflection possible? What potentially fraught topics might surface as a result of students reflecting out loud? And how might you prepare to facilitate and redirect if the conversation, as it often does, leads the class into tricky territory?

   When a student shares something out loud that might cause harm (unintentionally reinforces a stereotype, shares their discomfort, sorrow, shame, or disbelief), you might say something like:

- *This is really painful history and it can bring up a lot of big feelings.*

- *As Dr. Hasan Jeffries (2023) says, "No child living today is responsible for the institution of slavery but they are responsible for something, and that's tomorrow." You might say something similar: None of us in the classroom is responsible for any of this history, but it's important that we learn what happened so that we can be informed historians and better understand the world around us.*

- *It's OK to question what you're learning but I encourage you to keep listening with an open mind as we explore this history together.*

- *This is a really painful history, and it can be difficult to believe that something so sad actually happened.*

Now is a good time to revisit your classroom agreements and make any additions that could serve reflection around hard history. For example, you might consider adding and centering "Speak from the I-Perspective" and depending on the grade level, reminders around not repeating slurs or hate speech could be helpful.

3. **What's the goal of this reflection?**

    Should this reflection lead to students learning from each other's unique experiences and perspectives or is this more a time to process on a personal level? Occasionally, reflections can veer into dialogue. If dialogue does not serve your reflection goals, but social sharing does, you might try focused listening dyads, which allow students to speak without interruption from their listening partner.

But We Don't Teach Slavery in Kindergarten

If you're a primary teacher you might think to yourself, we don't cover or teach hard history, but the reality is children come into primary grades with knowledge about all sorts of historical people and heroes, information about concepts like slavery and freedom, democracy, America's founding (think Fourth of July, presidents, Constitution/Bill of Rights), human rights, fairness, and equality. Many textbooks and resources for K-2 include spotlight stories or biographies on figures like Harriet Tubman and Frederick Douglass, which might unexpectedly surface student questions about slavery. When these moments arise, it can be helpful to have developmentally appropriate ways of responding in the moment. And, it's especially important to use humanizing language when you are responding to questions because young children are so impressionable and we want to make sure they don't have to end up needing to unlearn dehumanizing language like "slave."

Some tips and language for responding in the moment:

- **Give context:** In our country's history, not all people were free. Some innocent people were forced to work without pay. This was wrong.

- **Name the resistance:** Not everyone was treated fairly in our country for a long time, and even though they were treated cruelly and not allowed to be free, they worked together to fight for their freedom and change the laws.

- **Define slavery:** "Slavery is when a person owns another person as property" (Learning for Justice 2018).

With biographies, start the story with their brilliance, not with their enslavement: If you notice the biography you're sharing doesn't do this, add your own prelude before you read from the book: Frederick Douglass was a brilliant speaker and writer who spoke out against unfairness and the idea that anyone should ever be enslaved. Harriet Tubman was one of the most courageous women in our country's history! She helped many people escape slavery to freedom and she took care of lots of people who needed help with injuries or sickness. She was even a spy in the Civil War!

THE ARTFUL APPROACH TO EXPLORING IDENTITY AND FOSTERING BELONGING

HISTORY CON: TELLING THE STORY OF US WITH A NEW TRADITION

After a year of engaging the fifth-grade team in all the practices and resources we outlined in this chapter, it was clear to everyone that Colonial Faire could no longer work as our culminating event. As we shifted our focus to a more all-encompassing study of early American history, the Faire could no longer serve our needs or provide the kind of substantive experience we wanted to give students. We hoped to design something new and fresh that would make it possible for students to bring their research to life, develop their leadership and public speaking skills, and be in community together—one last time as fifth graders.

As we started to think about what an event like this might entail, we wanted to make sure our process was a collaborative one. We didn't want to *tell* teachers how to change their tradition by single-handedly overhauling activities that teachers and families had participated in for years. We wanted to honor the expertise of our teaching team and create something together that would be just as loved, just as long-lasting, and just as special for the community. So, we started with a question that was surprisingly generative: *What do you love about this tradition?*

By listening first and acknowledging the love and energy that had fueled this day for years, even decades, we were able to capture the essence of the event. We discovered what mattered most to this team of teachers:

- Hosting a cumulative event that felt special to just the fifth graders, especially during their last month at elementary school

- Wearing special clothing, or outfits, that demarcated this day from all others

- Giving students independence to choose and design projects that matched their interests

- Making space for parents and caregivers to participate and connect with their child's learning

- Doing something fun and interactive!

After generating this list, we thought, "Wonderful! We can do all this!" Together with our team of teachers, we brainstormed. One cultural phenomenon kept coming up in conversation after conversation: the musical *Hamilton*! We had all seen or listened to the show and thought we might continue to use it as a reference as we planned for our own artful event that would attempt to grapple with honest history.

Ultimately, we created an all-day student-led conference that told "the story of US" and featured student projects like podcasts, doll making, dance, short plays and films, and stop-motion. The goal of these projects was to breathe life into the more commonly centered stories *and* speak to the legacy of contributions by enslaved people, Indigenous people, women in the colonies, and other identities that have been historically marginalized. And students would share their projects and learning by participating in panels centered around themes like Power and Resistance, Identity and Belonging, and Creativity and Technology. Finally, the day would close with a community-wide poetry reflection experience inspired by the poem "I, Too" by Langston Hughes.

After this creative collaboration and brainstorming, all our event needed was a name. We wanted a name that sounded both sophisticated and fun, and since we lived in San Diego, the birthplace of ComicCon, we didn't have to look far for inspiration. We decided we had to call our event: History Con! Just a few months later, we would order our first T-shirts with "History Con: A Student-Led Conference Celebrating the Story of Us" in huge letters. We're also proud to say that we even worked in a *Hamilton* moment: the inaugural History Con also included a student-choreographed flash mob to "Yorktown." As a result, History Con will always make time for a dance break!

While Colonial Faire might not be a tradition at your school, maybe there's another event or tradition you've wondered about shifting or reimagining. Maybe you've thought about some potential ideas but aren't sure how to even begin a conversation around something that has such a long history or deep hold on the community. We hope that sharing our story and process might inspire you to take a closer look at the special days, gatherings, and festivals at your school. And if you notice an event that could use some updating, you might also use the tips below to get started in your own reimagining.

How to Reimagine Your Own Community Event, Inspired by History Con

When we think about the work cut out for us as honest history educators, journalist/author Isabel Wilkerson and her "old house" analogy come to mind. In an interview for the podcast *On Being,* Wilkerson compares the reckoning that must happen around our country's history to living in an old house, "Our country is like a really old house" she tells host Krista Tippett. Wilkerson goes on to say, "I love old houses. I've always lived in old houses. But old houses need a lot of work. And the work is never done. And that's what our country is like. And you may not want to go into that basement, but if you really don't go into that basement, it's at your own peril . . . whatever you are ignoring is not going to go away. Whatever you're ignoring is only going to get worse. Whatever you're ignoring will be there to be reckoned with until you reckon with it. And I think that that's what we're called upon to do where we are right now" (*On Being* 2020).

Many of us who are teaching elementary school might not have an extensive background in teaching history specifically. As K–5 teachers, we're often expected to be able to adapt quickly from subject to subject, grade to grade, differentiating and personalizing for a new group of students every year—making it difficult to become a content area expert in any one historical period. Moreover, in the age of book bans, textbook censorship, and bad faith debates over what should be taught as the truth, teaching social studies has become increasingly trying. And yet, those very factors have made the need for honest history more paramount now than ever.

It is with these challenges in mind that we offer the following resources, whether you use them to learn for self-growth or as inspiration for curriculum building. Our hope is that these guides, templates, and writing prompts will help any of you who are interested in teaching history honestly (and artfully!)—wherever you are in that journey. (See Initial Brainstorming [OR 6–1], My Project Proposal [OR 6–2], and Thoughtful Representation [OR 6–3] templates in the Online Resources.)

Here are a few things to keep in mind before you get started:

1. **Start with an Opening Community Moment:** What will you do to create a community moment to set the tone for the day and start with intention? We have created video montages of multiple students sharing their project titles or quotes from their research, played a "stand up if your project is about _____" activity, and invited students into a 3, 2, 1 "Welcome to History Con" cheer!

2. **"Invite" a Special Speaker:** This can be a video or virtual connection or you might invite a local community member, history teacher from an older grade, or student family member with a connection to the content to speak to the students and light a spark for the day.

3. **Inspire Students to Be Creative Communicators:** In addition to teaching skills and helping students develop enduring understandings, this is also an opportunity for students to connect their learning with hobbies or passions that bring them joy. For example, students who love theater might want to create a short screenplay. Or students who love to cook might want to share some of their creations as part of their presentation.

4. **Find Time for Community Fun:** Will the day include a flash mob? A drum line? A slam poetry moment?

5. **Close with an Artful Reflection:** How can you come together as a community at the end of the event? Check out Chapter 10 for Artful Reflection ideas. Ultimately, students developed a question that would guide their research and their "Creative Communicator Project." Some questions from years past have included:

- How was sewing a source of self-expression and empowerment for women?

- How does King George III's medical problems affect his leadership and help us understand how we see him today?

- What were some of the games that Indigenous children played that played a role in American sports?

- How did enslaved African Americans use creativity to overcome the challenge of creating new food?

- What role did Alexander Hamilton play in the Revolution? What lasting impact did he have?

- How did Native American farming and technology affect today's America?

I, Too: An Artful Reflection on American History

For our reimagined event, we wanted to give students, teachers, and any caregivers who joined us, an opportunity to reflect and connect at the end of the day. Given that the content for History Con was rooted in early American history, we turned to Langston Hughes and his poem "I, Too."

I, Too
LANGSTON HUGHES

I, too, sing America.

I am the darker brother.
They send me to eat in the kitchen
When company comes,
But I laugh,
And eat well,
And grow strong.

Tomorrow,
I'll be at the table
When company comes.
Nobody'll dare
Say to me,
"Eat in the kitchen,"
Then.

Besides,
They'll see how beautiful I am
And be ashamed—

I, too, am America.

We created this guide to help students write their own "I, Too" poems and reflect on their learning and their potential roles as student historians. (Figure 6–2 is also available in the Online Resources as OR 6–4).

I, Too Poem Starter

I, too, sing America.

I am a ____ (role or identity you are claiming as a historian)

I ____ (things you did in your research that you now do)

I ____

I ____

Tomorrow, I will ____ (things you will continue to do as a historian/thinker)

I will ____

I will ____

I, too, am America.

Figure 6-2

CLOSING WITH A POEM

I, Too
MATTHEW

I too sing America
I am a Black boy trying to find himself
How will I make history?
Lost in my thoughts
Thinking about my past the present and the future
I too am America

I, Too
ANNA

I am an advocate
I search for hidden stories
I wonder what hasn't been told
I look beyond the textbooks
Tomorrow I will write my own stories
And I will listen to the tales of others

I, Too
JONAH

I too sing America
I am a historian
I uncover the forgotten secrets buried
and crushed under the lies and misconceptions of the past
I will seek the truths of the past
to make tomorrow even better.

7

RESPONDING WITH CARE

How to Empower Students with Letters of Love and Upstander Skills

Art is the prime expression of Love in action.
—Allison Russell

In any given school year, events from the outside world manage to find their way into the community. Maybe a student has seen something in the news and shared it with their classmates. Maybe a natural disaster has inspired a local community drive in which students are eager to participate. Maybe you're in the midst of an election year and bracing yourself for what the results will mean to your school's families. Or maybe the moment you're facing is not happening on the outside at all, but within the walls of your own school or even classroom. A family in your school might be suffering a loss or someone might be undergoing treatment for an illness. Or, given the rise in hate speech, antisemitism, and bias incidents across the nation, the likelihood that your community has had to address one of these painful situations has also increased in recent years. These moments all have the potential to create fissures in the community and threaten the sense of belonging you've been intentionally fostering amongst your students. Some of the time, we have systems or language in place that helps us respond to these challenging moments, but sometimes we are caught off guard. In these moments, teachers can use the arts to respond with care and in turn, empower students to process the moment restoratively.

In this chapter, we'll share some ideas that have worked well for us when addressing these types of challenging situations both in the moment and throughout the year. From developing a student advocacy group fueled by the arts called "The Belonging Lab" (see Chapter 8 for more on this) to responding with care to hate speech and other harmful moments to using poetry and design thinking to elevate the power of student-led campaigns, we have learned fresh and artful approaches that empower student leaders and help elementary children develop upstander skills and creative vision. But more than that, we have continued to look to art for what it can inspire, if, as Allison Russell (2021) says, "art is the prime expression of love in action."

A POEM, A LETTER, AND AN INVITATION: ARTFUL POSSIBILITIES FOR RESPONDING TO CHALLENGING MOMENTS

When challenging global moments arise, children are often eager to help, but it can be difficult to find realistic ways to support them in making a difference. It is always important to think first about what the genuine need is (community organizing, money or food, clothes or shelter, mental health support, and so on). And while children might be able to volunteer or join local organizations working toward meeting the genuine need, we also think it is important and empowering, to give them opportunities to offer something from their hearts. As a community, we can respond to the genuine needs and create space for children to express their support and love through words, poetry, and all kinds of artful advocacy. In this chapter, you'll find tools, scripts, poems, and other artful resources for responding to challenging moments with care.

Who Is This Chapter For?

While so much of this thinking and language is helpful for teachers of all grade levels, teachers should note that most of the content in this chapter is developed with grades 3-5 in mind. With that being said, some of these projects could be adapted for younger students, especially if you handle them with care.

A Word We're Sending You Is Hope: Poems and Letters of Support

As news reaches students, some may begin to ask teachers what they can do to help. As elementary educators, we might all be familiar with the challenges this kind of moment poses for our community. How can we support students who are looking for ways to help during a developing crisis, especially given their varying awareness around an event as violent, fraught, and political as war? How can we address and acknowledge tragedy without causing more anxiety or fear?

Unfortunately, we have found ourselves in this position several times over the years. One of our go-to poems that we use to help children tap into their own sense of inner calm is Naomi Shihab Nye's "Over the Weather," which invites us to think about words we love, words that make us feel calm—and then "slip" those words "into the atmosphere and rise." This poem has a way of setting a hopeful tone in the classroom and helping children think about what words they might want to lift up into the atmosphere and send all the way to the people in the midst of such uncertainty and suffering.

When we've used this poem with children, and even adults, we have found that it has helped them feel like they were offering something meaningful during a traumatic time, sending something comforting into the world even when they might have no control over the geopolitical dynamics or tragic circumstances. Writing these poems is an act of agency and support, and it can also correspond with other efforts to meet a genuine need in a community, locally or globally.

After reading "Over the Weather" once or twice, we invite students to think about words that make them feel calm, that give them a sense of hope or even courage, words that they love or that fill them up when they hear them. We model a few of our own. After modeling and sharing out a few words or phrases, we shift gears a bit. What words would you want to send to people that might help them feel supported, cared for, or seen? After giving students a bit of time to brainstorm or jot down some ideas, we share the following invitation:

A word I'm sending you is _____

I hope it makes you feel _____

The poems students write can be performed in the community and/or sent as letters of hope to local or global organizations connected with the challenging moment at hand.

ALL: "We Send You" by Fourth Grade

Jo: A word I'm sending you is friendship.
I hope it makes you feel supported.

PAUSE...

Ella: A word I'm sending you is support.
I hope this makes you feel heard.

Priya: A word I'm sending you is united.
I hope it makes you feel together.

Sam: A word I'm sending to you is light
I hope it makes you feel loved.

ALL: Because you are.

Ezra: A word I'm sending you is love.
I hope it makes you feel important.

ALL: Because you are.

Matt: A word I'm sending you is health.
I hope this makes you feel strong.

Jose: The words I'm sending you are, "We Love and Support You."
I hope they make you feel like you have friends from all over

PAUSE

Maris: A word I'm sending you is together.
I hope it makes you feel like you are not alone.

Jessie: A word I'm sending you is family.
I hope it helps you remember who is by your side

Ada: I also send you hope for a brighter future.
GROUP 1: We also send you bravery.
GROUP 2: We also send you courage.
GROUP 1: We also send you strength.   *ALL ↓*
Jo: We also send you love, **from all the way across the world.**

Figure 7-1 This annotated poem shows how we work with students and teachers to help them use their voice, their body, and their presence to convey the tone they are hoping to convey. In this case, we wanted to be sure our tone was gentle, reflective, and supportive. We were careful to stay calm, to leave space in between each stanza, and to slow our pace toward the end of the poem.

Letters of Love

Another way for students to express their support is to write a thoughtful letter. Whether you are responding to your students' concerns, or you are hearing a current issue pop in conversation around the classroom, or you are hoping to make a curricular connection with a current event, writing a "letter of love" might be a way to help students process what's happening and channel their feelings in a meaningful way. You might give them some guidance around phrasing and language, so that their letters honor the humanity of the people who receive them and convey a responsive tone. One way to ensure this activity is rooted in love, compassion, and tenderness is to offer some suggestions and share some possibilities for what students might include in their letters.

Letters of Love: Tips for Teachers

Introduce with care. Frame the project by sharing the "why" by keeping it simple and concise. Use language that is clear and developmentally appropriate without veering into too many details. Students might have questions that could pull the classroom conversation into tricky territory, so be prepared and practice your response for addressing those questions in the moment.

What teachers can say: *Many of you have been hearing about _____, and lots of you have been asking about how to share your support during this difficult time, so we are going to write letters to show that we care.*

In response to a student question: *I can tell that this is on your heart/mind and I can see that this is really important to you but we're not going into details today. I understand some of you might have a lot of questions or feelings, but today is about writing letters to show our support.*

The purpose of these letters is to let _____ know that we care about them and that they are supported. Before we get started writing our letters of love and support, I want to share some possibilities for what you might write or include in your letters. Let's look at the Letters of Love Writing Guide.

Keep tone in mind. Exclamation points, exaggerated expressions of enthusiasm, platitudes can be jarring during traumatic experiences. In their effort to be positive, it's easy for students to rely on phrases like, "Hang in there!! Be strong!! Everything is going to be great!!" which you should try to avoid.

What teachers can say: *Be careful about using exclamation points. The people who are going through this might be feeling sad or afraid so we want to make sure our tone is gentle to respect what they're feeling.*

Try not to assume specifics. Empathy is important, but you might not know exactly who will receive your letters, and we can't assume exactly what their circumstances are or what they're feeling. We also don't want to reinforce the trauma, nor are we typically sharing explicit details or the full context. Therefore, instead of: "I'm so sorry you lost everything," or "I'm so sorry you are in a war," try "I'm sorry for what you are going through" or "I'm thinking of you" or "I'm sending you (a healing and loving word)."

What teachers can say: *You might want to share your feelings about what's happening, but it's important to remember we probably don't know the specifics and so something supportive we could say is: "I'm thinking of you" or by sending them words of love, peace, or support.*

Figure 7-2

Letters of Love: Tips for Teachers

Avoid mentions of war, violence, or trauma.
It's important for us to help our students remember that people are more than the awful thing being inflicted upon them or that has happened to them. One way to do that is to avoid labels associated with tragedy. For example, students might try opening their letters with Dear "Families or Friends" (instead of "refugee" or "victim of _____"). Although people on the receiving end of these letters might be in the midst of tragedy, their identities and experiences include so much more than this time in their lives. Students in your class might also be experiencing their own trauma or something similar, or have close ties or personal connections to the region or conflict, so this is another reason not to dwell on or dig too deeply into the painful details.

Figure 7-2 *continued*

Letters of Love: Writing Guide

Before students write their letters, you could share some of these examples and have the following examples displayed on chart paper or projected on a slide.

Letters of Love: Writing Guide

Letter Opening

Dear Families,

Dear Friend(s),

Dear Community,

Words of Love and Support

I am sorry for what you are going through

I am sending you hope/We are sending you love/I'm sending you support

We are thinking of you/I am thinking of you

Even though we are far away/Even though we are not with you, we are thinking of you, and send you love

We hope you stay safe/We hope for peace soon/We hope you feel supported

Figure 7-3 *continues*

RESPONDING WITH CARE

Letters of Love: Writing Guide

Extra Artful Ideas

Colorful Drawings/Artwork

Pictures with loving, friendly symbols

Pictures that might have local significance (regional animals, colors, trees and flowers)

Quotes from poems we've written as a class

Letter Closings

Sincerely,

With Love,

Take Care,

Your Friend from _____

With Warm Wishes,

Figure 7-3 *continued*

How to Give with Care

Because children are often eager to help, they want to know what they can give or bring or do to make a difference. This leads us to launch a drive or set up a donation bin, which can be efficient ways to collect items quickly and help the community meet the genuine needs of the moment. When done thoughtfully, however, they can also be an opportunity to center the humanity of those in need and model for students how to give with care. If this is something that often surfaces in your community, you might consider launching your next community drive with a poem. Student leaders can read this poem at a school gathering, record a video to be emailed, or print artful flyers to accompany the bins around campus.

How to Give with Care

Ask yourself what is needed

Ask yourself how can we help

Many families can use

Blankets and bottles for babies
Maybe some pencils for school
A toy that brings joy
A letter of love
A colorful drawing
A favorite book
Soaps, shampoos, lotions, and combs
Think about how we can with care
Take your time
Show your love
Send some hope
Give with care

WORDS THAT STING LESSON: ADDRESSING HARMFUL WORDS AND HATE SPEECH

In addition to addressing challenging moments occurring in the world, you might find yourself navigating bias incidents in your own classroom or community, most of which relate to harmful words and hurt feelings. Many of you are likely working with young children and might rarely be confronted with straightforward hate speech intended to harm. However, these words do make their way into the community, and even if the intent is not to harm, we know that the impact is often harmful.

In our years of teaching, we've encountered several incidents of students sharing or mimicking harmful words, hate speech, or even repeating stereotypes they've picked up from online gaming and comment boards. When moments like these have arisen in our teaching lives, we've often found ourselves reacting and making rushed decisions instead of responding thoughtfully. Once we noticed this pattern, we decided to start planning proactively in order to give ourselves a moment of pause. When you're not in the midst of responding to a crisis, you can often think more clearly about how to react in a more grounded way that not only provides support, but also provides a sense of agency for children who are navigating these moments themselves. We've also found that crafting a response rooted in the arts is restorative and grounding for everyone.

As a result of addressing these situations year after year, we developed a "Words That Sting" lesson. Sometimes we teach this lesson proactively in grades 3–5, but other times we're using it to respond to something that has happened in the moment. It has helped us teach students how to:

- Name what they are experiencing, noticing, and feeling

- Differentiate between harmful words and hate speech

- Understand the gravity of hate speech and how its connection to identity makes it all the more painful and serious

> **Handle with Care**
>
> Lessons and discussions that delve into the topic of hate speech benefit greatly from intentional preparation and thoughtful planning. We recommend giving yourself time to loop in your classroom caregivers and prepare yourself mentally and emotionally for heavy content. Make a list of any student questions that might surface and practice how you can respond in the moment. As you begin your lesson, take the time to recenter your classroom agreements and, perhaps depending on the grade level and group of students, consider adding a reminder like the following: *When we are learning and sharing about hate speech, we can use the term* hate speech *in place of the actual words so that we don't cause any harm to each other by repeating words that can really sting.*

- Be an upstander when they encounter harmful words or hate speech

- Seek support from an adult when they think they have been the target of hate speech or encounter language that makes them feel unsure, unsettled, or uncomfortable.

Words That Sting Lesson: A Step-by-Step Guide

We have found that having a slide deck for this lesson at the ready has made it possible for us to respond right away when an incident occurs. The following visuals are available as an online resource (see OR 7–1 in the Online Resources, Words That Sting).

First, we define the terms: Harmful Words, Bystander, and Upstander.

Important Words to Remember

HARMFUL WORDS
Words that are hurtful, unkind, mean. These words put people down or hurt people's feelings.

BYSTANDER
Someone who hears harmful words and does not say or do anything.

UPSTANDER
Someone who hears harmful words and speaks up in the moment or tells an adult.

Figure 7-4

Then, we differentiate between Harmful Words and Hate Speech.

Harmful Words vs. Hate Speech

HARMFUL WORDS
Words that are hurtful, unkind, mean. These words put people down or hurt people's feelings.

HATE SPEECH
Cruel words that attack a person's identity.

Figure 7-5

RESPONDING WITH CARE

Next, we remind students of what makes up our identity and show the identity graphic shared in Chapter 2 (Figure 2–1).

What Do We Mean by Identity?
Things That Make Us Unique

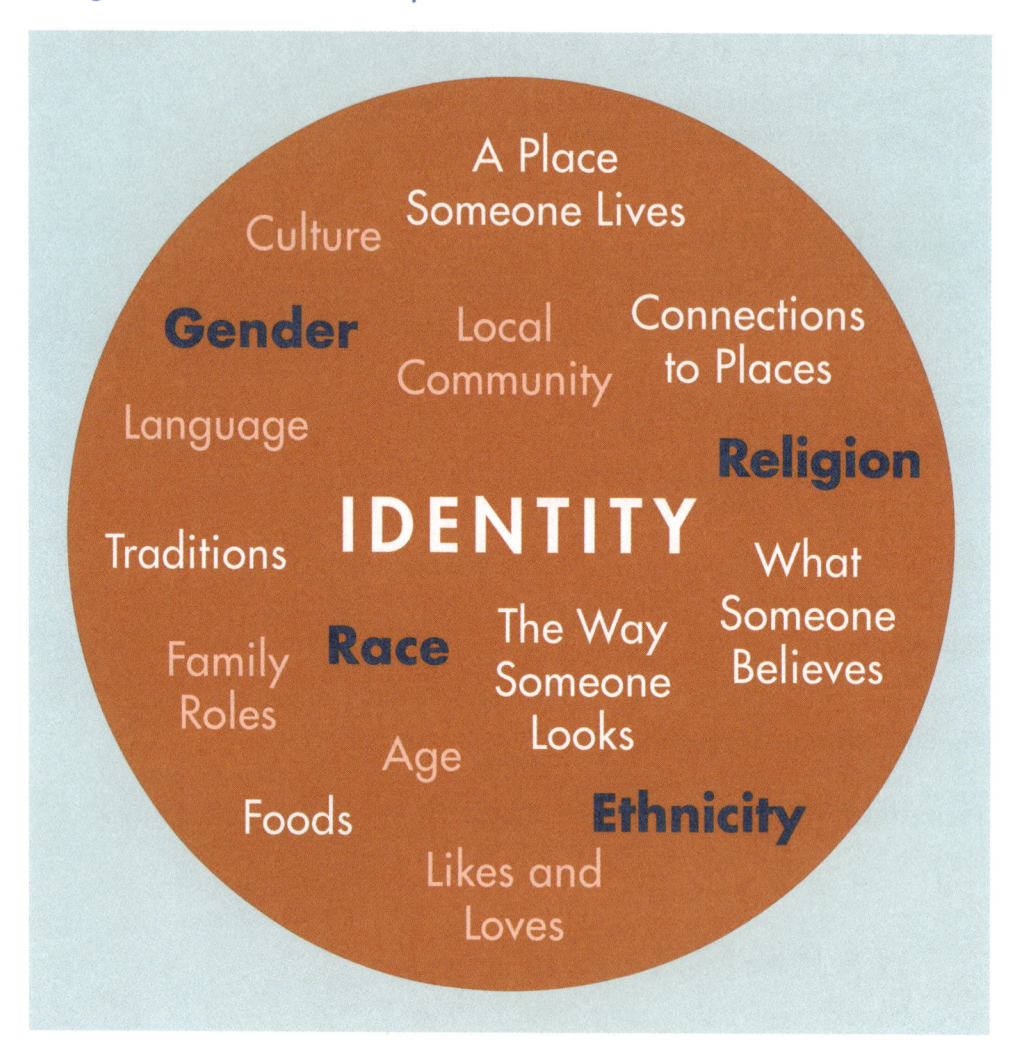

[Identity graphic with terms: A Place Someone Lives, Culture, Gender, Local Community, Connections to Places, Language, Religion, Traditions, IDENTITY, What Someone Believes, Family Roles, Race, The Way Someone Looks, Age, Foods, Ethnicity, Likes and Loves]

Figure 7-6

Then, we reinforce that hate speech includes cruel words that typically target aspects of a person's identity, which is what makes it especially cruel and hurtful. Depending on the specific hate speech you're addressing, you might add something like, "There's actually a long history of people saying and doing hurtful things to people of color/Black people/Jewish people/women/LGBTQ people so while hate speech can be hurtful for anyone to hear, it's especially painful for people who share that identity."

THE ARTFUL APPROACH TO EXPLORING IDENTITY AND FOSTERING BELONGING

Hate Speech
Cruel Words That Attack a Person's Identity

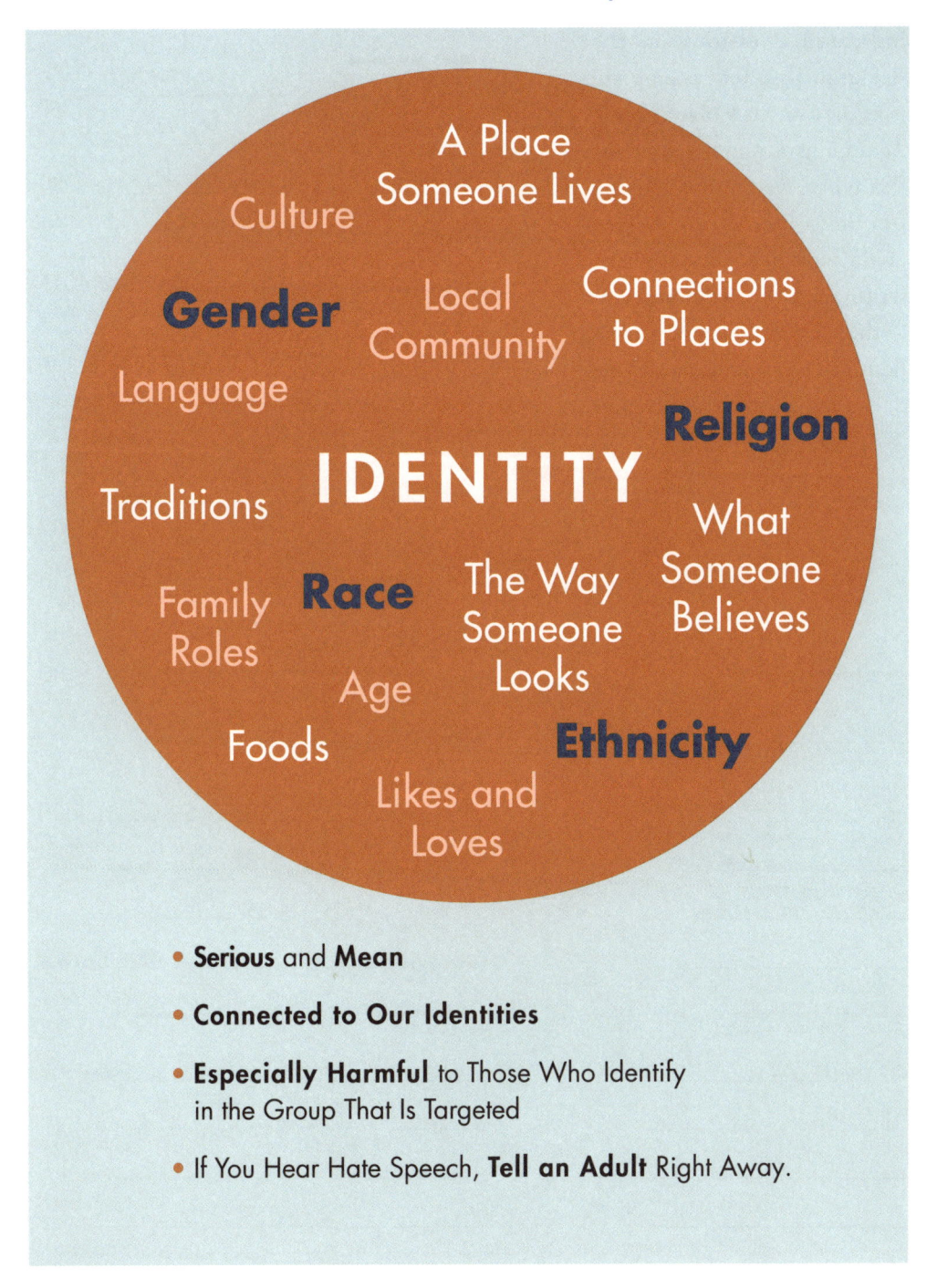

IDENTITY

- A Place Someone Lives
- Culture
- **Gender**
- Local Community
- Connections to Places
- Language
- **Religion**
- Traditions
- What Someone Believes
- Family Roles
- **Race**
- The Way Someone Looks
- Age
- **Ethnicity**
- Foods
- Likes and Loves

- **Serious** and **Mean**
- **Connected to Our Identities**
- **Especially Harmful** to Those Who Identify in the Group That Is Targeted
- If You Hear Hate Speech, **Tell an Adult** Right Away.

Figure 7-7

RESPONDING WITH CARE

Next, we invite students to take a moment to reflect and process their thoughts, feelings, and questions on the Being an Upstander template (see OR 7–2 for a blank copy). Again, this is another time for flexibility. We are not looking for uniform responses. This might look like some students writing a thorough paragraph of thoughts and lingering questions and other students sharing only a feeling word (see Figures 7–8, 7–9, and 7–10).

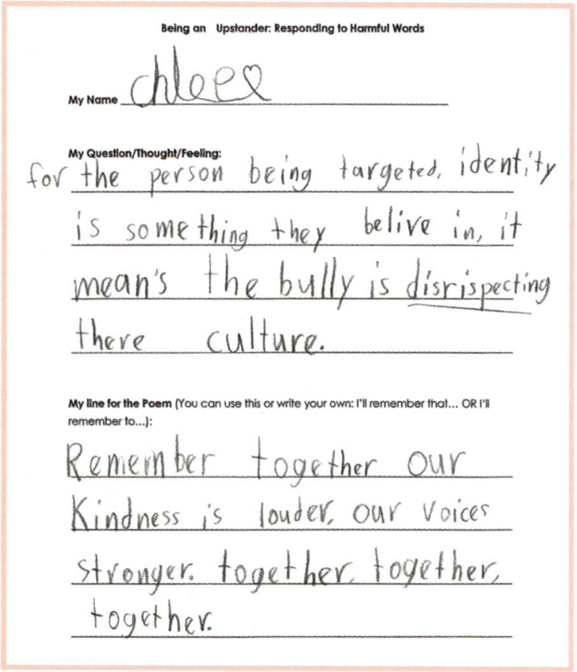

Being an Upstander: Responding to Harmful Words

My Name: chloee

My Question/Thought/Feeling:
for the person being targeted, identity is something they belive in, it mean's the bully is disrispecting there culture.

My line for the Poem (You can use this or write your own: I'll remember that... OR I'll remember to...):
Remember together our Kindness is louder, our voices stronger. together, together, together.

Figure 7-8

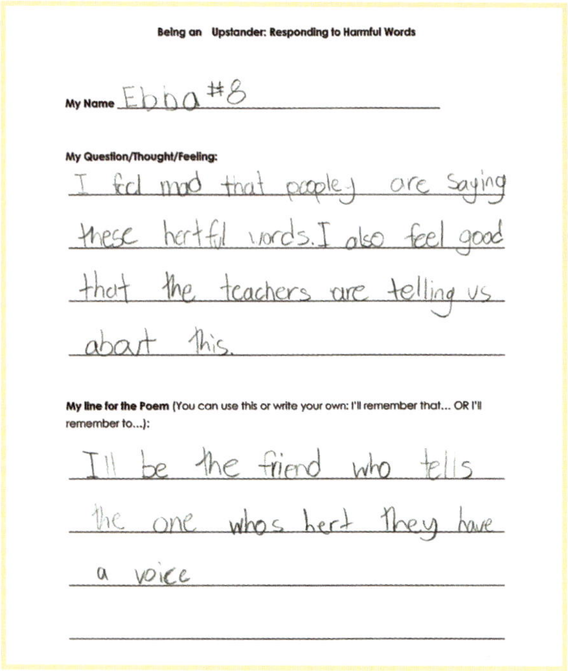

Being an Upstander: Responding to Harmful Words

My Name: Ebba #8

My Question/Thought/Feeling:
I fel mad that peopley are saying these hertful words. I also feel good that the teachers are telling us abart this.

My line for the Poem (You can use this or write your own: I'll remember that... OR I'll remember to...):
I'll be the friend who tells the one whos hert they have a voice

Figure 7-9

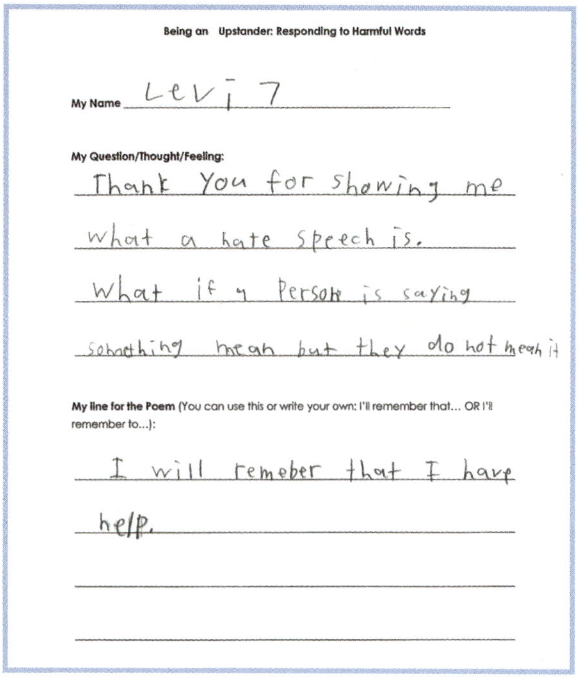

Being an Upstander: Responding to Harmful Words

My Name: Levi 7

My Question/Thought/Feeling:
Thank you for showing me what a hate speech is. What if a Person is saying something mean but they do not mean it

My line for the Poem (You can use this or write your own: I'll remember that... OR I'll remember to...):
I will remeber that I have help.

Figure 7-10

THE ARTFUL APPROACH TO EXPLORING IDENTITY AND FOSTERING BELONGING

Finally, we read aloud a poem that Veronica wrote called "Words That Sting" as a way to bring all of these ideas together, calm the energy, feel connected as a classroom community, and transition into a closing.

Words That Sting
VERONICA

Some words sting like fire ants
And feel like tiny sharp pains happening all at once
Some words smell like a pile of old garbage
They make my stomach turn
Some words bark like a loud mean dog
They make my ears ring
Some words burn like poison ivy
They make my cheeks hot
Some words sound like a sad song
They make my heart hurt

Some words make me think
Why do people use these words that sting?
Where do they come from?
What do they mean?
Why do some words hurt like this?

But when the words that sting
Come my way
I'll remember to speak up
That I have a voice to say no to hate
I'll remember never to repeat
The words that sting like fire ants
I'll remember to ask for help
From the people I trust

Words That Sting

Have you ever thought about what you would do?

Will you remember to reach for help?
Will you remember to find your voice?

Will you remember . . .

That you are supported
By the people around you

That you are cared for
By the teachers rooting for you

That you are loved
By your family and friends

Will you remember . . .

That together we're stronger
And our kindness is louder

And we can drown out
The words that sting

By lifting out voices
And speaking up when it counts?

Will you remember . . .
That we are not alone?

Because we are not alone.
We are not alone.

I'll remember that I am not alone
That I am supported by my friends
That I am cared for by the teachers around me
That I am loved by my family
That together we are strong
Together we are kind
Together we are a community
I am not alone

We wanted to give students the opportunity to own these words themselves, so we turned this poem into a choral reading experience. Most of the time, we split the class in half, with one half reading the orange lines, the other half reading the blue lines, and everyone reading the final two green lines together. The phrases in red are read by the teacher or facilitator.

For our closing moment, we invite students to write a line of their own by using the stem, "I'll remember that," "I'll remember to," or their own phrasing (see OR 7–3 in the online resources for a blank template).

Finally, we string their lines together to create a community poem called "I Will Remember" that uplifts all the student voices and ideas.

Figure 7-11

CLOSING WITH A POEM

I Will Remember
THIRD GRADERS

I will remember
That we are a community
That I should always stick up for my friends
That I can ask a teacher if I am scared

I will remember to support others and myself
To never use the fire ant and garbage words

I will remember
I know people who love me no matter what
And I should do the same
Everyone deserves a chance
Even in the darkest times

I will remember
That an attack on an identity
Is an attack on a soul
Culture, language, religion and heart

I will remember that I have a voice
That can drown out the worst hurtful words
That can drown out the hate speech
I HAVE A VOICE

I will remember
That we are peace
We aren't hate
We are kind
Together we are strong
We are friends
We are community
We are family

8

DESIGNING YOUR OWN BELONGING LAB

A Space for Student Leaders, Poets, and Public Speakers

> *I long, as does every human being, to be at home wherever I find myself.*
>
> —Maya Angelou

We created *The Belonging Lab* to support conversations about identity and belonging while also lifting up student voices. When we thought about what our dream student advocacy group could look like, we imagined a place where students could gather to connect, design projects, and collaborate artfully. We wanted to incorporate some of the disciplines that bring us the most joy and fuel our work together: literacy, the arts, educational technology, design thinking, and of course, belonging. We decided to call it a *lab* because we imagined it to be a place for new ideas and workshopping our upstander skills. By calling it a lab, we also hoped to underscore the idea that belonging work is never finished. We're always improving upon ourselves and theorizing about how to build a more inclusive community.

We created the Belonging Lab with three explicit goals in mind. First, to develop what we call "Belonging Ambassadors" for our school, young people who are committed to speaking up and reaching out. Second, to empower students to design and lead their own annual campaign that serves a genuine need in the community and supports belonging for all students. And third, to give children opportunities to practice behaviors that help them create a sense of belonging for the students around them: practicing active or "generous listening," showing curiosity about one another, and reflecting on small actions that make a big difference in people's lives. Small actions like saying a friendly hello back, welcoming someone to sit with them, or noticing who might need a little extra support.

Another implicit goal for us as facilitators is to intentionally foster belonging within this group. While it seems obvious in retrospect, we hadn't realized that the Belonging Lab would attract students who were feeling a heightened sense of belonging uncertainty themselves. When we noticed that students who were signing up to join us were not only interested in advocacy work but were also hoping to find connection and belonging through the lab space, we started to incorporate even more community-building time into our meetings.

SETTING UP A BELONGING LAB

Before you launch your first meeting, here are four steps to get you started:

1. Plan your meeting times
2. Make an announcement
3. Establish community agreements
4. Create an agenda and meeting structure

Plan Your Meeting Times

We typically meet for thirty minutes during lunch once or twice a month because that way, students don't need to get to school earlier or stay later. Of course, you could decide to meet anytime but we encourage you to think about finding a time when as many students as possible are able to attend. While each meeting has a consistent structure, there is an organic, even informal vibe to our gatherings. Students are typically eating lunch and trickling in for the first few minutes. This informality is intentional. We want to create a "come as you are" feeling in the room, which, for some kids, is a welcome break from a more academically focused day.

Make an Announcement

We intentionally created a visually appealing slide to share with students that explained the club using vibrant colors to help grab their attention and get them interested in this new gathering. Think about ways that you can stir up some buzz around your own Belonging Lab and make your announcement feel special and exciting. Is it a slide? A fun and quick video? A live announcement from a few interested students?

You're Invited to Join the Belonging Lab!
An Invitation Template to Get Started

THE BELONGING LAB

Where we:

- Create, write, and share stories
- Use the arts, design, and technology to express ourselves!
- Workshop ideas for schoolwide projects
- Ask big questions
- Engage in courageous conversations about justice and equality
- Celebrate identity and diversity
- Lead with courage

Figure 8-1

Establish Community Agreements

Before we dive into work, we start with our community agreements. This will be a space where identity is centered, which means it's even more important for us to begin this way. We also take a brief bit of time for students to share what most resonates with them and offer suggestions for us to add. See Chapter 2, p. 46 for agreements you might adapt for your own belonging lab.

Create an Agenda and Meeting Structure

Our meetings typically include:

- **A Community Check-In**: Refer to Chapter 2's Check-In Guide, "20 Questions for Each Season" (5 min.). As you might already know, we are big on check-ins. You can use check-ins as more than just a fun way to get started or focused. When done with intention, they offer a consistent ritual that supports the work of belonging. In fact, the Stanford design school lists ritual as one of the four "levers" of design that contribute to a strong sense of belonging in any community.

- **Artful Reflection**: Doing an artful reflection can look a lot of ways: discussing big ideas, writing and sharing our thoughts (lines of poetry, journal reflections, answers to prompts) (10 min.).

- **Project Collaboration**: Depending on where we are in the design process, this could include: defining the need by reviewing survey data, brainstorming and seeking inspiration, creating a rough draft or template, gathering input and making revisions, testing things out, or creating and implementing (10 min.).

- **Closing**: In a similar way to the check-in, our closing ritual matters too. Sometimes we do a collective breath or movement, a final one-word share-out, or a mindful moment (5 min.).

- **Celebrating Our Work and Each Other (Occasionally)**: We love to take time for joy and noticing our impact on the community. We might play a fun playlist, have a dance party, and maybe share some snacks!

GETTING STARTED: SAMPLE AGENDAS

The following are a few sample agendas from our Belonging Lab across the year that you can adapt for your own needs. You'll also find some of the tools (such as surveys, scripts, and brainstorming questions) we used to design and implement one schoolwide project for fostering belonging in our community.

Sample Agenda: Day One

- **Community-Building Check-In:** This or That! (Low Stakes for Day One)

- **Values Affirmations Activity:** Building Community

- **Artful Reflection:** Belonging Backpack

- **Project Collaboration:** Initial Campaign Brainstorm

- **Closing:** Belonging Lab on 3!

Community-Building Check-In: This or That!

Read aloud this list (or make your own) and have students quickly indicate their choice.

This or That!

Video games or board games

Homework before dinner or after dinner

Tacos or burritos

Pasta or pizza

Candy (sours and gummies) or chocolate

Vanilla or chocolate

Cats or dogs

Spooky movies or funny movies

Play sports or watch sports or no sports

Read the book or watch the movie

Beach or park

Ice cream cake or regular cake

Values Affirmations Activity: Building Community

On our first day of Belonging Lab, we always start with a "Values Affirmation" (Cohen 2022b) exercise, which you can find on Geoffrey Cohen's website. Not only does this help students reflect on what values matter to them most, but it helps them begin to develop a sense for the way our actions, choices, and responses are rooted in what we value. After students choose two or three values that are most important to them, we look through their choices, calculate the data, and share out our findings with the group. They always find this big reveal fascinating, and the values that emerge as the most important help guide the goals of the schoolwide project that Belonging Lab leads.

Artful Reflection: Belonging Backpack

We introduce our mentor "Belonging Backpack" poem and then invite students to add their own line by journaling and then sharing it out loud.

Belonging Backpack Poem
MS. BELLINGHAM AND MS. SCOTT

I'm bringing an open mind

So that I remember to stay curious

I'm bringing a heart that cares

So that everyone feels included

I'm bringing my love of stories

To encourage everyone to share their own

I'm bringing my dad's advice that it's okay to make mistakes

So that people feel free to take risks!

I'm bringing my unique self

So that other people feel safe to bring theirs

I'm bringing my curiosity in others

I'm bringing The Rabbit Listened

To help us remember the power in listening

I'm bringing my mom's lentil soup, my family's favorite comfort food

Invitation to Journal: What is in your Belonging Backpack? What can you offer the people in our community to help everyone feel like they belong?

Project Collaboration

Announcement of initial campaign brainstorming: Be on the lookout for spaces and places in our community that might need a little extra support and would benefit from some Belonging Lab attention.

Closing

Whole-group cheer: "Hands in wherever you are! Belonging Lab on Three!"

Sample Agenda: Day Three

By our third session, students had decided they wanted to focus their attention on making sure everyone felt they belonged on the recess field. In this meeting we continued to build community and created a campaign name to generate excitement for the work ahead.

- **Community Check-In:** Most Yourself

- **Artful Reflection:** Museum of Me

- **Project Collaboration:** Name the Campaign (brainstorming in small groups/journaling/pitching)

- **Closing:** Whole-Group Share-Out

Community Check-In: Most Yourself

In a pair and share, discuss: When do you feel most yourself? What kinds of activities make you feel super happy, excited, or special?

    Rebecca: *When I'm singing along to one of my favorite songs*

    Veronica: *When I'm having a dance party with my family*

Artful Reflection: Museum of Me

Create a quick collection of sketches or word clouds that represent the times we feel most ourselves. Share with a partner.

REBECCA

Word cloud 1: "This little light of mine I'm gonna let it shine" (lyrics from the iconic song, "This Little Light of Mine" with music notes)

Word cloud 2: Free, fast, strong, alive, energized, powerful (words that express how I feel when I go for a run)

Word cloud 3: pine trees, sky, sunshine peeking through, green, blue (what I see on a walk through the woods)

VERONICA

Sketch 1: Books with hearts (love of reading)

Sketch 2: Tacos on a table (dinner with family)

Sketch 3: Dancing stick figure with music notes (dance party)

Closing: Whole-Group Share-Out

Share with the whole group something new, interesting, or special that you learned about your partner. Maybe it was a commonality or maybe it was a surprise!

Sample Agenda: Day Five

In the next couple of Belonging Lab meetings, you'll decide upon a focus for your group project—in our case students determined that the recess field could use a little extra Belonging Lab support to help everyone feel included. Once we had established a need, we led students through a design-thinking process that included the following steps: **collect data** (in our case, we created a survey), **review data and decide on a focus** (in our case, students decided that the recess field was the community space they wanted to focus on), **name** your campaign (in our case, Friendship Field!), and **brainstorm** artful projects. For a detailed look at our design process, see OR 8–1, Design Process to Develop a Belonging Lab Campaign, in the Online Resources.

By the time we gathered for day five, we had reviewed data from our survey and brainstormed ways to market the campaign.

- **Community Check-In:** True for Me Too
- **Artful Reflection:** True for Me Journaling
- **Project Collaboration:** Table Read
- **Closing:** Friendship Field together on 3 . . . 1, 2, 3 . . . Friendship Field!

Community Check-In: True for Me Too

This is meant to be a values affirmation, a community builder, and a get to know you better activity. Feel free to use these, remix, and add your own. Or invite your students to submit their own ideas.

> *If this is true for you too, raise your hand/give a signal and say, "True for me too."*

I like to keep my room organized.

I love to sing along to music in the kitchen or the car or wherever! Sometimes exercising, playing, or moving my body gives me a real positive energy boost.

I love family traditions, like pizza night on Fridays.

Sometimes I get the Monday morning blues.

Making people laugh is something I love to do.

I like helping out around the house.

I like to cook with my family.

Sometimes I feel unsure about how to express myself.

I really appreciate it when people reach out to me because it can be hard for me to reach out first.

It's important to me to feel understood by and connected to my friends.

I like listening and learning about my friends' experiences and traditions.

Sometimes it's hard for me to say I'm sorry even though I know I probably should.

I love playing games like board games, video games, all sorts of games!

I love dessert and sweet treats.

Artful Reflection: True for Me Journaling

Invite students to choose one of the "True for Me" statements and do a brief free-write to say more!

> **Veronica:** *I love to cook with my family because it's a tradition we've always had together ever since I was little. One of my favorite foods to make with them is breakfast tacos. My mom makes the tortillas on the comal and I scramble the eggs and sometimes my dad fries up some bacon. Whenever I smell delicious breakfast tacos cooking in the kitchen, I feel like I'm home!*

> **Rebecca:** *I love listening and learning about my friends' experiences and traditions because it makes me feel more connected to them. I also learn so much about them when they share with me, and I love hearing all their stories!*

Project Collaboration

If you decide to announce the campaign out loud, you might have collaborated on an announcement script like we did (see OR 8–2 Sample Script in the Online Resources). You might use this session to read through your announcement script and work through any confusions or line distributions. Practice saying the lines smoothly!

Closing

Whole-group cheer: "Friendship Field on 3 . . . 1, 2, 3 . . . Friendship Field!"

Sample Agenda: Day Eight

At this point, we were well into the school year. You might notice that our artful reflection "True for Me" journaling builds on the community check-in and invites students to dig a little deeper into what makes them unique and share a little more of their identity stories. Our closing "Try One Thing" encourages students to continue acting as "Belonging Ambassadors" around campus by being powerful noticers and thinking about how their own small actions and words can contribute to a community of belonging.

- **Community Check-In:** What We Wish Someone Had Said
- **Artful Reflection:** Acting It Out
- **Project Collaboration:** Campaign Posters
- **Closing:** Try One Thing

Community Check-In: What We Wish Someone Had Said

When you're feeling left out or unsure you belong, what's one thing someone has done for you or something you wish someone would do for you? (Teachers might share "We want you to listen carefully because we will be coming back to this.")

1. A parent listened to me and gave me comfort.
2. A friend noticed that I was sad and asked me about it.
3. Someone on the field told me I played well.
4. I wish my friend would have checked in with me.
5. Someone asked me questions about something I shared.
6. Someone smiled at me that I thought didn't like me.
7. I wished someone started the conversation first.
8. Someone asked me if I wanted to sit with them.
9. Someone smiled at me.
10. I wish someone had helped me feel better when I didn't score.

Artful Reflection: Acting It Out

Work with a partner to write a few examples of what you could say to help someone who is feeling left out and then practice saying those lines out loud to each other. Some students might want to perform their lines (or mini skits) for the group.

Project Collaboration: Campaign Posters

In pairs or small groups, create a poster for high traffic areas that reminds your community about how to be a friend and an uplifter on the field. *At this point in the year, we would be in the midst of our schoolwide project and could use our time together to collaborate on that.*

Closing: Try One Thing

What's one thing you will do or say to help people feel included and that they belong? It could be something you heard or learned about today or an idea you've tried before. For our next Belonging Lab check-in, we will share out one thing we tried!

Figure 8-2

Figure 8-3

Students Collaborating on Belonging Lab Campaign Posters

Sample Agenda: Belonging Lab Party

We believe in finding ways to celebrate wins! The work of advocacy and allyship is lifelong and often change takes years to enact, so it's important that we teach student advocates to notice, acknowledge, and celebrate the progress they've made in their community. Celebrating small shifts and making time for joyful moments doesn't mean the work is finished! Students are often the first to notice that one campaign will not resolve every kickball conflict on the field or game of tag gone awry. One way to counter "all or nothing" thinking and potentially curb what could one day become social justice fatigue, we recommend teaching students how to process what they're feeling in those moments, notice and recognize the progress they've made, and envision what role they might play moving forward. End-of-year celebrations can be the perfect time to invite this kind of reflection and support students as they imagine how they will continue fostering belonging in all their communities as they move through school and life.

> ### Belonging Shout-Outs Idea
>
> Create a "Belonging Shout-Outs" bulletin board or set aside a little time at a weekly gathering to share examples of belonging around campus. This can help reinforce for Belonging Lab students that part of being in this group is being an ambassador of belonging and noticing when they see students supporting each other. You might encourage students to offer shout-outs to groups without using individual names, so that they don't become a popularity contest.
>
> - "We noticed the third graders sharing the field this week!"
> - "We noticed our class was listening really closely to the guest speaker today!"
> - "We noticed fourth graders being kind with their first-grade buddies on the playground!"

- **Community Check-In:** Words for the Bench
- **Project Collaboration:** Painting the Bench
- **Closing:** What's a Legacy of Belonging That You Want to Leave? What's one of the Belonging Lab ideas or projects that you hope lasts forever at our school?
- **Surprise:** Popsicle® party!

DESIGNING YOUR OWN BELONGING LAB

Community Check-In for Belonging Lab Party: Words for the Bench

We've had a "buddy bench" for years on our playground, but it had gone unnoticed for quite a few years, in part because it needed a fresh coat of paint, some updated designs, and a touch of color! This became part of our celebration.

Whole-group share: Think about what you hope to add to the bench today. When you're ready to share out loud, share: What's one word or symbol you want to add to the bench today?

Project Collaboration for Belonging Lab Party: Painting the Bench

As the students painted the bench, lots of children gathered around and asked questions about the project, which brought some awareness to this important spot on the field.

Figure 8-4

Figure 8-5

Figure 8-6

Painting the Bench for Friendship Field

THE ARTFUL APPROACH TO EXPLORING IDENTITY AND FOSTERING BELONGING

Closing for Belonging Lab Party: What's a Legacy of Belonging That You Want to Leave?

What's one of the Belonging Lab ideas or projects that you hope lasts forever at our school?

> Student response: I hope more kids feel comfortable playing together on the field.
>
> Student response: I hope students look out for each other more.
>
> Student response: I hope everyone remembers our video for Friendship Field!
>
> Student response: I hope kids remember to stick up for their friends when someone's being mean.

Surprise: Popsicle Party!

Even though Belonging Lab students only met with us once a month, and the projects that we designed were relatively small in scope, the impact of this work has surprised, and frankly, moved us. When we encounter Belonging Lab kids out in the world, they often inquire about the ongoing legacy of their campaigns, their projects, and the work of belonging at the school. "Are you still doing Belonging Lab?" they will ask, or "What is the Belonging Lab campaign this year?" What matters most to us is that we have planted a seed. We have helped these students develop a lens for being the kind of people who have learned how to notice differently, how to take steps to make big changes or even just small shifts. We have worked together to become more attuned to the ways our words, actions, and presence can support people in our community, so that everyone feels welcome and everyone feels they belong.

DESIGNING YOUR OWN BELONGING LAB

CLOSING WITH A POEM

Belonging Feels Like

Belonging feels like friends waving hello
Laughing at the lunch table
Being part of a team
Belonging feels like working together to get a job done
Creating something that makes you feel really happy
Catching a ball from all the way across the field
Belonging feels like getting to spend time with my family
Helping out at home
Belonging feels like singing in my choir
Fitting in with my baseball team
Cooking tacos with Dad
Belonging feels like being understood
Someone saying, "sit here!" when I'm looking for a seat
A rainbow heart pinned to my teacher's shirt
Belonging feels like watching TV on the couch with my family
Sunday afternoon phone calls with Grandma and Grandad
And my dog's smell after a bath
Belonging feels like knowing you are loved wherever you are
Like coming home after a long day
Like being greeted with open arms
Belonging feels like you're home

9

MEETING FOR WINDOWS, MIRRORS, AND COFFEE

A Children's Literature Book Club for Parents and Caregivers

> *Stories help us ask and navigate the big, scary questions in our lives. How do we find our place in the world? How do we support and care for the people we love? And a pressing question in almost all middle grade books: how do we bridge the gap between childhood and adulthood? Stories are a safe space to explore these ideas, and in my own life, I have always turned to them for hope and reassurance.*
> —Tae Keller

WHAT IF WE READ CHILDREN'S BOOKS

When we began working together in the fall of 2020, teachers and families were hanging on by a very thin thread (kindergartners on Zoom, homemade masks, so much disinfectant, and the one household always forgetting to mute!) With all the distancing, the masking, and the Zooming, we found ourselves just trying to keep up, and it became increasingly challenging to make space or find energy for the artful moments that had fueled our work for years. As anyone who started working at a new school in the fall of 2020 might have also experienced, building relationships with new colleagues felt practically impossible.

In addition to the reality of Covid, in response to a history of racism, racial injustice, anti-Blackness, and police brutality, people were joining in protest in unforeseen numbers across the world, making the need for local conversations about race all the more important. We wanted community and conversation, but it felt like a struggle to make either of those things possible. If *we* were feeling this way, we imagined our school's families must have been yearning for connection too. We had heard from caregivers who were looking to learn more about race and identity in America or seeking connection and solidarity with fellow allies and co-conspirators or hoping to begin a family conversation about what was unfolding in the news. We knew we wanted to support families during this time, but kept returning to the question: *How could we create a space that meets all these parents' needs?*

Then we thought to ourselves, *what if we read children's books together?* We combed through our growing collection of contemporary kid lit, pulling graphic novels and chapter books off the shelves and stacking a little tower of books by Jacqueline Woodson and Kelly Yang and Tae Keller and Renée Watson and Jerry Craft. Book by book, we flipped through the pages and began to talk through what these gorgeous stories could make possible. *Inside Out and Back Again* (Lai 2013) could offer insight into a family's refugee experience. *Efrén Divided* (Cisneros 2021) could provide perspective on what families with mixed immigration status might experience in their day-to-day lives. *Prairie Lotus* (Park 2022) could illuminate the history of anti-Asian hate in the American West. *Hurricane Child* (Callender 2019) could bring to light the many intersecting identities young people are navigating. *El Deafo* (Bell 2014) could help launch a conversation about disability, deaf culture, and diversity within deaf identity. *A Duet for Home* (Glaser 2023) could help us humanize the experience of unhoused young people and their families. While these were all books for young people, they were just as layered, sophisticated, and wise, especially in the hands of such extraordinary writers. And they wouldn't take as long to read.

THE ARTFUL APPROACH TO EXPLORING IDENTITY AND FOSTERING BELONGING

We also knew we would be giving these adults an opportunity few of us had growing up: reading books that centered BIPOC and LGBTQ+ characters, written by BIPOC and LGBTQ+ authors, exploring themes like Black joy, and the enduring power of cross-racial coalitions. Centering these kinds of themes using contemporary children's literature felt like a way to meet everyone where they were at, without prioritizing white comfort. We felt the "windows and mirrors" framework that serves so well in the classroom would extend beautifully to the broader community.

> ### What's Your AND ___?
>
> What's the vibe you want to create with your family community? For us, Windows, Mirrors, and *Coffee* felt fresh and fun. But there is nothing sacrosanct about coffee! You could have a Windows, Mirrors, and Tacos Book Club or Windows, Mirrors, and Jazz! It could be that you are spotlighting specific identities. A focus on LGBTQ+ books might inspire a Windows, Mirrors, and Rainbows Book Club. Think about the ways in which you connect with the families at your school. What tagline could you use for your book club that might inspire participation and engagement?

Our "windows and mirrors" themed book club was finally coming into focus, but the framework alone didn't capture the whole vibe we were hoping to create. We knew we wanted the book club to prioritize learning, but we also wanted to leave a little space for something extra—for checking in, for artful moments, for building community. Inevitably, the book club would help families support their children's reading lives, but we also wanted to signal that this was also something for caregivers themselves. We wanted this experience to feel like more than a book club. We wanted this experience to feel like something communities all over the world have some version of—deep conversations over coffee. And thus, *Window, Mirrors, and Coffee Book Club (WMC)* was born.

Finding Ways to Make Sunshine: Our First WMC Book Club Meetup

We chose *Ways to Make Sunshine* by Renée Watson (2020) as our first book. It stars Ryan Hart, an optimistic Black girl full of spirit and moxie navigating everything from friendship and big sisterhood to beauty standards, race and identity, and slumber parties. As soon as we opened our first meeting for discussion, it became clear that so many people saw themselves inside the book—whether it through family dynamics, relationships with siblings, searching for belonging as a young person, or the changing tides of friendships. One parent said that up until reading this book, she had never seen a family like her own so authentically portrayed: the Sunday trips to church, the family dinners, Ryan getting her hair done by Grandma and taking in some wisdom and a little extra love along the way. Not only is this book full of joy and mirrors for Black parents and caregivers, but it also led us into a nuanced conversation about being "color brave" (Hobson 2014). The conversation that unfolded turned out to be a powerful one about race. Some caregivers let us know it was the first time they had broached the subject in a safe interracial space. Others mentioned appreciating being able to delight over a character who didn't exist in their childhood or gaining a better understanding of a lofty equity concept or framework by seeing it play out in a children's book.

PLANNING YOUR OWN WMC BOOK CLUB!

As you begin to think about planning a WMC (or a Windows, Mirrors, and Tacos! or Windows, Mirrors, and Pizza! Or whatever you choose!) book club of your own, you'll want to think about what the needs of your community are and how to use a book club like this to build relationships with families. In your initial year, you might consider starting small, only hosting one event a season or a semester, and leaning on books that support the kinds of issues you want to surface for learning and discussion. While we give suggestions for books to read across a year, we recognize that it may be impossible to launch a monthly book club right off the bat. Take it slow! Make it work for you and your families.

Because our WMC was born in the pandemic, all our meetings were held online for the first year. In the subsequent years, we continued to meet online for most of our monthly gatherings, but we initiated a few in-person events that ended up being special opportunities to connect in person with caregivers. Depending on the needs of your community, you might start with online gatherings, or you might have the capacity to meet in person (with snacks and mingling!) to build community in person right away. What we loved about hosting our sessions online was the flexibility it offered all our caregivers; sometimes they even joined as they drove home from work or cooked dinner! But, of course, there's nothing like face-to-face interactions, so you might consider hosting at least one community gathering in person as well.

One important consideration to keep in mind as you plan your first meetup, is launching with a book that will engage and excite your families. For us, that book was *Ways to Make Sunshine* (Watson 2020). What might that book be for your community?

Brainstorm Your Reads for the Year

For children's literature superfans like us, there is nothing more exciting than thinking about our annual book lineup! We generally choose one per month across the school year. We take several factors into consideration before choosing and announcing our lineup:

> Which identities are represented in the characters and authors?
>
> What's happening in the world or in our community?
>
> What new books are on the horizon?

Host Your First WMC: Structuring the Meetups

All our Windows, Mirrors, and Coffee sessions include the same consistent features for each gathering. The following table (see Figure 9–1) gives you a sense of this structure, as well as examples that bring each component to life. A blank copy of this planning template is available as OR 9–1 in the Online Resources along with a complete plan for our meeting about the book *Ways to Make Sunshine* (OR 9–2).

Windows, Mirrors, and Coffee Book lineup

This is just one example of books chosen for the year. You'll base your decisions on your own community and what new books you're hearing about.

September: *Ways to Make Sunshine* by Renée Watson (2020)

October: *Mexikid* by Pedro Martín (2023)

November: *In the Footsteps of Crazy Horse* by Joseph Marshall III (2015)

December: *A Duet for Home* by Karina Yan Glaser (2023)

January: *El Deafo* by Cece Bell (2014)

February: *When Winter Robeson Came* by Brenda Woods (2022)

March: *Star Fish* by Lisa Fipps (2021)

April: *Other Words for Home* by Jasmine Warga (2021)

May: *When You Trap a Tiger* by Tae Keller (2020)

June: *King and the Dragonflies* by Kacen Callender (2022)

Windows, Mirrors, and Coffee Planning Guide

What we do	How it might look
Welcome This is an opportunity to set the tone for the gathering.	We play music connected to the book or that speaks to a message or feeling we're hoping to convey and welcome each person as they join the virtual meetup.
Invitational Opening/Check-In If you've made it this far in this book, you know we love a check-in! Just like we would with students, or each other, we always start with one low-stakes, engaging question tied to the themes of the book or the time of year. A question helps set the tone and invites people to share important connections to culture, family, or identity.	Drop in the chat or share out loud: • What's a food that reminds you of home? • One word that reflects how you are feeling today or in this moment? • What is a song that is giving you life or joy right now? • What's a regional love you have? (Drop in the chat: I love ____. It's a ____ thing. E.g., Veronica loves sweet tea. It's a southern thing.) • What would be your cupcake creation? (Zoe loves to bake in *From the Desk of Zoe Washington* by Janae Marks [2021]) • For *New Kid* by Jerry Kraft (2019), what was a popular (or embarrassing!) middle school fad when you were growing up? • For *First Rule of Punk* by Celia C. Perez (2018), "What makes you a little bit "punk"?
Agreements For our first few meetings, we read through these, but once the group is familiar with the routine, we usually give a moment for participants to read and acknowledge before we transition.	*See Chapter 2, p. 46 for agreements you can use or adapt* For a book club that delves into hard history, we might say something like, "This book is heavy and rooted in a violent past. Given what might come up today, let's remember to honor each other's experiences and to speak from the I-perspective—which means to only speak from your own experience."

Figure 9-1

What we do	How it might look
Why We Chose the Book We usually explain our reasoning for why we are discussing *this* book in *this* moment. Sometimes it aligns with a cultural month, or perhaps it's a book that's fresh off the press and might help us surface themes that are particularly relevant.	Why We Chose *Front Desk* by Kelly Yang (2019): "We both love this book so much! It delves into so many intersectional issues, which we'll discuss later this evening. The book is full of complex characters whose stories help disrupt stereotypes. *Front Desk* is also in 'own voices' because the author pulled from her own life experiences to write this story. And, of course it's set in Southern California so there are some local connections as well. The Houston connection in the opening chapter was also a reflective mirror for Veronica. Finally, this book illustrates the power of writing and collective action to make change."
About the Book You might simply read the book jacket or an excerpt from an article about the book to give book clubbers a sense for the plot, themes, and main characters. Some books might need a little extra historical context that you could sprinkle throughout the meetup, or you could provide supplemental materials, as well. We also recommend finding a pronunciation guide for any names, historical events, and places that you will be saying aloud as you summarize the story and prepare for discussion.	Before diving into *When Winter Robeson Came* (Woods 2022), we showed some images and played videos that featured LA and some of the communities and landmarks connected to the book to give a little context around the setting: Baldwin Hills, which is often referred to as the Black Beverly Hills, and the iconic Watts Towers, which are featured on the cover of this book as well. We also played a one-minute video that showed the Watts Towers because often the media fails to spotlight Black neighborhoods or poor neighborhoods in a way that uplifts the art and beauty that exists in them.
Read-Aloud During every book club, we always read aloud a page or two. As Rebecca likes to say, "we don't age out of the read-aloud experience" and nothing creates a mood or sets a tone like reading aloud. Just like it does in a classroom, it settles the group, connects us to one another, and helps get conversation flowing. And for parents who have not had a chance to read the book, it gives a sense of the themes we will be discussing and makes it possible for them to join in the discussion.	For a book like *When You Trap a Tiger* (Keller 2023), we know we are going to surface the idea of disrupting stereotypes, so we know we would read aloud a section or two of the book where those stereotypes show up in the book.

continues

What we do	How it might look
Discussion Questions Questions that surface the book's DEIB themes: How does the book explore identity? Race? Gender? What are some textual connections that help us think about systemic injustice or historical movements? Where are you noticing examples of intersectionality? What important frameworks, concepts, or terms (e.g., color brave, intersectionality, model minority myth, equity vs. equality, single-story narratives, and belonging uncertainty) could you bring to life or help illuminate through this story, or these characters?	Our questions range from, "How does Thanhha Lai [2023] explore identity through the role of food in *Inside Out and Back Again*?" to "How do the characters in *Prairie Lotus* [Park 2022] uphold white supremacy in both subtle and explicit ways?" After reading *Ghost Boys* by Jewell Parker Rhodes (2020), we asked parents to grapple with the truth of a complicated and violent history of police violence: "What is the difference between something feeling true versus being true?" And for many of the books: "What do you think this author is exploring about what it means to be American and who is allowed to be American?"
Additional Resources Before we announce our next book and transition into a closing, we share podcasts, films, other books (for young people or adults) that connect to the topic, text, or author. Often, these books surface identity topics (e.g., deaf culture, Black joy in literature, LGBTQ+ history, multiracial identity, and body positivity) and important issues (e.g., immigration, the housing crisis and homelessness, mass incarceration, forced assimilation, and white supremacy) without fully exploring the context in a way that a documentary or a nonfiction text would. Sharing clips and excerpts of paired texts and resources throughout your meetups can help book clubbers draw contemporary and historical connections and find resources to learn more.	After reading *Prairie Lotus* by Linda Sue Park (2022), we shared the following resources to help parents and caregivers extend their learning about many of the topics we addressed in our gathering: **Picture Books** *Bee-Bim Bop* by Linda Sue Park (2008) *Eyes That Kiss in the Corners* by Johanna Ho (2021) *Amy Wu and the Perfect Bao* by Kat Zhang (2019) **Chapter Books** *When You Trap a Tiger* by Tae Keller (2020) *Where the Mountain Meets the Moon* by Grace Lin (2019) *A Single Shard* by Linda Sue Park (2011) **Articles** NBC News (2019) "How 1800s Racism Birthed Chinatown, Japantown and Other Ethnic Enclaves" *New York Times* (2021) "Separate but Equal, the Court Said. One Voice Dissented"

Figure 9-1 *continued*

What we do	How it might look
Announcements We might use this moment to announce what our next book will be, share about local community events related to themes of the book, or even give insight to any student projects or learning connected to topics we discussed.	For *Mexikid*: There is a community tour happening next weekend at Chicano Park! For *Front Desk:* Kelly Yang will be on *Good Morning America* tomorrow introducing the sequel to the book we just read. For *When You Trap a Tiger* by Tae Keller: The fifth-grade students just finished a read-aloud of this book and we thought we would show you a few of the "star story" jars they crafted as a way to reflect on the book in class.
Closing Reflection We love closing out our time together with a brief, artful moment. Depending on how book clubbers are feeling, we might take the moment to connect in a joyful way, write a bit, or simply reflect on what we've learned.	After our book club on *Mexikid,* we closed with a question inspired by the role Abuelito plays as an elder: Who is one person that came before you and helped you become your authentic self? After discussing *Prairie Lotus* by Linda Sue Park, we lifted up a lovely line that Hanna remembers her mother saying: "Tea with friends is a feast for the spirit" (Park 2022, 242). We asked participants, "What is your feast for the spirit these days?" and invited them to respond to the following prompt: My feast for the spirit is ____.

Bring Families Together with a Special Event

Something that struck us in the process of planning was how wonderful it is to have one or two experiences a year that are focused solely on joy and connection. Our conversations throughout the year are often deep and threaded with loss and hard history, which makes these lighter moments important and impactful. Here are some tips to make those events feel special:

- **Launch with a Book Club "Meet and Mingle"** to get to know your parents and caretakers and build community before diving into content and conversation. Decorate the room with chart paper and questions like: What's your favorite genre? (Thriller/Mystery, Sci-Fi/Fantasy,

MEETING FOR WINDOWS, MIRRORS, AND COFFEE

Poetry, Memoir, Historical Fiction, History, Contemporary Fiction, Nonfiction, Other _____). Vote: read the book or watch the movie, book you loved as a child (or anytime!), and What's your favorite morning drink?

- **Add a theme:** For a holiday gathering, you might choose something like "Windows, Mirrors, and Cocoa" or "Cozy Reads." In June, you might have a Pride-themed WMC Family night (and Rainbows!) Never underestimate the power of a tagline! Naming your event costs nothing and it's a creative way to make it feel special.

- **Create an invitation!** Even if you're meeting at the same time and location, you can set your special event apart from your monthly book club meetings by designing a quick and cute digital invite using apps like Canva or PicCollage.

- **Set the vibe with music!** For our holiday gathering, we played our "By the Fireplace" playlist of winter songs, jazz, and music that made the space, even over Zoom, feel cozy.

- **Add a family game!** Invite the kids to play a low-stakes community-building game like "This or That" You can ask fun questions like: hot cocoa or cider? Stay up till midnight or go to sleep early? This helps welcome the kids into the book club space.

- **Invite the kids to take the lead!** Offer them the opportunity to have their own book club experience by sharing their favorite page or moment from a picture book they brought to Family Night.

LEAVE ROOM FOR HOPE

Children's literature—stories told through a child's eyes—helps open all of us up, brings us closer together, and encourages vulnerability and tenderness. As Ann Patchett reminds her adult readers in a *New York Times* article ode to Kate DiCamillo and children's literature, "Don't miss out. Do not make the mistake I nearly made and fail to read them because you are under the misconception that they are not for you. They are for you" (Patchett 2020).

The stories in many of the books we read for Windows, Mirrors, and Coffee do not end in tidy or resolved ways. All of them help us to bear witness, and to begin reconstructing a more honest story about who we are, as individuals and as a country. Despite the emotional work this process can require, caregivers left our book club eager for more. In fact, one parent referred to our meetups as a place to "feel challenged" and "fill her bucket" all at the same time—even over Zoom. One of the great things about children's literature is that while it tells the truth, it also leaves room for hope.

CLOSING WITH A POEM

This poem could work as a closing or an opening. What more fun and artful way to launch your own Windows, Mirrors, and Coffee Book Club than with a poem?

What If We Read Children's Books

What if we read children's books together
Even though we're grownups now
What if we could see ourselves
In the stories and the settings
Even if we never had before
What if we gathered around the rug for a read-aloud
Just like we did in kindergarten
Even though it's been a while

What if we bore witness
To the stories that haven't been told
Even though sometimes they're harder to find
Even though sometimes they might make us cry
What if we saw those stories
As stars to light our way
And became readers of the pages
Readers of the world

What if we took time for ourselves
Even when the days feel nonstop
What if we made a little space
A little space for conversation
A little space for coffee
A little space for hope

10

REFLECTING ARTFULLY

The Power of Closing Moments

> *This little light of mine. I'm gonna let it shine, let it shine, let it shine!*
>
> —Children's Folk Song and Civil Rights Anthem

At the end of any meeting, lesson, or even day, it can be tempting to wrap up quickly and rush right into the next thing on our task list. Sometimes we're even mentally preparing for the next thing in the final moments of the present thing, keeping us on this ouroboros treadmill of overlapping things. As Oliver Burkeman, author of the book *Four Thousand Weeks: Time Management for Mortals,* reminds us, "the modern world provides an inexhaustible supply of things that seem worth doing" (Burkeman 2023). In other words, the never-ending checklist will always be there. So, let's try to resist that urge to rush and instead take a minute to pause and make space for reflection—a little beat to acknowledge, to soak in, to process, before we jump into the next thing.

As we bring this book to a close, the work of exploring identity and fostering belonging feels both increasingly crucial and overwhelmingly scrutinized. In this polarized landscape, the stakes are high, and how we lead this work feels like it matters more than ever. When our world seems to be spinning out of control, our instincts might tell us to scramble to meet the urgency of the moment. Or to disengage. Taking the time to reflect and go inward might feel counterintuitive, but it is essential. It's important to note that *pausing* is not *stopping*. An intentional pause, planned ahead of time, reduces the risk of overloading our systems and can help prevent a more permanent shutdown. Not only does pausing fuel our teaching, our leading, and our activism, but it also gives us a chance to breathe, connect, and come back to ourselves. And when we take the time to pause, we give ourselves space to reflect. When we feel our lights beginning to dim, artful reflection is a sacred and generative practice to which we can always return.

Whether we are attempting to support students grappling with unjust realities or trying to inspire our colleagues in challenging times, artful reflection is key. It can offer us perspective and help us remember that we exist within a larger context of movements for change. Reflective moments enable us to tap into the strength of the collective and remind us that when it comes to changemaking, we are not alone. That the only way forward is together. Just like us, young people sometimes feel overwhelmed and unsure about the role they can play in this march toward a more equitable future, and they too need a reminder that they are part of a greater whole.

That's where reflective moments come in. They can help students feel like they are connected to something bigger than themselves, which might in turn motivate them to stay engaged and work toward more sustainable, long-term efforts for change. We like to think that artful reflection can be both grounding and galvanizing, for our students and for us.

As the pace of society continues to speed up, the art of slowing down might very well become a rare, yet vital, practice for our students. We imagine that in the future, there will be no shortage of virtues to signal, or endless opinions to scroll through, or stories of injustice to quickly caption and repost. But the brevity and volume to which we're all growing accustomed doesn't always result in meaningful movements. Increasingly sophisticated technologies marketed as tools to connect us also enable us, even encourage us, to pick up a megaphone whenever we like. As a result, it's practically impossible to resist the urge to take a stand or pick a side, and to do so quickly and loudly. But, rushed responses will likely not bridge our greatest divides. Amplifying our voices online can be an important part of conveying allyship, but it's important to notice how often we're on the speaking side of the megaphone. While these virtual tools have democratized the media landscape and made grassroots organizing possible in unprecedented ways, their potential impact on the *real* world makes learning how to harness their power for good all the more important. Teaching students the skills to pause intentionally, listen generously, and reflect artfully will help them learn how to use their voices not only to make a point, but to make a difference—especially when it comes to advocating for the

---

Artful Reflection

Taking a moment to pause, look inward and use an artful medium to take note of what's on your heart and mind. Artful reflection helps us refuel, replenish, and reconnect with ourselves, our work, and our community.

causes closest to their hearts. Not only that, but these skills will deepen our capacity for noticing nuance, not only in contemporary causes and complex histories, but in each other as well. But here's the thing, we can't teach students any of these skills if we aren't in the habit of making space for reflection ourselves. While this book is chock-full of prompts, poems, and invitation for student reflection, we created these artful reflection ideas with all of you in mind.

COLOR, SOUND, AND WORDS TO HOLD ON TO: ARTFUL REFLECTION IDEAS FOR TEACHERS AND TEAMS

Whether you are reflecting on your own or with a group, the ideas in the following table (see Figure 10–1) can help you get started with artful reflection. Take five to fifteen minutes to create using whatever you have: scissors, craft paper, or a freshly sharpened pencil. And we recommend freeing yourself from the pressure of a polished product, so that you can just enjoy a little artful experience that on its own can be so rejuvenating and restorative. While these reflections were designed with teachers in mind, many of these ideas adapt easily for students! We've done a student version of "Color Moods" with fifth graders and "Jazz Break" (listening to music for a mindful moment) with kindergartners.

Artful Reflection Ideas for Teachers and Teams

Get started	Prompts to think about, journal, or share	With a group: Add-on for group settings
Name jot Jot down a list of inspiring names, maybe those who came before you or those alongside you, to remind you that you are not alone in this work.	What's your personal connection to the names you wrote? How does their work, life, story inspire you? What words of wisdom might they have for you?	Invite each person to share out one name from their list (and maybe some words of wisdom from their person) and string them together to create a community poem. Try this stem: _____ who reminds me _____.

Figure 10-1 continues

Get started	Prompts to think about, journal, or share	With a group: Add-on for group settings
Jazz break Take a few breaths while listening to jazz (or whatever kind of music feels right!)	What are you breathing in? What are you letting go of that no longer serves you? What affirmations or reassurances do you need right now?	As a whole group, take some collective breaths as you listen to a song that brings the group together. After your first few breaths, you might invite people to share some affirmations out loud.
Color moods Swirl together some colors to represent your moods. You might just use an index card (which may feel less daunting to fill up with color) to create a mini piece of artwork.	Give your colors mood names. Maybe the blue-green swirls represent quiet-calm or the orangey-fuchsia splatters represent your neon-energy.	Take an informal gallery walk and notice what's coming up for the group. Discuss: How does seeing all these colors and moods make you feel? How do these mini color stories make you feel connected?
Words to hold on to Use colorful sticky tape (or colorful sticky notes) to create a "Words to Hold On To" collage filled with things you want to remember. Write down a word or phrase on each sticky note or piece of tape. You might display it in a place it'll serve you best (at your desk when writing emails, on your nightstand to see after a long day).	How can we hold on to what matters when we are feeling overwhelmed, uncertain, or exhausted?	Take an informal gallery walk and notice what's coming up for the group. Share out one line from your collage with the group, or swap collages with a partner to discuss. You could also create a Community Collage using one sticky note or piece of tape from each person. You might display it in a shared space, or photograph it and send it out to the whole group!

Figure 10-1 *continued*

Get started	Prompts to think about, journal, or share	With a group: Add-on for group settings
Personal anthem Hit play on your personal anthem and have yourself a one-minute (or longer!) dance party.	Remember what brings you joy! What role can joy play in working toward change? How can joy fuel you to keep going? Where else can you find joy and how can you spread it around?	Collect personal anthems from each person in the group and turn them into a group mixtape (playlist) of your anthems. This playlist can be a source of joy and connection for the group.
Found poem reflection Cut out some clippings of words and phrases that help you process what you're learning, reflect on how you're feeling, and envision what you're hoping to create.	Why did you choose the word clippings you included in your found poem? What words are popping out for you? What do they represent for you?	Each person contributes a line of their own found poem to create a fun mash-up of words and phrases that represent the group's learning, reflection, or vision.

Which of these ideas do you think would help you feel replenished? Sometimes, finding time for a full reflective experience (even just fifteen minutes) can be a challenge, so we suggest jotting down a short "top three" list of potential go-to practices that can help you return to yourself next time you're feeling overwhelmed. Feel free to draw from our list and add some of your own for a handy go-to list of reminders!

BRINGING IT ALL TO A CLOSE (ARTFULLY)

We've all been there before. The final moments of a meeting or lesson are unfolding and it's time to wrap up, but one glance at the clock reveals that once again, we are out of time. But, how we close out really matters. Even Shakespeare, perhaps an unlikely source of inspiration for our book so steeped in the contemporary, knew the power of the closing moment. He often ended his plays with an epilogue, sometimes even a

Figure 10-2 Rebecca's "Words to Hold On To" collage

Figure 10-3 Veronica's "Words to Hold On To" collage

musical one, as a way to wrap significance around those last beats and draw the audience's attention to the complexity of our human lives, and our human stories. And, if the play was a tragic one, this moment might offer some levity for the audience as they made their way back into the world.

Anyone who has been lucky enough to see the Broadway show *Hadestown* might remember the moment after the curtains close (spoiler alert), just seconds after the tragic fall of Orpheus, when the actors reconvene center stage to offer the audience a song filled with peaceful, joyful imagery: sun shining, wine pouring, birds flying. This closing moment doesn't only conclude the story, it lifts the spirits and acknowledges to the audience that we all just experienced something heavy, but we experienced it together. And there's something hopeful in knowing that despite the heaviness, we all showed up anyway. This is how we like to think about our closings as well. It's a way to thank whoever has joined us, a chance to center connection, and an opportunity to gather our students, colleagues, or families for one final beat.

An artful closing doesn't require tons of time, printed handouts, a special setup, or a fancy screen. An artful closing can take a few minutes (or a few seconds, as you'll

THE ARTFUL APPROACH TO EXPLORING IDENTITY AND FOSTERING BELONGING

see!) and can look different (fast-paced and out loud or calm and quietly to ourselves) depending on the needs of any group (a nourishing moment for anxious students, an energizing feel for an exhausted team, or a restorative space for classroom families). It can be the sing-along to a crowd favorite at the end of a concert, the standing ovation after the dancer's last leap, or the supportive snaps after a second grader shares the first lines of her very first poem. It's a way of saying to the group, *let's hold on to this feeling we just shared, let's continue to lift each other up, and let's remember we can come back to this moment when we need it.*

Creating Artful Closings with Any Group

Whether you're closing out a morning meeting with students, a back-to-school night with families, or a planning session with your teaching team, this little guide can help you bring the experience to a close in a way that deepens connection and builds community.

Artful Doesn't Always Equal Serious: How to Close It Out Whitney Houston Style

Artful closings can also be about having a good time! And what better way to connect than through a timeless pop song? Once, we were tasked with closing out the final moments of a conference and thought it would be fabulous to send everyone off to the iconic music of Whitney Houston. We thought we might play a bit of one of her songs that was having a moment that year and then ask the audience (of almost three hundred teachers and administrators) to repeat back the final line with us in unison. As we were planning this moment, we remember thinking: *Are they going to think we've totally lost the plot here? Is anyone going to actually do this?* We decided we would give it our all and hope for the best. Because even if no one chimed in, we would still get to end the day dancing to Whitney Houston.

As it turned out, the audience didn't let us down. Maybe because we gave it our all, maybe because there's courage in numbers, maybe because it was Whitney Houston, people enthusiastically chanted that final line. It was the greatest and most unconventional choral reading we'd ever experienced! We left feeling uplifted, like part of a community, and something we can't ever remember feeling after a long conference day: energized, even ready to dance. If a fun and pretty simple pop-song-closing can do this for us teachers, imagine what a similar moment can do for our students.

Five Five-Second Closings

(Okay maybe closer to twenty seconds, but still!)

In the teacher spirit of making every second count, we've created five ideas for closings similar to our Five-Second Check-Ins from Chapter 1. Next time you're pressed for time, try adapting one of these five-second closings to craft an ending that is both artful and quick! We designed these to not only be quick but also be open enough to work for any group—students, colleagues, and families too.

1. **Echo:** Version 1: Let's all repeat back the final two lines of _____ (this could be a poem you just read, a song you played or sung, or text you shared together). Version 2: After someone in the group shares out a piece of writing, invite the group to echo back some of their words to the group. Think of a word or phrase that resonated with you in that piece and echo it back to the group. For the next five seconds, let's just fill the space (or drop in the chat!) with some of those words popcorn style.

2. **Final Word Send-Off:** Think of one word you want to send to the group or out into the world in this moment. To start us off I'll say, "We send (word here)." And when we get to you, you can add your word by saying, "And (word here)." This might sound like: "We send community . . . and wisdom . . . and care . . . and support . . . and listening . . . and compassion . . . and generosity . . ."

3. **Sunset Stretch:** Let's all imagine the gorgeous colors of a sunset and reach high toward the top of the sky (soak up those warm golden hues!). Lower your arms and stretch them out to your sides (swirl your fingers through the cotton candy pinks and purples!). Keep bringing your arms down toward your sides (and breathe in those final moments of blue . . .). You could take a few collective breaths after this final line.

4. **Two-Line Poem:** In the here and now, we soak up _____. As we make our way out, we take with us _____. This might look like: In the here and now, we soak up the collective creativity all around us. As we make our way out, we take with us the courage to keep going.

5. **Community Toast:** Let's take a moment to honor _____ (maybe something or someone you've just learned about) with a festive toast. So let's raise our (cups of sparkling water or mugs of morning coffee) and think of one thing you want to toast. "Here's to _____!"

   Small group version: Kick off the share with your own "Here's to _____!" and then invite people to share back-to-back without interruption.

   Large group version: Kick off the share with one "here's to" and then invite the whole group to share their toasts in unison (which might sound like a little fun chaos!). Or you can invite everyone to turn to a partner, or a few people, and "toast" with *them*.

A Quick Guide to Help You Artfully Close

1. **What's your intention?** What do you hope your group will feel as a result of this closing? Are you attempting to counter a potentially challenging conversation with a closing moment that feels nourishing or healing? Or should this feel like a celebratory moment? Maybe you're hoping to make space for a little joy or to leave your participants feeling energized and inspired.

2. **What artful content aligns with your intention?** For a healing moment, you might turn to some acoustic soul or a calming poem. For a more energizing closing, you might incorporate movement, call and response, or play a fun song that people can't help but sing or dance along to.

3. **How will you make this feel like a *moment*?** For these closing moments to be effective, we try to lead with openness and confidence, even if it takes us a little outside of our comfort zone. And if we want these moments to *feel like moments,* we have to set the tone—whether it be playful and upbeat or heartfelt and full of gravitas. For a more serious closing, sometimes we invite people to share a single word, phrase, or line of writing without interrupting in between each person, which creates a bit of a rhythm and makes it feel like a poem. Other times, we might want to create a more lighthearted send-off, which might mean cheering people on in between, echoing certain phrases, or inviting people to chime in throughout with encouraging words or the connections they're making.

In these last few moments together, we thought we might say goodbye artful closing–style with one final poem. This is an extended version of one of our Five-Second Closings called "Community Toast" that celebrates the creativity living inside every classroom and the scrappy spirit living inside all of us. If we can let enough light into our classrooms for creativity and connection to flourish, then we can help our students feel truly seen, valued, and free to be their unique selves. If we can tap into our own radical imagination for what's possible, we can inspire this next generation of young people to do the same.

FINAL CLOSING WITH A POEM

We invite you to raise your glass of sparkling water, your mug of morning coffee, your most festive paper cup and join us for a community toast.

Here's to community
To hellos in the hallways
To tacos on Tuesdays and coffee in the lounge
To dreams just starting to take shape

Here's to curiosity
To taking it slow sometimes
To listening with an open heart
To making space for multitudes

Here's to possibility
To future makers of music that'll one day move us
To future writers of words that'll someday stir us
To holding onto hope for one day and someday

Here's to sharpened pencils
To rainbow stacks of paper
To the creative mess at every desk
To glitter and gravitas

Here's to wonder
To all that kid energy
To the hugs and high fives
To creativity hiding in a pencil pouch

Here's to laughing
To drafting
To concocting
To crafting
To dreaming up a lesson from scratch
To waking up at 5 am
To making it work and fitting it in
To getting into good trouble
To taking the time
To lifting them up
To pulling it off
To that
Glorious
Scrappy
Spirit
Inside

Here's to us

WORKS CITED

Acevedo, Elizabeth. 2018. *The Poet X*. New York: Quill Tree Books.

ADL (Anti Defamation League). n.d. Books Matter™ Children's and Young Adult Literature. Online bibliography at ADL.org.

Ahmed, Roda. 2020. *Mae Among the Stars*. New York: HarperCollins.

Alexander, Elizabeth. 2016. *The Light of the World*. New York: Grand Central Publishing.

Alexander, Kwame, Chris Colderley, and Marjory Wentworth. 2017. "Majestic." In *Out of Wonder: Poems Celebrating Poets*. Somerville, MA: Candlewick Press.

Alexander, Kwame. 2019. The Crossover series. New York: Clarion Books.

Baldwin, James. 1962. "As Much Truth as One Can Bear; to Speak Out About the World as It Is, Says James Baldwin, Is the Writer's Job as Much of the Truth as One Can Bear." *New York Times*, January 14, sec. Archives. https://www.nytimes.com/1962/01/14/archives/as-much-truth-as-one-can-bear-to-speak-out-about-the-world-as-it-is.html.

Band's Visit, The. 2016. "The Concert," song from musical. Music and lyrics by David Yazbek and book by Itamar Moses, adapted from 2007 Israeli film of same name.

Banneker, Benjamin. 1731–1806. "The Puzzle of the Cooper and the Vintner."

Bedini, Silvio A. 1999. *The Life of Benjamin Banneker: The First African American Man of Science*. Baltimore: Maryland Historical Society.

Bell, Cece. 2014. *El Deafo: A Graphic Novel*. New York: Abrams.

Bellingham. Rebecca. 2019. *The Artful Read-Aloud: 10 Principals to Inspire, Engage, and Transform Learning*. Portsmouth, NH: Heinemann.

Beyoncé. 2015. "Formation" from *Lemonade*. Produced by Mike Will Made It. Video 3:26. New York: Quad Recording Studios.

Brantley-Newton, Vanessa. 2020. *Just Like Me*. New York: Random House Children's Books.

Brooks, Brittany. 2022. "The Hidden Power of Read-Alouds." ASCD, March 16. https://www.ascd.org/el/articles/the-hidden-power-of-read-alouds.

Brown, Brené. 2020. "The Courage to Not Know." Brené Brown, February 13. https://brenebrown.com/articles/2020/02/13/the-courage-to-not-know/.

Bryan, Ashley. 2019. In *We Rise, We Resist, We Raise Our Voices,* edited by Wade Hudson and Cheryl Willis Hudson. New York: Yearling.

Bullard, Lisa. 2021. "Tae Keller on Bridging the Gap Between." Mackin Community blog, October 25. www.mackincommunity.com/2021/10/25/tae-keller-on-bridging-the-gap-between/. Accessed 9 Jan. 2024.

Bunch, Lonnie. n.d. "Knowing the Past Opens the Door to the Future: The Continuing Importance of Black History Month." National Museum of African American History and Culture. https://nmaahc.si.edu/explore/stories/knowing-past-opens-door-future-continuing-importance-black-history-month.

Burkeman, Oliver. 2023. *Four Thousand Weeks: Time Management for Mortals*. New York: Farrar, Straus and Giroux.

Callender, Kacen. 2019. *Hurricane Child*. New York: Scholastic Press.

———. 2022. *King and the Dragonflies*. New York: Scholastic Press.

Canellos, Peter. 2021. "Separate but Equal, the Court Said. One Voice Dissented." *New York Times*, May 18.

CBS Mornings. 2023. "Author Jason Reynolds Says Latest Children's Picture Book Is an Ode to Literary Legends." Video 6:07, October 3. https://www.youtube.com/watch?v=-C-nRq7i4X8.

Chenoweth, Robin. 2019. "Rudine Sims Bishop: 'Mother' of Multicultural Children's Literature." Ohio State University, College of Education and Human Ecology, September 5. https://ehe.osu.edu/news/listing/rudine-sims-bishop-diverse-childrens-books.

Cherry, Matthew A. 2019. *Hair Love*. New York: Penguin.

Cisneros, Ernesto. 2021. *Efrén Divided*. New York: Quill Tree Books.

Coates, Ta-Nehisi. 2015. *Between the World and Me*. New York: Random House Publishing.

———. 2017. "Imagining a New America." Chicago Humanities Festival, November 16. The On Being Project, Chicago, Illinois. https://onbeing.org/programs/ta-nehisi-coates-imagining-a-new-america/.

Cohen, Geoffrey L. 2022a. *Belonging*: The Science of Creating Connection and Bridging Divides. New York: W. W. Norton.

———. 2022b. "Surveys and Interventions." Geoffrey L. Cohen, September 13. https://www.geoffreylcohen.com/surveys-and-interventions.

Coleman, Valerie. n.d. "Umoja Anthem of Unity." Valerie Coleman Flutist and Composer. https://www.vcolemanmusic.com/umoja-anthem-of-unity.html.

Colorin Colorado. 2022. "Matt de la Peña: The Story Behind 'Milo Imagines the World." January 20. https://www.youtube.com/watch?v=tEdxmTv70Nw.

Crenshaw, Kimberlé. 2016. "The Urgency of Intersectionality." TED Talks. https://www.ted.com/talks/kimberle_crenshaw_the_urgency_of_intersectionality/transcript.

Crews, James. 2021. "Over the Weather" by Naomi Shihab Nye in *How to Love the World: Poems of Gratitude and Hope*. New York: Storey Publishing.

de la Peña, Matt. 2018. *Love*. New York: G. P. Putnam Books for Young Readers.

———. 2021. *Milo Imagines the World*. New York: Penguin Young Readers Group.

Davis, Viola. 2022. *Finding Me*. New York: HarperOne.

Deggans, Eric. 2018. "How the Civil Rights Movement Transformed 'This Little Light of Mine.'" *All Things Considered*. NPR.org, December 24. https://www.npr.org/2018/12/24/679895682/how-the-civil-rights-movement-transformed-this-little-light-of-mine.

Dias, Marley. 2015. #1000BlackGirlBooks. Website.

DiTerlizzi, Angela. 2020. *The Magical Yet*. New York: Little, Brown Books for Young Readers.

Dorling Kindersley. 2020. *A World Full of Poems: Inspiring Poetry for Children*. London: Dorling Kindersley.

Dockterman, Eliana. 2023. "A Major Hollywood Diversity Report Shows Little Change—Except for One Promising Stat." Time.com, August 17. https://time.com/6305012/hollywood-diversity-report-asian-representationo/.

Dunbar, Erica Armstrong. 2020. *Never Caught: The Story of Ona Judge*. New York: Aladdin.

Edwards, Nicola. 2018. *What a Wonderful Word: A Collection of Untranslatable Words from Around the World*. Powder Springs, GA: Big River Books LLC.

Eggers, Dave, 2018. *What Can a Citizen Do?* San Francisco: Chronicle Books.

Engle, Margarita. 2015. *Drum Dream Girl*. Boston: Clarion Books.

Eno, Brian. 2008. "Singing: The Key to a Long Life." *Weekend Edition Sunday*. NPR.org, November 23. https://www.npr.org/2008/11/23/97320958/singing-the-key-to-a-long-life.

Fipps, Lisa. 2021. *Starfish*. London: Nancy Paulsen Books.

Fisher, Douglas, James Flood, Diane Lapp, and Nancy Frey. 2004. "Interactive Read-Alouds: Is There a Common Set of Implementation Practices?" *The Reading Teacher* 58 (1): 8–17. https://doi.org/10.1598/rt.58.1.1.

Ford, Ashley. 2021. *Somebody's Daughter*. London: Flatiron Books.

Ghibli Park. 2022. Ghibli Park website. http://ghilbi-park.jp/en/.

Gilio-Whitaker, Dina. 2018. "How Native Americans in the Arts Are Preserving Tradition in a Changing World." *Los Angeles Times*, November 29. www.latimes.com/entertainment/arts/museums/la-et-cm-native-american-artists-20181129-htmlstory.html.

Giovanni, Nikki. 2008. "Art Sanctuary" from *Quilting the Black-Eyed Pea*. New York: HarperPerennial.

———. 2014. *The Sun Is So Quiet*. London: Square Fish.

———. 2018. *I Am Loved*. New York: Atheneum/Caitlyn Dlouhy Books.

Glaser, Karina Yan. 2023. *A Duet for Home*. New York: Clarion Books.

Goodman, Diane J. 2001. *Promoting Diversity and Social Justice: Educating People from Privileged Groups*. Winter Roundtable Series. Thousand Oaks, CA: SAGE. https://doi.org/10.4135/9781452220468.

Gorman, Amanda. 2021. "Inaugural Poet Amanda Gorman Delivers a Poem at Joe Biden's Inauguration" and "The Hill We Climb." YouTube video, January 20. https://www.youtube.com/watch?v=Jp9pyMqnBzk.

Gray, Gary R., Jr. 2023. *I'm From*. New York: HarperCollins.

Great Big Story. 2017. "The Chef Bringing Native American Food to Your Table." YouTube, August 21. https://www.youtube.com/watch?v=ocm6DRIF9oU.

Gross, Terry. 2023. "'Reservation Dogs' Co-Creator Says the Show Gives Audiences Permission to Laugh." *Fresh Air*. NPR.org, August 18.

Hammond, Zaretta. 2014. *Culturally Responsive Teaching and The Brain: Promoting Authentic Engagement and Rigor Among Culturally and Linguistically Diverse Students*. Thousand Oaks, CA: SAGE.

Hannah-Jones, Nikole. 2019. "The 1619 Project." *New York Times*, August 14. https://www.nytimes.com/interactive/2019/08/14/magazine/1619-america-slavery.html.

Hannah-Jones, Nikole, and Renée Watson. 2021. *The 1619 Project: Born on the Water*. New York: One World/Random House.

Harjo, Joy. 1996. "Perhaps the World Ends Here" from *The Woman Who Fell from the Sky: Poems*. New York: W. W. Norton.

———. 2021. *Poet Warrior: A Memoir*. New York: W. W. Norton & Company.

Harris, Aisha. 2016. "Stevie Wonder Wrote the Black 'Happy Birthday' Song." Slate, December 20. slate.com/culture/2016/12/stevie-wonder-wrote-the-black-happy-birthday-song.html.

Hasso Plattner Institute of Design at Stanford. 2010. "An Introduction to Design Thinking Process Guide." Stanford University. https://web.stanford.edu/~mshanks/MichaelShanks/files/509554.pdf.

———. n.d. Design for Belonging. K–12 Lab. https://static1.squarespace.com/static/57c6b79629687fde090a0fdd/t/5cc7baefe79c7092be2eae94/1556593394623/Design+For+Belonging+Web.pdf.

Henry Ford Museum (blog). 2020. "Walt Disney and His Creation of Disneyland." Donna Braden, Curator of Public Life at Henry Ford Museum. The Henry Ford, July 13. https://www.thehenryford.org/explore/blog/walt-disney-and-his-creation-of-disneyland.

Hempel, Jessi. 2021."Transcript: Episode 101: Brené Brown on Getting It Right." *Hello Monday with Jessi Hempel* @ LinkedIn, March 22. https://www.linkedin.com/pulse/transcript-episode-101-bren%C3%A9-brown-getting-right-jessi-hempel/.

Hinojosa, Maria. 2020. *Once I Was You: A Memoir.* New York: Atria Books.

Ho, Johanna. 2021. *Eyes That Kiss in the Corners.* New York: HarperCollins.

Hobson, Mellody. 2014. "Color Blind or Color Brave?" TED Talks, www.ted.com/talks/mellody_hobson_color_blind_or_color_brave?language=en.

Holmes, Linda. 2021. "'Beckett' Is a Perfectly Average Chase Thriller." *Pop Culture Happy Hour*. NPR.org, August 18. https://www.npr.org/transcripts/1026804821.

Hudson, Wade, and Cheryl Willis Hudson, eds. 2019. *We Rise, We Resist, We Raise Our Voices.* New York: Yearling.

Hughes, Langston. 1926. "I, Too." *The Weary Blues.* New York: Alfred Knopf.

Immerwahr, Daniel. 2019. *How to Hide an Empire: A History of the Greater United States.* New York: Farrar, Straus and Giroux.

Innovation Press. 2023. "Your Name Is a Song." November 21. https://www.youtube.com/watch?v=ZmXqJGherE8.

Jaouad, Suleika. 2021. *Between Two Kingdoms.* London: Bantam Press.

Jeffries, Hasan. 2023. "Teaching Hard History Presentation" for *Learning for Justice.* Personal, July 17.

Johnson, James Weldon. 1900. Song lyrics from "Lift Ev'ry Voice and Sing."

Kandil, Caitlin Yoshiko. 2019. "How 1800s Racism Birthed Chinatown, Japantown, and Other Ethnic Enclaves." NBC News, May 13.

Katz, Karen. 2002. *The Colors of Us.* New York: H. Holt and Co.

Keats, Ezra Jack. 2012. *The Snowy Day.* New York: Penguin Young Readers Group.

———. 2023. "Ezra Jack Keats: A Life Creating Books for Children." Accessed November 21, 2023. https://www.ejkf.org/wp-content/uploads/2015/03/Ezra-Jack-Keats-Bio-for-Kids.pdf

Keller, Tae. 2020. *When You Trap a Tiger.* New York: Random House.

Kennicott, Philip. 2018. "Review: A Powerful Memorial in Montgomery Remembers the Victims of Lynching." *Washington Post*, April 24. https://www.washingtonpost.com/entertainment/museums/a-powerful-memorial-in-montgomery-remembers-the-victims-of-lynching/2018/04/24/3620e78a-471a-11e8-827e-190efaf1f1ee_story.html.

Klein, Ezra. 2022a. "Transcript: Ezra Klein Interviews with Ada Limón." *New York Times.* May 24. https://www.nytimes.com/2022/05/24/podcasts/transcript-ezra-klein-interviews-ada-limon.html.

———. 2022b. "This Is Your Brain on 'Deep Reading.' It's Pretty Magnificent." *New York Times.* November 22. www.nytimes.com/2022/11/22/opinion/ezra-klein-podcast-maryanne-wolf.html.

Kleinrock, Liz. 2021. *Start Here, Start Now.* Portsmouth, NH: Heinemann.

Lai, Thanhha. 2013. *Inside Out and Back Again.* New York: HarperCollins.

Lavoie, Fin. 2021. "Why We Need Diverse Books Is No Longer Using the Term #OwnVoices." *We Need Diverse Books* (blog), June 6. https://diversebooks.org/why-we-need-diverse-books-is-no-longer-using-the-term-ownvoices/.

Lazarus, Emma. 1883. "The New Colossus." *Historic American Documents* (Lit2Go Edition). Retrieved March 26, 2024, from https://etc.usf.edu/lit2go/133/historic-american-documents/4959/the-new-colossus/.

Learning for Justice. 2012. "Speak Up at School." July 26. https://www.learningforjustice.org/magazine/publications/speak-up-at-school.

———. 2018. "A Quick Reference Guide to Teaching Hard History: A K–12 Framework for Teaching American Slavery." https://www.learningforjustice.org/sites/default/files/2022-12/LFJ-Quick-Reference-Guide-Teaching-Hard-History-K-12-Framework-December-2022-12092022.pdf.

———. 2023. "Centering Student Experiences." May 26. https://www.learningforjustice.org/magazine/publications/critical-practices-for-social-justice-education/culture-and-climate/centering-student-experiences.

Limón, Ada. 2023. Personal communication, March 23.

Lin, Grace. 2019. *Where the Mountain Meets the Moon.* New York: Little, Brown Books for Young Readers.

Lindstrom, Carole. 2020. *We Are Water Protectors.* London: Roaring Brook Press.

———. 2023. *Autumn Peltier, Water Warrior.* London: Roaring Brook Press.

Livingston, Donovan. 2016. "Lift Off." Harvard Graduate School of Education. Convocation, May 25. https://www.gse.harvard.edu/ideas/news/16/05/lift.

Maillard, Kevin Noble. 2019. *Fry Bread: A Native American Family Story.* London: Roaring Brook Press.

Mallenbaum, Carly. 2015. "Tim Gunn Didn't Always Use the Mantra 'Make It Work.'" *USA Today*, April 14. https://www.usatoday.com/story/life/entertainthis/2015/04/14/tim-gunn-make-it-work/77563526/.

Marks, Janae. 2020. *From the Desk of Zoe Washington.* New York: Katherine Tegan Books.

Marshall, Joseph, III. 2015. *In the Footsteps of Crazy Horse.* New York: Amulet Books.

Martín, Pedro. 2023. *Mexikid.* New York: Dial

Miller, Chanel. 2020. *Know My Name.* London, UK: Penguin.

Moon, Kat. 2019. "How One Woman's Story Led to the Creation of Asian Pacific American Heritage Month." *Time*, May 23. https://time.com/5592591/asian-pacific-heritage-month-history/.

Mora, Oge. 2018. *Thank You, Omu!* New York: Little, Brown Books for Young Readers.

———. 2019. *Saturday*. New York: Little, Brown Books for Young Readers.

McMurdock, Marianna. 2022. "Bringing 1619 Project, Black History to Life for Young Readers." The74million.org, February 22. https://www.the74million.org/article/painting-black-history-in-the-time-of-censorship-for-young-readers-a-conversation-with-nikkolas-smith-illustrator-of-1619-projects-born-on-the-water-childrens-book/.

Miranda, Lin-Manuel. 2019. "The Role of the Artist in the Age of Trump." *The Atlantic,* December. https://www.theatlantic.com/magazine/archive/2019/12/lin-manuel-miranda-what-art-can-do/600787/.

Morris, Wesley, and Nikole Hannah-Jones. 2019. "Episode 3: The Birth of American Music." *New York Times*, produced by Andy Mills and Annie Brown. September 6. Podcast. https://www.nytimes.com/2019/09/06/podcasts/1619-black-american-music-appropriation.html.

Muhammad, Khalil Gibran. 2019. "The Barbaric History of Sugar in America." *New York Times Magazine*, August 14. https://www.nytimes.com/interactive/2019/08/14/magazine/sugar-slave-trade-slavery.html.

National Park Service. 2022. "Language of Slavery." Underground Railroad website (U.S. National Park Service), January 28. https://www.nps.gov/subjects/undergroundrailroad/language-of-slavery.htm#:~:text=Enslaver%20versus%20Master%2C%20Owner%2C%20or.

Newton, Maud. 2022. "Y'all: The Most Inclusive of All Pronouns." *New York Times Magazine*, October 18. https://www.nytimes.com/2022/10/18/magazine/yall.html.

Ngugi, Evelyn. 2016. "Beyoncé Said Drink This #Lemonade, Heaux!! | VEDA Day 24 of 30 @EVEEEEEZY." YouTube. www.youtube.com/watch?v=3NI3ZjcLbe8. Accessed 27 Nov. 2023.

NPR. 2016. "Hold Up! Time for an Explanatory Comma." *Code Switch*, December 14. https://www.npr.org/2016/12/14/504482252/-hold-up-time-for-an-explanatory-comma.

———. 2022. "How Can Museums Honor Both the Extraordinary and the Everyday?" *Ted Radio Hour*, November 4. https://www.npr.org/transcripts/1134049361.

Nye, Naomi Shihab. 1998. "One Boy Told Me" from *Fuel*. Rochester, NY: BOA Editions.

Obama, Michelle. 2021."Amanda Gorman and Michelle Obama in Conversation." *Time*, February 4. Interview. https://time.com/5933596/amanda-gorman-michelle-obama-interview/.

On Being with Krista Tippet. 2016. "Isabel Wilkerson: This History Is Long; This History Is Deep." June 18. Podcast. onbeing.org/programs/isabel-wilkerson-this-history-is-long-this-history-is-deep/. Updated 2020.

On Being with Krista Tippet. 2017. "Ta-Nehisi Coates: Imagining a New America." November 16. Podcast. https://onbeing.org/programs/ta-nehisi-coates-imagining-a-new-america/.

Othering and Belonging Institute. 2023. Institute website. https://belonging.berkeley.edu.

Ó Tuama, Pádraig. 2020. "Meleika Gesa-Fatafehi: Say My Name." The On Being Project, October 26. Podcast. https://onbeing.org/programs/meleika-gesa-fatafehi-say-my-name/.

———. 2022. "A Poem Is a Made Thing." *Poetry Unbound* (blog), December 11. https://poetryunbound.substack.com/p/a-poem-is-a-made-thing.

Park, Linda Sue. 2008. *Bee-Bim Bop!* New York: Clarion Books.

———. 2011. *A Single Shard*. New York: Clarion Books.

———. 2022. *Prairie Lotus*. New York: Clarion Books.

Patchett, Ann. 2020. "Ann Patchett on Why We Need Life-Changing Books Right Now." *New York Times*, March 30. https://www.nytimes.com/2020/03/30/books/review/kate-dicamillo-ann-patchett.html.

PBS NewsHour. 2016. "Christian Robinson, Illustrator." September 8. Video clip, 2 min 31 sec. https://www.pbs.org/newshour/brief/192310/christian-robinson#:~:text=They%20need%20to%20see%20their.

———. 2023. "The Legacy of Hawaiian Swimmer and Surfer Duke Kahanamoku." May 7. Video clip, 2 min. 26 sec. https://www.pbs.org/video/hidden-histories-1683486821/.

Pearlman, Robb. 2021. *Pink Is for Boys*. Philadelphia, PA: Running Press Kids.

Petry, Ann. 2018. *Harriet Tubman: Conductor on the Underground Railroad*. Foreword by Jason Reynolds. New York: Amistad Books for Young Readers.

Pulitzer Center. 2022. "The 1619 Education Conference Keynote Discussion: Born on the Water." March 3. https://www.youtube.com/watch?v=a7O65KE_QLw&t=367s.

Quintero, Isabel. 2019. *My Papi Has a Motorcycle*. New York: Penguin Young Readers.

Reynolds, Jason. 2017. *Ghost*. New York: Atheneum/Caitlyn Dlouhy Books.

———. 2023. *There Was a Party for Langston*. New York: Atheneum/Caitlyn Dlouhy Books.

Reynolds, Jason, and Ibram X. Kendi. 2020. *Stamped: Racism, Antiracism, and You: A Remix of the National Book Award–Winning* Stamped from the Beginning. New York: Little, Brown Books for Young Readers.

Rhodes, Jewell Parker. 2010. *Ninth Ward*. New York: Turtleback Books.

———. 2019. *Ghost Boys*. New York: Little, Brown Books for Young Readers.

Ringgold, Faith. 2020. *Tar Beach*. New York: Random House Children's Books.

Robertson, Campbell. 2018. "A Lynching Memorial Is Opening. The Country Has Never Seen Anything Like It." *New York Times*, April 25. https://www.nytimes.com/2018/04/25/us/lynching-memorial-alabama.html.

Robertson, David. 2021. *On the Trapline*. Toronto, CA: Tundra Books.

Robinson, Christian. 2016. "Christian Robinson, Illustrator." PBS NewsHour, September 8. Video clip, 2 min 31 sec. https://www.pbs.org/newshour/brief/192310/christian-robinson#:~:text=They%20need%20to%20see%20their.

———. 2020. *You Matter.* New York: Atheneum Books for Young Readers.

———. 2021a. "Artist Christian Robinson Demonstrates His Resilience Through Illustrating | TODAY," video 6:43. February 1. https://www.youtube.com/watch?v=Fn-JtDm3I_4.

———. 2021b. Summer Learning 2021: Meet Christian Robinson! New York Public Library, May 26.

Russell, Allison. 2021. "Allison Russell on the Shero with a Thousand Faces and the Rise of the Rainbow Renaissance." *No Depression*: Posted on May 21. https://www.nodepression.com/spotlight-allison-russell-on-the-shero-with-a-thousand-faces-and-the-rise-of-the-rainbow-renaissance/.

Saturday Night Live (SNL). 2016. "The Day Beyoncé Turned Black." Season 41, Episode 13. 3:24. February 14. YouTube. https://www.youtube.com/watch?v=ociMBfkDG1w.

Schwartz, Sarah. 2023. "What Is Background Knowledge, and How Does It Fit into the Science of Reading?" *Education Week*, January 30. https://www.edweek.org/teaching-learning/what-is-background-knowledge-and-how-does-it-fit-into-the-science-of-reading/2023/01.

Searls, Damion. 2015. "Write Tight." *The Paris Review*, April 21. https://www.theparisreview.org/blog/2015/04/21/write-tight/.

Sehgal, Kabir, and Surishtha Sehgal. 2018. *Festivals of Color.* New York: Beach Lane Books.

Sheinkin, Steve. 2023. Personal email from author, October 31.

Shubitz, Stacey. 2015. "Creating Classroom Environments: Starting the Year with Empty Walls." *Two Writing Teachers* (blog), August 5. https://twowritingteachers.org/2015/08/05/emptywalls/.

Simmons, Dena. 2020. "6 Ways to Be an Antiracist Educator." YouTube. August 7. https://www.youtube.com/watch?v=UM3Lfk751cg.

———. 2021. "Why SEL Alone Isn't Enough." ASCD Abstract, March 1. https://www.ascd.org/el/articles/why-sel-alone-isnt-enough.

Smith, Charles R., Jr. 2018. "Allow Me to Introduce Myself Basketball Poem by Charles R. Smith Jr." Video, July 31. https://www.youtube.com/watch?v=Vf2185xss6o.

Smith, Clint. 2021. *How the Word Is Passed: A Reckoning with the History of Slavery Across America.* New York: Little, Brown.

Smithsonian Afrofuturism Series. n.d. "Claiming Space Symposium." Accessed November 21, 2023. https://airandspace.si.edu/afrofuturism/claiming-space-symposium.

Sorel, Traci. 2021. *We Are Still Here!* Watertown, MA: Charlesbridge.

Spinelli, Eileen. 2020. "How to Love Your Own Little Corner of the World." In *A World Full of Poems: Inspiring Poetry for Children*. London: DK Children.

Stanford University Design School. 2017. "Getting Started with Design Thinking." February 21. dschool.stanford.edu/resources/getting-started-with-design-thinking. Accessed February 1, 2024.

Tallchief, Maria. 1994. September 19 Broadcast. WNIB 50, Chicago, IL.

Taub, Shaina. 2019. "Huddled Masses." YouTube. https://www.youtube.com/watch?v=uifSBQOGCHc&list=RDuifSBQOGCHc&start_radio=1.

Thompkins-Bigelow, Jamilah. 2020. *Your Name Is a Song*. Wheeling, WV: The Innovation Press.

Tippett, Krista. 2017. *Becoming Wise: An Inquiry Into the Mystery and Art of Living*. New York: Penguin Publishing Group.

Tretheway, Natasha. 2021. *Memorial Drive*. New York: HarperCollins.

Warga, Jasmine. 2021. *Other Words for Home*. New York: Balzer + Bray.

Watson, Renée. 2020. *Ways to Make Sunshine*. London: Bloomsbury Publishing.

Wilkerson, Isabel. 2010. *The Warmth of Other Suns: The Epic Story of America's Great Migration*. New York: Random House.

Williams, Elliot. 2021. "Historians Are Searching for Stories of Enslaved People Who Built the White House." NPR.org, July 2.

Woods, Brenda. 2022. *When Winter Robeson Came*. New York: Nancy Paulsen Books.

Woodson, Jacqueline. 2018. *The Day You Begin*. New York: Penguin Young Readers Group.

Yang, Kelly. 2019. *Front Desk*. New York: Scholastic Press.

———. 2022. *Yes We Will: Asian Americans Who Shaped This Country*. New York: Penguin.

Zhang, Kat. 2019. *Amy Wu and the Perfect Bao*. New York: Simon & Schuster Books for Young Readers.

Zauner, Michelle. 2023. *Crying in H Mart*. New York: Vintage.